RECLAIMED
Turning an uneventful life into an adventure

Dedicated to two beautiful daughters
Gemma and Melanie

INTRODUCTION

Is this all there is?

Many of us arrive at a stage in our lives when we ask this question...

When life leaves us unfulfilled and looking for something more...

When who we've become, is a stranger to ourselves.

This is exactly where I found myself at 47 when after months of 'wake-up calls,' I finally decided to listen! Taking a massive leap out of my 'comfort zone', I took an unpaid career break to start the journey back, to reclaim a Lost Self. This is the true account of the amazing adventures, self- explorations and discoveries that I had. It documents the 'magic' that manifested in my life, as I learnt to 'play' with a new-found energy tool called the Law of Attraction.

Everything you will read actually happened.

Some names have been changed for privacy reasons, but the sequence of events and details are taken from personal diaries and journals kept during the four months I travelled alone, across both islands of New Zealand.

CHAPTER 1

Looking back, I can see how it all kind of started with a rescue dog called Harvey.

I was definitely not out for getting a dog that day. I was out for a bike ride, with the hope of blowing some heavy cobwebs out of my mind and a man out of my life. Earlier that morning I had begun serious consideration of how to end (yet another) relationship that was just not working out for me.

So there I was cycling along furiously with sun and wind on my face and mind deep in thought, when a strong 'pull' unexpectedly drew my focus to the Animal Rescue Centre I was fast approaching on my left. A random thought popped suddenly in and kept playing over and over *just go have a look*... So I did and there he was.

In the washhouse being deloused, de-tangled, scrubbed and de-matted. His nails so long and broken they had almost turned back into the tiny pads of his little feet. The dog's pink tongue tip rested on the outside edge of his mouth, giving him such a cheeky look! Despite his terrible physical condition, this tiny miniature terrier appeared calm and relaxed in the young attendant's arms; displaying an innocent trust and gratitude for their gentle care.

Instantly, I felt a connection and movement within my heart and without thinking, I found myself enquiring about his circumstances. And in that one crazy moment, I just knew I'd be coming back here, again.

Five days later a vet check-up confirmed this dog was old (but healthy) and we arrived to take him home. Sitting alongside my teenage daughter Melanie, the tiny dog whimpered anxiously as he glanced nervously back at the Rescue Centre, his last place of safety since abandonment. Mel fell in love instantly and from that time on they were inseparable. Whenever she was home, he was with her.

We named him Harvey.

After being deliriously excited every time he saw me during those first days, his loyalty quickly transferred to Mel as she indulged him with cuddles in bed, sweet smelling shampoos and doggy-dressing up sessions. Harvey loved it! So quickly he settled into our lives, bringing much love, joy and laughter. And how beautiful an experience it was for me, to share 'something special' like this with my two daughters - after seven difficult years of post-family breakup and single parenting through a double dose of 'adolescent angst'. Then, almost as suddenly as he came into our lives, Harvey got ill and left.

Yet but one sweet walk down the park did I have with him scampering along daintily beside me; my heart bursting with pride and happiness. Such deep feelings of love and a depth of tenderness that I'd not felt for a long time. How deeply and joyously I loved him. How quickly these newly ignited beautiful feelings were joined by my old 'friends' confusion, grief and inner chaos. Why, oh why did I get to feel such an intensity of love and sharing; only to experience such suffering and the pain of loss after a few short weeks of joy?

Life seemed cruel…

The nightmare began with signs of blood in Harvey's urine, followed by a week of sudden and progressive illness. Bewildered and helpless, we watched Harvey bravely suffer and struggle to recover. A large vet's bill later and then those dreaded words, "I'm so sorry, we can do no more, it would be kindest to let him go."

Hard as it was for me to make the decision to be there at that final moment of Harvey's life, I was certainly not about to let him die alone feeling abandoned once again, as he left this earthly plane. I could not give him life but I could surround him with love, at his death. As the vet's injection left him floppy in my arms, it felt like my heart was ripped into a million pieces. And yet strangely, at the same time, it stayed open and outpouring with love for dear little Harvey as his weary spirit left that tired, thin, sick body, laying limp and warm in my arms.

We took him home, and buried him under his favourite 'pee patch' in the garden.

Harvey's passing left an enormous black hole in my heart. A gaping abyss and a loss in my life that I could neither comprehend or know how to deal with.

How strange the lessons of life are…

The relationship I was considering ending the day that Harvey and I found each other had ironically, been my strongest source of support love and care throughout Harvey's illness and the period immediately after his death. My gratitude to this man was immense. Yet, how utterly confusing for me, as I tried to make sense of my earlier decision to end the relationship. And so it was, that as I learnt about giving from a place of unconditional love and heart-flowering for a small lost dog, I also received the gift of love and unconditional support, from a man (probably for the first time ever) through this little dog's passing. Harvey's farewell gifts to me were immense.

I was no longer the same person, nor would be ever again…

CHAPTER 2

A great restlessness comes over me and begins to course its way through my veins and spills out into all areas of my life. It is no longer satisfying or enough to exist in this way I used to call *life*.

I begin to question everything.

What am I doing? Where is my life going? Who am I?

And again (alarmingly) I question anew the relationship I'm still in. These are confusing times and I debate fiercely within myself. One 'resident' argues that this relationship may well be my last opportunity to experience love, whilst yet another voice inside rebels. It warns of the fear of being overwhelmed by (what feels like) dependency. Then, a third voice argues, *Maybe it's because you still have the need to understand and experience yourself and your own uniqueness, outside of relationships with men, before you'll be ready for another long term relationship, with one.'*

The inner debate continues. Many questions parade across my mind:

What are the qualities that are necessary for me to be happy in a relationship?

Can I ever truly find happiness that sustains beyond the early stages of romantic love? Have I ever known real happiness and fulfilment in an intimate relationship?

The urgency of life runs before me and I feel a hunger for more. More than this safe conventional life, with its job, mortgaged house and new car. I want adventure! New experiences and new beginnings! I want to know what it feels like to live in the mountains or near an ocean. To explore new places and cultures and more than anything I want to test and explore my own inner limits and find out about my true strength as a woman who stands alone.

Stopping one day to reflect again, on the *mystery of life* I realise that other growth periods (that prompted personal and spiritual yearnings in me) had come after difficult life events. And, that heightened awareness and consciousness often followed periods of extreme emotional suffering and confusion – such as the year after my difficult decision to divorce.

I began to recall that uncomfortable roller coaster of feelings which triggered an intense search for deeper meaning. Trying to find some sense and meaning to all the emotional pain that followed the death of a marriage and loss of my social identity as a 'safe and respectably married woman'. Year after year I searched for healing, exploring different spiritual practices, self-help books and workshops. Slowly, I began to move into a new place of self-awareness, after what felt like a deep sleep and a life lived through other people's values.

Around the time of Harvey's death, I recall hearing about an 'off the card' new thing called the Law of Attraction. First, through Esther and Jerry Hall's book *Ask and it is Given* and then in a new DVD given to me by a friend called *The Secret*. Feelings of excitement and fascination shot sky high, after slipping that unassuming little shiny disk into my DVD player one evening. I watched with wonder as the screen danced with inspirational and famous faces of past and present. All informing me that the power to attract and manifest whatever I want in my life was actually inside me! This powerful notion, that I can actually become a painter on the canvas of my own life (rather than helpless spectator) feels so attractive to me. Somewhere deep inside, it resonates loud and clear.

I decide to test out this radical new universal Law of Attraction. I start paying more attention to what's going on in my head and become more conscious of the army of negative mind chatter that I find living there, I start to focus on flipping worry thoughts to positive ones; based on what I want to experience, rather than what I don't! And I start to follow up more on my gut feelings rather than ignoring it.

CHAPTER 3

So much of what I'm thinking and reading at this time, really does support this 'alternative' philosophy of living in a state of natural abundance. One that's created by what you manifest through your own thoughts and emotions. However, my social conditioning and ego does not want to agree with it at all! Yet even though my highly educated and analytical mind tries to refute it, I find a stronger place inside me that senses the time has come to move away from all this professional 'babble' and intellectualism that's leading me absolutely nowhere. It's time to take a big step towards something new. So my first big manifesting move is to write up a *Wish List* of the new things I now desire to experience, in my life. Then I set an intention to have a go at attracting and manifesting some of them through this new 'wacko' way! Well, that was how this experiment started off (initially) anyway; kind of playful and loose. But then my 'harmless' little game seemed to take on a whole new life of its own!

At work one day in my safe and well paid public sector job, I see an advertisement in a professional journal from a colleague in New Zealand requesting UK networking connections. I email, on an impulse to connect with faraway places and others working in similar areas of work. I've never been much interested in NZ before, but a chain of email replies rouses a curiosity and appetite for more knowledge of this mysterious land. Each email that bounces back and forth across the world gathers its own energy and momentum. I find myself drawn along a path of imaginings, of adventure in a foreign land, as I visualise majestic images of New Zealand scenery.

All of this, through one random email (made on impulse) to a faraway stranger – who I later discover has a wife with the same unusual name as my own! Then, out of what seems like nowhere, other connections to NZ begin to start to line up thick and fast; propelling me further towards my journey of adventure and deeper personal discovery.

CHAPTER 4

The desire to step out of my professional and full-time working life gets stronger. Energy draining and soul-destroying activities like driving through city rush hour traffic every morning, starts to grate on me more than usual. I begin to long for the experience of starting each day in a more leisurely, peaceful way. As I work on my manifestation ideas I visualise the details of an ideal life and place in my mind's eye:

- A peaceful place to write and a garden with flowers and vegetables

- A simple wooden house with a veranda looking onto sea or mountains

- A leisurely start to each day without driving through busy rush hour traffic

The vision continues to grow. I see myself now working the hours I want to work, not the hours working me. I'm exploring new countries, free to be me and making interesting new friends. My two grown up daughters are still connected and close to my heart, but getting on with their own lives, and no longer dependent on me. Further along in my 'daydream', I see a together-kind-of-mate who wants to share it all. Building a life and a home that's full of love, we live a happy and a peaceful life. I experience harmony, well-being and a sense of belonging. I'm connected, yet free. Free to find my place in the world based on who I am and why I'm here. I have the ability to love deeply without fearing loss or rejection, or the need to control.

This is the new life that I paint on the canvas of my mind and set out to attract into my reality. I begin to believe that I can have this wonderful life! I tell myself I'm worthy and deserving of it and begin to affirm that it's mine by Divine Right. And after spending time in my 'creative workshop' I say, "Thank you Universe" as if it's already here.

Somewhere, on this long self-development road of mine, I once remember reading, *'As soon as you decide who and what you want… everything unlike it will come into that space'*. And so it was that a couple of weeks later the Universe sent me a second 'wake up' call, just to help me get real focused and clear about what I want...

I'm driving and I'm late. Rushing to get to a work location where I'm lead facilitator on an adult group work programme. I'm feeling really tired, juggling too many roles and extra responsibilities of staff who are off sick. My mind is troubled and distracted with the thought of being late, as I speed along dark country lanes trying to find a short cut. Suddenly there's a tight bend right in front of me. It's dusk and the light is poor. I'm going too fast. I brake. I swerve! There's nothing I can do as my beautiful cabriolet sports car veers off the road and into a ditch. The entire length of the driver's side is pounded, beaten and battered as it travels through shrubs, bushes and foliage. As fast as it happens it's all over.

I regain control of the steering and the car swerves back on to the road. I continue on to my destination (without stopping) like I'm in some sort of a bad dream! Work is still waiting and I am still late. Acting like a zombie I arrive, brief the other staff on their roles and take up my place (smiling) in front of the group. Quite bizarrely, almost like nothing had happened. Apart from being aware of a mild feeling of shock and inconvenience, I find myself experiencing little distress. It's like I'm almost too tired to even bother wasting any energy on it all.

A few hours later, I drive slowly home, minus one electric wing mirror with some very sorry looking bumps and scratches scored along the length of my car's (previously) gleaming paintwork. I start to think about the events of the day. *What on earth was that all about?* As I reflect, I realise that I'd been rushing and going too fast. That I had been prioritising work needs over my own needs for safety and wellbeing. I'd been driving too fast, in an area with no street lights. And as I desperately searched for a short cut, I had started to feel lost.

How symbolic of my current feeling about life! *Where the hell am I going?* It's dark and I feel lost and alone. It's like the Universe is speaking to me in metaphors. Slow down! Stop sacrificing your own needs at the price of helping others. For God's Sake Lynette, you are a human *being* – but one that's become lost in *doing*.

The driving 'wake-up' is followed directly by another one, when I arrive home to an enormous mess in the kitchen; that my youngest daughter has created. To make it worse there she sits waiting, impatiently. Her beautiful eighteen year old face (now looking twenty five) all made-up, ready for a night out clubbing and asking sweetly for a 'taxi' into town! Devoid of enough energy to make a stand over the kitchen, (a far too regular battle to mention) I silently drive into town, again on automatic pilot.

On the return journey home the 'inner voices' start up again, *I don't want this life anymore. It's all give, give and give. I'm fed up of years of living with teenagers' whose focus is mainly on their needs. What about me?*

CHAPTER 5

In the midst of the full-blown adolescent years of my two daughters' lives, I have now come to the sobering realisation that maybe I contributed to the creation of this adolescent angst; through my inability to balance and communicate my own needs with those of my children in a healthy enough way. Did I give them too much choice in the earlier years of their lives? Have I been 'over-giving' in the pre-teen and post-divorce years? And how much of this guilt-giving has been from a place that's trying to make amends for 'putting them through it all'? The last question echoes a sad truth, as I sit cradling a mug of comforting coffee, back home but too tired to rustle up anything to eat. A silent tear plops down into cold coffee dregs.

The yearning to experience 'something else' returns. It just won't go away.

Oh, God! I so want to do something different with my life! Something that's just about me. I've worked hard at being a dedicated mother, loyal daughter, reliable employee and responsible citizen. But right now none of that seems worth much. I just want to go away, far away and experience something other than this unfulfilling life of mine.

The idea of taking a career break and heading off to New Zealand to escape a UK winter pops up in my head. I share it with my (still hanging in there) boyfriend who jumps in enthusiastically and tells me that he wants to come too. Very soon he's talking of how we could drive around New Zealand together, in a camper van. And before I can decide if this is what *I* really want, I find I'm going along with the plan (so as not to hurt his feelings). *Argh!*

Still uncertain about this relationship in my deepest core, I know I'm pushing these feelings down, as I feel closeness (on one level) to this kind and caring guy – and a part of me still desires to be in a relationship. I'm really trying to put these nagging doubts out of my mind and tell myself to, s*top being so bloody ungrateful!*

We seem to be heading into a difficult phase again. The old niggling feeling of wanting to leave the relationship surfaces and tell me that lovely as this guy is, he's not my life partner. I remind myself that I've been here before (prior to Harvey). I return to thinking about the importance of getting to know myself and learn about my own needs and how to meet them in healthier ways. Maybe I need to have an inner love affair with me, before I can 'do' an outer one?

How complicated this relationship game is…

I find myself growing tired of trying. And oh, how hard it is not to become lost in compassion for the anguish this sweet man expresses when I try to tell him it's not really 'working'. I can't bear to see his sadness and despair, as I sense his fear of aloneness rising up. Being the gentleman he is there are no angry words. He gives me the space to decide for myself what to do. But I 'chicken out' again. It's so hard.

CHAPTER 6

Despite relationship confusions many beautiful and amazing things begin to flower in my life around this time. My eldest daughter Gemma, who's been on such a rocky and rebellious road for most of her adolescent years, begins to blossom in confidence, gets a part time job and starts to do well at university. She seems full of life, energy and focus! It's beautiful to behold. For the first time in years it feels like I can breathe an inner sigh of relief that Gemma is finally moving forward. Then my youngest daughter Melanie informs me she's decided to take a year out from studies after A levels, as she wants to work in Europe. A big internal shift in the weight of financial responsibilities as a single parent suddenly comes about. It opens up a space of freedom for me to seriously consider my own needs. Slowly, slowly I see the manifestation of my dream becoming reality...

A New Year arrives and new resolutions are made. The (now familiar) desire for new beginnings still lingers on. And so, after the New Year's break, I decide to *JUST DO IT!*

To take action in the moment! I fill out the necessary paperwork at work and inform my manager I want to take a mini career break for four and a half months. My adventure moves a big step nearer. But at the same time, without any further discussion, my boyfriend starts to finalise his own plans to take a career break too. He talks again of buying a camper van and travelling around New Zealand together. *Gulp*!

Ashamedly, I have not yet been brave enough to end our relationship. I've been coasting along with his plans and needs (avoiding my own) but now something inside of me speaks loud, urgently and clear. I can no longer ignore it. It nudges and demands me to ask what *I* want from the trip, not just the 'easiest way' to do it, or what my boyfriend wants. I'm forced to go deep within to inquire and I start to come up with my own wish list for this trip.

CHAPTER 7

Almost as soon as I put pen to paper it's crystal clear to me what *I* want.

There's a wish to experience being a 'free spirit', visiting new places, meeting new and interesting people. To experience living in another culture. I discover I want to spend time living in NZ, not just as a tourist, but living some of the time with locals. I also want to meet with other travellers and finally, I discover a desire to experience living and working in a spiritual community.

More than anything I find a wish to push out comfort zones, to connect with (and discover) any hidden strengths and gifts within me. In my mind's eye I imagine what making such a trip with my guy might be like. I 'see' us travelling around in a campervan and it feels very safe and cosy but sadly, very un-stimulating. I imagine myself being in some sort of a tourist-bubble. Being in New Zealand but not really touching, smelling or feeling it – a bit like dipping my toe in a swimming pool of delicious water. Spending time exclusively with my bloke but not really meeting locals or fellow travellers. (He's not a great lover of strangers). It doesn't feel good. It's a gnawingly uncomfortable feeling that I try to cancel out by focusing on positives of travelling with him. Yet when it comes to meeting the needs of my own growth, I realise they cannot be met by doing this trip together. There's a strange and disturbing feeling that I need to (and on a deeper level) *want to*, do this trip alone. Somehow I have to tell him.

There's a hard lump in my throat as I explain this, in the best way I can. But he can neither understand nor comprehend what I'm saying. It's just not in his orbit to even consider the idea that I'd want to go alone. But in his true loving fashion, my guy accepts what I say. Yet I fight with a demon inside that tells me what a rotten, selfish, bitch I am for disappointing him like this. It's so clear now though, that if I can't feel excited with the idea of travelling with this man, then this is definitely not the right relationship for me. He knows it's coming, but desperately wants to hide from the painful truth that it's finally over.

There really is no easy way to do this. I care about this guy. In our last hours together, as he gathers up his weekend possessions from around my house (trying to delay that final hour) I feel his pain so deeply. Once more I'm back in that seemingly 'win-lose' situation of meeting my own needs and those of others. I go out to his car to say goodbye and find him head in hands, sobbing like a child. I know that I can do nothing to comfort him. I can't give him what he wants. It tears at my heart to hurt this sweet and gentle guy but I need to be strong enough this time. To set us both free.

The weeks that follow are painful and intensely lonely. It's hard, knowing that I only have to pick up the phone and tell him I want him back and he'll be here. Only a few weeks pass and I hear that he's already looking for a new relationship via the Internet. That hurts! I wonder what happened to a time of mourning. Was I really so special to him after all? It feels like I'm easy to replace, like a commodity bought in a shop. Within a month there's a new girlfriend and in eighteen months, he's married.

I experience my own stages of grieving. I grieve the loss of our good times and a return to weekends, alone. It's hard. Yet still, I feel gratitude for the gifts this relationship brought; whilst at the same time carrying an inner knowing that it was the right decision to make. Holding on tight to the attitude of gratitude, I focus my mind on future dreams and wishes. Very quickly, the 'darkness' shifts as this new way of grieving for me ends and a brand new energy of anticipation replaces it.

CHAPTER 8

Enthusiastically, I start exploring options and ideas for my lone trip that are now springing up like new buds after wintertime. In a passing conversation at work, a new colleague tells me about an Internet site I can register to find NZ work-trade opportunities. So I press the buttons, join and post a profile of myself and of the type of skills I could offer a few hours of work in – for return of food and lodgings. Wow!

In no time at all emails from far away people start dropping into my inbox offering work-trade opportunities on farms, private homes and spiritual centres. What a gift! How easy! I have such fun cherry picking from the dozen or so offers I get. I start to shape my first few weeks in NZ. A young Kiwi family want a mother's helper for their five year old daughter, in return for food, lodgings and use of their second car. I check out the website's list of retreat centres that are offering work-trade opportunities on both islands, and arrange the final part of my trip work trading for a month on a hillside spiritual community in the Coromandel. As soon as I enter The Mana Retreat Centre's website to check out details further, something about the place jumps right out at me. I know immediately it's *the one*.

I've decided to leave the middle period of my trip open, to allow for places and plans to manifest and grow themselves. I want to spend some time backpacking across both islands. Taking each day as it comes, like a free spirit. Staying a while or moving on at my leisure. The whole process of planning my trip seems to come together effortlessly, thanks to the Internet! I feel pretty proud of myself for making it all happen! Another passing conversation gives me information on a webpage called Budget Backpacking Hostels that offer loads of places to stay across NZ. I register and receive a booklet full of interesting sounding hostels. Some even have their own hot tubs and swimming pools. Wow! The site offer ratings by past travellers on hostel cleanliness, location and facilities. Perfect!

Everything I need to create the trip of my heart's desires seems to be being provided; it's amazing, exciting and almost magical. The abundant manifestations through the Law of Attraction continue to blow my mind when a random enquiry sent over the Internet, to another NZ professional in my same field of work, in Youth Justice offers a work shadow opportunity for my first week in New Zealand. The gifts continue to flow in. I then receive an invitation to stay with him and his wife! My English employer's bless this unexpected gift further by agreeing to pay my wage for this work-shadow week. It's all totally unexpected!

Abundance! Abundance! It's everywhere.

My air tickets are booked easily online and I even get the offer of an airport pickup on arrival by my professional contact's wife, Rona! *What else is possible?* It's like living in the enchanted forest picking fruits off the trees. But, to be honest, it's both a mixture of exciting and scary all rolled into one. Almost too easy (not at all how life has been up until now) and soon old fear thoughts start popping in. They try to pull me back into old ways of thinking around limitation and lack.

That familiar 'worry monster' pops up too and reminds me, *you're going half way around the world on your own!!* (gulp!) *You know you haven't saved for this trip and your wage will be suspended for most of the time away...* (gulp!) *And all your plans are being made via the Internet and with strangers. (Don't you remember what your dad taught you about strangers, Lynette?)* (double gulp!!)

11

On one level fear comes up when these thoughts surface but deep down there's such a strong sense of inner 'knowing' that this is all coming together perfectly for a reason and that I just need to trust. So my antidote, whenever the *fear voice* pops in is to remind myself that the Universe is with me. I'm not alone. And, surprisingly, the fear feeling falls away shortly after. I guess this 'mantra' helps sooth and reassure it...

I do so want to learn to trust in the Universe. To believe in the Law of Attraction and the abundance that it says is simply waiting for me to 'claim'. I try hard not to focus on money, which has always been a big 'fear of lack' area for most of my life. Because of the work-trade parts of my trip I feel kind of reassured that those weeks won't have food and accommodation expenses. I also remind myself that I don't really need much money to enjoy myself and have fun...

Renting my house could generate extra funds but I don't really want to let to a total stranger, as I plan to leave all my furniture in. However, I'm reminded by an inner voice that I do want to become more trusting and so I decide to leave the matter of the house let to the Universe. I set my intention that if any potential contacts come into my 'orbit' for a short-term let, I'll be open to explore it.

The very next week as easy as a summer's breeze blows though, I receive a call from my sister's ex-husband saying he has a manager at work whose marriage has broken up and is looking for a short term rent until his divorce settlement is through. I agree to meet the guy for an informal chat. Very quickly I intuit that he's okay and offer him the house for less than its rentable value, in return for him taking extra love and care of my home and its contents. The deal is done. It's a win-win situation and I like that.

The canvas is almost full. There is such a feeling of inner calm and 'knowing' about everything – despite it all being completely unknown! I'm determined to fully embrace and make the most of this wonderful opportunity to explore not only a new country but also a chance to cast off the last bit of residue of a 'me' that grew up feeling I couldn't trust in my own ability. That old thread hangs onto a half hidden belief that I can't cope with 'big' things on my own. And this ties itself to the *I-need-a-man* belief that was put in me (maybe by mum) as a child! The one that says a woman can't really be happy without a man in her life. So it's a real opportunity to challenge these old limiting beliefs, once and for all!

They no longer serve me and are so outdated. Yet they still lurk around, like shadows in my mind. The time that I was 'needy' and dependent on a man, for financial security, happiness and a sense of self-worth is behind me now. I've been living and financially standing alone for seven years. *So for goodness sake Lynette, let's wash this old crap out of the system once and for all.*

Let's go girl!!

CHAPTER 10

<u>Wednesday 7th November 2007</u> So here I am, 47 years old, a divorced and single mum, setting off to travel half way round the world on her own. The magical departure date is finally here. Everything is in place. House rented. Car stored with friends, career break approved. Youngest daughter's alternative living arrangements all sorted and a few basic connections established in New Zealand.

As my two daughters drive me to Manchester airport, I'm not at all sure how that last parting moment will feel. Will there be tears or last minute jitters at leaving them?

It's always a bit unknown on the emotional front at times like these but no, there's complete calmness within. No stress. It feels right. (I think the girls are more worried than I am!) They kiss me goodbye at the drop off point as I push little angel pictures scripted with tender words of love, into their hands. Gemma gives me a small guardian angel and murmurs, "To keep you safe." I guess it helps her feel that 'mad mum' might have some protection in the months that lie ahead!

I walk towards Check-in and Departures with my heavily laden back pack and bright new red canvas holdall. It carries the carefully chosen contents of what will become my whole world and wardrobe for four and a half months. My feet clomp noisily with the heavy walking boots I'm wearing – to save on precious baggage weight. Once through check-in, I plan to change into flip-flops tucked tidily into my backpack and attach the walking boots by their laces to it. Even down to little actions like this, I love the way I've had to stretch my mind and problem-solve to achieve best outcomes for my trip.

Sitting in the departure lounge complete with coffee and a croissant, texts of good wishes and goodbyes start coming in. A growing feeling of anticipation, liberation and excitement begins to creep over me. It feels like I'm shedding an old worn out skin, like as a snake! A text comes in from Melanie, *look in your note book!* I rummage inside my rucksack to find a good luck card hidden there, with words of love and encouragement for my trip. Bless her. A text from my sister and a friend come in. Before I know it we're boarding!

I'm travelling on the highly acclaimed long-haul fight company, Singapore Airlines. Another challenge to value my need for comfortable travel, along with the old fear of spending money on myself! In the seat next to me on my first flight, to Singapore is a guy called Mark. We smile, introduce ourselves and are soon chatting away. I feel happy to have such a friendly person to talk to on the long flight ahead and it appears he feels the same. Mark is 41, from Blackpool, owns a taxi company and tells me he's going on holiday for the first time alone too. I sense some apprehension. It's a last minute decision he's made to take a month in Phuket to join friends who are out there. He thinks that what *he* is doing is pretty brave and is amazed when he hears what I'm up to! Very soon my professional coaching skills come out (can't help myself!) as I start to coach Mark around his fears and negativity. A few hours of air time and a three course meal later, he tells me how much better he feels about the whole trip. Mark confides that his last relationship ended badly only a few months ago and he's still trying to recover from after effects.

Our flight passes pleasantly, lots of quality food and drinks and hot relaxing flannels to pamper and refresh jet-weary skin. The toilets have exquisite moisturisers and perfume in them to sooth my travel parched skin. I give myself another silent *well done* for valuing me enough to purchase this quality experience, to start my adventure with.

CHAPTER 11

On arrival in Singapore, and with a sudden realisation that his 'in-flight life-coach' is now leaving his life Mark lapses back into feelings of uncertainty, again. We check in to a transit hotel in the airport to await our separate, onward flights; only to find there's a one hour wait for rooms to become available.

Mark and I spend an hour drinking coffee in a beautiful little orchid garden in the middle of Singapore Airport, perched on tiny ornate benches amidst profusions of colour and coy carp. Once again I coach him back into a place of positive expectation, growth and change. His optimism rises as the negative mind loosens its grip. I say goodbye and wish him well. He thanks me and says I must look him up if ever in Blackpool. We hug and kiss as friends, next to a mini waterfall in the orchid garden. Mark holds on to the security of our hug, as if reluctant to let me go. I gently break his hold, smile and say goodbye.

Checking into my transit room I set an alarm and sleep for a few hours, then shower and eat. Compliments of Singapore Airlines I take a short bus tour of the city and round off the wait for my connecting flight with a lovely neck massage by a sweet middle aged masseur who chatters about her years spent in massage. Working intensely on my neck, Lola tells me how family who holiday with her like to sightsee or shop – but her own holiday treat is to take a foreign massage!

Boarding my final flight to Christchurch I find myself in the window seat next to a prim and proper looking middle aged couple. The woman eyes me up and down suspiciously. I figure it might be kind of hard for her to understand what a woman of my age is doing travelling alone with backpack and walking boots as hand luggage! There's no conversation on this flight. But it's mainly a night flight, so I try to rest. Breakfast is served by smiling petite oriental ladies, as the first images of New Zealand come into view through a window on my left. I peer out of the tiny portal onto my new world in awe, as virgin snow-capped mountains whizz past! A strong emotion rises up inside. I did it! I'm here! My new home for the next four and a half months.

We touchdown and brilliant sunshine greets our arrival. Endless fields, green plains and hills are beyond the busy airport landscape. Wow! Immigration Control seems to take forever as I join a long queue to have my walking boots inspected and washed. Finally, I make it through arrivals and glance around, (a little nervously) then see a stranger waving a black and red sign. It reads: *Welcome to New Zealand Lynette*. This is Rona, Andrew's wife. Andrew is the youth justice contact that I made over the Internet when I had the idea of combining my first week with taking a look at Family Group Conferencing – a good practice model that originates here. Andrew had not only set up for me to 'shadow' a co-ordinator for a week in Christchurch Youth Justice but is 'putting me up' at his home and taking me in to the office, each day!

So here is Rona, an American. As she drives us along in her little red Mini, she tells me how she came here eight years ago, to do research for a Master's degree. How she met Andrew and they married soon after. It's a nice little fairy-tale story to start my trip. I love it! In half an hour we're at a lovely village called Sumner. Their home is high above sea level, looking out onto the very sea that Captain Cook sailed gloriously over, hundreds of years ago! The house is shaped like a ship's front with many terraces and balconies. The room I'm to sleep in has a sea view. Heaven! Soon, I'm sitting in their pretty garden looking out onto a glistening ocean and enjoying warm sun on my jet lagged skin. Rona goes back to work for the afternoon and I doze in and out of sleep. Later I unpack and then shower.

Rona is cooking in the kitchen. We chat politely; stranger to stranger, until Andrew returns home from work. Soon we are all talking about our shared passion of Family Group Conferencing and within a few hours of knowing me, Andrew is offering paid work in his office – if I want it! It's tempting but not for long, as I remember my reasons for being here. Freedom from responsibility, work routines and schedules, along with the opportunity to go where life takes me! I decline. That first evening passes gently. I find I'm experiencing a strange kind of rolling feeling as I move about the house. I expect it's due to all the flying and changes of season. I've left winter behind and moved right into late spring in New Zealand. I text my girls to say I've arrived. It feels awesome knowing how far the messages have to travel to get to them. It's kind of hard to believe I'm half way around the world. Wow! You did it Lynette. What a girl! Awesome!

I retire to bed early, but it's a long time before I settle off to sleep.

CHAPTER 12

The next day Andrew has offered to take us into Kaikoura if the weather is good – but its drizzle and mist this morning, so he decides against it. Later it begins to clear and I'm anxious to be outside exploring my new world. From the kitchen window there's a panoramic view of gently rolling cliffs, down to the sea. It calls to me and I can't resist. Not really knowing where I'm heading, I take a walk and explore the cliff tops down into Taylor's Mistake Bay. Later, I learn that this is the area that Captain Scott brought *The Endeavour* through, and mistakenly took it to be Lyttelton Bay. What a lovely walk! Beautiful clear views of sea and hills. Tropical plants adorn the paths and quaint little beach shacks (called batches) are intermittently tucked into cliff coves with trailing, magical green furry creepers dangling and draping about them.

How sweet!

Later in the day, Rona takes me into Lyttelton, their nearest port. She's curious to hear my life story so I share it over a beer and this seems to prompt her to share too. Rona tells me about her life, back in America, of an unhappy marriage to an ex-veteran scarred by the Vietnam War. Of a childhood with a mother who pushed her to dance; (in Hollywood) wanting to make Rona another Shirley Temple. She tells the story of breaking free of her old life when she came to New Zealand and married Andrew. The sharing of our stories and Rona's hearing of my own childhood and marriage difficulties seem to form a common bond between us. I sense her relax a little. Perhaps she was wary of me, a single woman coming like she'd done. Maybe she thought I might be after her man? Absolutely not!

Rona proposes a toast with our beers, "To new beginnings" and we clink glasses. I feel for the carved Maori symbol hanging around my neck, given to me years ago by a friend. In recent months I'd learnt the meaning of its beautiful mysterious shape to be the symbol of 'new beginnings.' Now here I am, in the country of the necklace's origin and purchase, toasting just that! I feel the hope of new beginnings stirring in my heart.

The evening is spent quietly watching a DVD about a French girl whose sweetheart goes to war and doesn't return. The story is about how she never gives up hope that he's alive. Rona says goodnight early. She leaves Andrew and me to finish watching the sad tale, together.

Sunday I awake to brilliant sunshine and after breakfast do hand washing then swing lazily in a sun hammock in the garden. After lunch Andrew Rona and I take a drive around the area. We climb high up, in Andrew's car and take in stunning views across the area. Then down into Christchurch to have a look around. Andrew points out the office that I'll be based at during my work shadow week, starting tomorrow. It feels exciting, if not somewhat strange, and completely alien as to what work culture I'll be part of. We enjoy a cold beer in a Belgium beer garden and I experience the very English-ness of Christchurch with its river punts and willow trees. It reminds me so much of Cambridge. Then it's home for one of Rona's thrifty dinners and early to bed, in readiness for tomorrow.

CHAPTER 13

Monday 12th November So here I am, with Christchurch Youth Justice Team. Andrew has come in briefly, to introduce me to a few people before he leaves for various meetings across the city as a Regional Manager. I spend the day with Malcolm (Mal) one of the co-ordinators here. It's a quiet and orderly office and I soak in its energy and the characters who work in it from my safe viewing position at the rear of the office, by Mal's desk. We discuss family group conferencing, solution focused approaches and its spiritual aspect in relation to unexpected conference outcomes. I've not thought of this before, but it's true. These kinds of meetings seem to be imbued in a spiritual energy that often brings unexpected forgiveness and healing.

At lunchtime I walk into the city centre to buy food and 'feel out' Christchurch. The afternoon is full of meetings with other workers. They are as much as interested in me and my work in the UK as I am in theirs! After work I stand outside the grey office building and wait for Andrew to pick me up. He's kindly offered to collect me, but as I wait and wait, I wonder if this is a lot of trouble and not really practical for him to fit in to his busy working day. Over an hour passes. As I stand there, a strong wind begins to chill me and I start to feel a little lost, alone, cold and tired. I try Andrew's mobile phone but it's not connecting. I have to work hard to focus on pulling myself out from the negative and fearful place that my mind wants to go. Then Andrew pulls up and it's suddenly okay again. I realise how very, very mentally tired I am. After eating, I check emails on their home computer. There's one from both daughters. That feels nice. I head off to bed early, as not much else seems to be happening. Boy, what a cold house! There seems to be no central heating to warm the cool evening air. I don bed socks and fleecy pyjamas and turn on a little heater in my room for a while, before drifting off to sleep.

The next day I'm in work early today as Andrew is dropping me off before he leaves for a trip up North. Rona kindly comes too, to show me how to use the Metro. I will be travelling home by bus tonight (little gulp). I buy a bus credit strip and hear that the system is pretty straight forward. I feel fairly confident I know how to get 'home' tonight. I have breakfast in the city and drink my first cup of chai latté. I like it! Mal's not in today and as he seems to be the one who's assigned to look after me, I spend a long morning (mostly alone) in the office. I had thought my own team back in the UK was laid back, but this one takes the biscuit! I fill my time eaves dropping on a social worker as she chatters on the phone for hours to her boyfriend, her daughter, and then a garage about car repair arrangements. I gaze out of the large office windows and contemplate the majesty of some snow-topped mountains I see at eye level. What a view.

It's sunny over lunchtime. I buy a book called *Leaving the Enchanted Forest* and enjoy swigging sarsaparilla in a chunky glass bottle. Guess it's time to try out a cash machine... Much to my relief it works and presents me with crisp green New Zealand dollars. One more mission accomplished!

Navigating the NZ bus system to get myself home is the biggest challenge of the day. But I pull it off great, even if the *what-if* monster did manage to creep in at various points to create pockets of anxiety over, *what if I'm on the wrong bus?*

What if I get off at the wrong place?

What if Rona's not there to pick me up at the other end?

Somehow I manage to push them out and in the end everything works out just fine. I'm fast realising that the worry-way of thinking is such a habitual programme. But I'm just not having it anymore! Before long I'm back at their sea view look-out and changed into warmer clothes for another evening above sea level.

CHAPTER 14

Great morning! Mal is back at work and it's a different world when he's here. Such a nice guy, he does a lot to make me feel welcome and included. This morning I go with him to a training event in the city for newly qualified social workers. Mal gives a presentation about using Family Conferencing with Care and Protection cases and works hard to instil a solution-focused approach into his training. It's a privilege to listen and I feel fortunate to be able to share his expertise in this empowering approach. There's torrential rain when we come out of the building, but we dodge the showers as Mal drives us speedily back to the office. It's great fun! By the end of the day the sun is out again, so I wander slowly back through city streets towards the bus station, taking in shops on the way. I buy a pair of groovy Indian style sandals for $19. Feeling more relaxed today, I *know* I'm on the right bus and I *know* where to get off! I enjoy the ride home. From the window, I'm treated to coastal views bathed in sweet, spring New Zealand sunshine.

Evenings are pretty much about emailing or TV. This couple seem to have a slow routine and steady life. But one that's nice for me to be cocooned in, as I adjust to my new world. There's an email from the Catch family, offering to pick me up on Saturday. I'll be doing work-trade for them in New Brighton (down the coast) for the next month. This arrangement was part of my *Wish List*. To have a cultural experience of living with locals, but it's also about moving comfort zone slowly enough for me to handle. There's no emails waiting from back home and that feels kind of hard. Guess I'm still feeling a bit in transition and needing contact with the familiar and known. No worries - it is as it is. I have a reassuring conversation with myself about how great I'm doing and how its early days in the adjustment process – after being catapulted into a whole new world.

Mal talks a lot the next day about his personal life. I find myself beginning to like him. He's very in touch with his feelings and also his spiritual side. For a second, I wondered if we might share anything other than professional time together. But then he's telling me about how he's met a woman through a friend of his and what a great relationship it is. Ah well. At lunch we eat a *hungi* together (traditionally cooked Maori meal). Its speciality lies in that it's cooked slowly in the ground, wrapped in giant leaves that allow meat and vegetable flavours to really come out. Mal chats away as we eat in the large central cafeteria, sharing lots of his personal stuff again with me. Then off he goes, for a coffee with 'her'!

I go out too, mainly to get over the disappointment that I'm surprised I feel. On reflection, I asked myself why? Sure, he's a nice guy but nothing more. I surprise myself on how easily the mind starts the 'connection game'. There was no energy of attraction around him at all, really - just a nice guy telling me his story. I think it's probably a sign from the Universe to show me that there are guys with a spiritual side - still out there. I buy myself a pair of groovy sunglasses at lunchtime and I'm soon over it. Ah, the balm of retail therapy!

A good last hour of my time with this team is spent with Kendra, a funky Australian manageress. She's really interested to hear about my work in the UK. Mal and I exchange email addresses and phone numbers. He promises to let me know if he has any interesting conferences I can 'observe' in the next few weeks. After a few goodbyes I leave the building and it looks like I'm done here, as it's a national holiday tomorrow (Friday). There's some sort of horse racing event on and Mal is taking the day off to attend. I set off walking across the great bridge that straddles the Sydenham end of the city when Kendra passes by, pedalling frantically on a pushbike. She waves and shouts, "Goodbye Lynette!"

I wave back enthusiastically, and smile to myself. That was nice. I take a reflective stroll back to the bus station and stop off for a Chai Latté, en route. Once back in Sumner I walk the coastal route home, taking pictures of the panoramic views as I walk. It feels good to be here. All is well and all is well indeed.

CHAPTER 15

It's a holiday day in NZ and the weather is really warm and sunny. I decide to get my walking boots out and walk along the cliff tops again. It's so expansive and wonderfully exhilarating! The thought that I'm walking along, quite happily, almost half way around the world on my own and doing just great, gives me a feeling of enormous satisfaction. I have another well-done conversation with myself, *you pulled it off girl! No one else did it for you; using all your own skills and determination.* I feel relaxed and open. On the return walk, I fall in step with a middle aged woman. We start to chat. I've been looking for somewhere to buy an ice-cream or get something to eat, but haven't found anywhere yet. She's a local and offers to give me a lift in her car, down into Sumner village. I'm touched by her kindness. Once in Sumner I get an ice cone and walk along the beach. It feels good to be out in the sunshine. As I walk, I reflect.

So my first week here is nearly over and tomorrow I move to the Catch family's house in New Brighton by the Sea. It feels time to move. I'm ready to meet my new family with its English mum Dorota, Kiwi dad Gordon and their daughter Lovejoy, aged 5. The Catch's contacted me to say they were interested in me living with them for a couple of weeks in return for a few hours of childcare and general help around the home. I'd thought it would be a nice way to settle into NZ gradually, before hitting the backpacker's scene. By living with a local family, I hope to gain a bit of insight into modern Kiwi lifestyle. I also like the idea of having use of their second car for a bit of sightseeing – along with the experience of living by the ocean.

It's my last evening with Andrew and Rona. We all change into smart clothes, Rona puts on bright red lipstick and Andrew drives us into Christchurch for a farewell meal at Valentino's their favourite restaurant. I make it my treat as a way of saying thank you to this couple for all their kindness and hospitality. I'm determined to not look at prices tonight or worry about the cost. I just want it to be a nice time. The place has a relaxed feel and gentle ambiance about it. After a huge malt beer Andrew is much more chilled and the conversations flow freely between us. Later, full of Italian goodness we take a slow ride home through the softly lit streets of Christchurch, before climbing the coastal road home. Up, up onto the headland above Sumner we go. Back at the house Andrew shows old video footage of Rona and when they first met. I think about how her life must have changed and her decision to leave America to join him. It's a lovely story. I wonder if my own relationship story will have such a happy ending…

CHAPTER 16

I really love the opening I have here for the unknown and unexpected to happen and that my own past is far away in the UK. Here, I can be who I want to be and the liberation of that feeling makes my spirits soar. I reflect on how surprisingly easy my first week has been and how relaxed and confident I've felt. Yes a little lonely, with some feelings of strangeness but this has been such a small aspect of the week. My sea legs have calmed and I am slowly easing into the rhythm of life on the other side of the world. I feel reassured that my intuition about coming here was right. I feel guided and safe. Even the old fear and worry-monsters seem to have taken a bit of a break...

<u>Saturday</u> Today Dorota Gordon and Lovejoy come to collect me. There's that awkward formality when strangers meet for the first time and are not really sure what to say or what small talk to make. Lovejoy stays in the car and it's not until I go out with my bags and sit in the back with her that we get to really meet. As the car moves away I wave goodbye to Rona and Andrew, giving them back their quiet routine – before the English woman came to stay!

The Catch family have a nice relaxed vibe about them as we make small-talk about this and that on the short drive back. Lovejoy is quiet for most of the journey, checking me out with sideways glances when she thinks I'm not looking. I know she's had a few mother's helpers come and go and I'm guessing it might be a bit hard, in some ways to have strangers coming and going in her life I give her space to come towards me in her own time. Dorota is full of chatter, but in a friendly, bubbly sort of way. Gordon seems older than his wife and has a relaxed, soft energy. I guess they complement each other nicely. Pulling into their driveway I see a modern detached bungalow sitting neatly in the middle of a fairly large estate. The rooms are bright and airy and out back there's a bulging vegetable patch that Gordon tends lovingly. A swing hammock and outdoor hot tub complete their lovely garden.

It's another sunny day in New Zealand and Dorota insists I just 'chill' for my first day. I enjoy the sunshine and watch Lovejoy whizzing from climbing frame to Wendy house, showing me tumbling tricks and her favourite toys. We have a barbecue. The pace is much more relaxed and informal than Andrew and Rona's. The beers flow and so does the food. The Catch's have friends staying overnight, and I find it tiring adjusting to new people again in such a short time. I have a beer, then a wine, to help ease those uncomfortable and strange feelings that change brings. But I know I'm probably in for a headache in the morning, after mixing my drinks. Still, I can't resist the dampening down effects of alcohol.

My room is a sweet little single. Very clean and comfortable (much warmer than my last one) although not as characterful a location! From the safety of my bed, I listen out to all the strange noises of this new house. I hear Gordon and Dorota talking in their bedroom further down the hallway, before I drift off to sleep on my first night in New Brighton.

Sunday The family have a computer in an open plan lounge area that I can use. There's an email from Melanie! Again, it feels comforting to have 'virtual' contact from loved ones. This on-going adjusting to my new environment and trying to find out what's expected of me in my role as mother's-help, is proving a little tiring. Gordon shows me the car (an automatic) which I am not at all sure about using. Well, at least they're on the same side of the road here! (This makes the thought of driving a little easier). Gordon drives me around the local area before pointing out a pushbike in their garage that's also available for me to use. That's more tempting...

The sun is out and soon I'm cycling along, exploring river paths that run up and down the area. Eventually I find one that leads to the sea. Parking up the bike, I have my first encounter with New Brighton Pier.

Sitting in silence for a long while, I simply listen and listen to the sound of the ocean. I make a mental note to visit the cute café called *Salt on the Pier* which sits next to an impressive public library, whose windows look out onto the sea.

Back at the house, I'm slowly getting to grips with household routines and my place within them. Dorota's nervous energy makes it more tiring to adjust and I find it difficult to know what she wants from me. She seems reluctant to say outright what my jobs are and is clearly a little shy. I learn that most of their other home-helps have been Japanese students and a lot younger. I'm guessing she hadn't realised the challenges that employing an older mother's helper might bring. There appears to be a lot of very structured routines set up for Lovejoy to follow, which probably helps Dorota feel more in charge of the parenting game. Lovejoy however, has other ideas! She's a very intelligent little girl, often lost in an imaginary world of toys and dreams with little interest in sticking to boring schedules. She seems to have more of Gordon's laid back temperament than her mum's. I hope that somehow Dorota will begin to relax around me. I work hard to help her feel at ease and non-threatened. It's pretty tiring however, and I seriously wonder if I'll stay here the three weeks I'd originally planned. I have a book with me called *The 7 Spiritual Laws of Success*. I make a commitment to myself to explore one new Law each day of the week.

CHAPTER 17

<u>Monday</u> Lying in my bed I hear the family going about their morning routines. Dorota is bustling about shouting out instructions to Lovejoy, who is amazingly organised for a little girl of 5! Eventually the clang of the electric garage door falling back into its groove signals they have left for the day and the house falls silent around me. After a gentle start and breakfast I complete the few chores that I've been left and take the bike out again. It's a lovely fresh day so I cycle down the river path towards the coast. Parking up the bike, I walk along the pier and feel the gentle morning sun caress my skin.

Later, I explore the library with its comfy chairs, foot stools and headphones that pipe a range of soothing music into my ears while I gaze out through big glass windows onto crashing surf. I sit for hours, watching surfers rise and fall on the waves. This process of slowing down the pace of my life, which feels to have been going ridiculously fast for too many years, is strange but deliciously sweet. Taking time for me, to reflect on what I want for my life, feels so good. Learning how to trust and relax into the rhythm of life.

I walk barefoot on the beach for miles and miles, looking across a horizon of sand dunes. Waves are crashing in. Surfers are riding them. The sun is shining, shining, shining. There's nothing to do and nothing to have to think about. Just a gentle unfolding of each new day, as it unwraps and shapes itself. Delicious! I take a malt beer at a local bar. The locals' make friendly gestures in my direction and move a vacant chair at the bar for me to sit down, but I go outside. This day is too glorious to be inside! I do love the friendly vibe here, though. After the beer, back I go to the awesome library by the beach; back to my comfy chair with its sea-view. Relax. Relax. Read. Read. Munch a few sweets. Is this real? Am I dreaming? Through the panoramic window I watch the waves break and join. Break and join. Hours roll by and suddenly a glance at the clock tells me it's time to cycle home to collect washing off the line and set the table for dinner.

Gentler connections with the family are slowly forming. Dorota seems hungry for relationship and connection. There is kindness, warmth and generosity here. She begins to relax and offers me the freedom to be 'me'. I begin to think about what's next on my trip, after here. It's Christmas in a few weeks' time. Where shall I go for Christmas? I consider catching a bus to a place called Queenstown. The Catch family are enthusiastic. Dorota tells me the story of how they were married in Queenstown and returned later with Lovejoy as a baby and were given the same room at the hotel that they'd had on their honeymoon! Their stories are full of the energy of Queenstown. They fill me with a curiosity and an interest to explore this area. It's looking like it might be Christmas in Queenstown...

I ring Melanie, back in England. It's her birthday yet her voice sounds flat and low in energy. I try not to worry or attach to this. My girls have their own journey now as young adults and need to experience their brilliance away from their mother's shadow – and I away from theirs. *I can still love them and be supportive whilst also meeting my own needs*, I tell myself. I need to believe this now.

The days roll gently along. I ride the bike almost daily. Some days I head one way down the coast and some days I go the other way. Sometimes I park the bike and walk the sands, other times I ride along sand dunes until the sand gets so thick in the wheels, it pulls my bike to a halt and I need to get off and push. The strong aromatic, sweet perfume of wild flowers delights my senses along these rides across the dunes. I watch a paraglider set up his equipment and glide off across the waves, free as a bird. I think about taking a surfing lesson. I buy calendars and postcards to send home and inexpensive things from shops around me. I still find I can't let go of the 'purse strings' and stop 'watching' my money. (Still a work in progress that one.)

I'm reading Deepak Chopra's *7 Spiritual Laws'* daily and reflecting on the spiritual law of each day. Creative ideas are beginning to pop into my head. I start to jot them down in a notebook. I get sick with a tummy bug. Retching up horrible bile as my stomach turns and turns its contents over. The family are kind, buying me flowers to cheer me up and ice lollies to sooth my aching tummy. I feel cared for. Better than at home!

CHAPTER 18

Christmas is coming. There's to be a 'Party in the Park' to celebrate Christmas in a park in Christchurch. Lovejoy, Dorota and I attend. It's strange seeing sunshine alongside dancing Santa's and Christmas trees! There's live music, Christmas lights and fireworks. Thousands of people sit on the ground, eating yuletide picnics, and not a single Christmassy feeling in any part of my being can I find!

I research my next stop Queenstown, and begin to put together the threads of the first stage of my backpacking. It feels good to be doing this by myself. Not a minute of serious home sickness and its two weeks in. I'd expected it, but no, just a feeling of being at home, right here. I drive the automatic car and baby sit for Lovejoy. It's all going as easy as a summer breeze.

Two vivid dreams haunt my sleep one night. I'm back at work. I am informed there are clients to see me. I'm busy and forget they're still waiting. They are angry. I explain honestly that I forgot. Then, I say that I'm afraid to see them in case I can't help. They calm down after this, and I am glad I was honest. Then there's an awful part with aggression, violence, blood and torture. I can't seem to remember now how this fits in to the dream or how it all ended. Then, a second dream…

I'm back at my old marital home but yet it doesn't quite look the same. I am working in the house and a male comes in. Unexpectedly, we kiss. Then suddenly he looks like an ex-boyfriend of mine and yet this seems okay. Everything in the house seems to be breaking down. Roof and pipes are leaking and I try to get a bucket to catch water. The telephone isn't working and when I look around the whole house is shabby and neglected. The man sits down and puts coal on the fire (there hasn't been a coal fire at that house since my eldest child was a baby). I notice him doing this but I'm not worried about him taking control of things, like I used to be. I find another male asleep on the bed, a man I only met once and don't know why he's here. I wake him up and ask him to leave.

I explain to my friend that I didn't invite this man and he accepts this. I'm not dressed very well but I don't seem too concern. I don't know why he's come, but I sense that I must leave this house and go with him; rather than begin to put my energy into renovating it. The dream ends. It's a vivid and strange one. I'm not sure what it means...

I book my journey to Queenstown for the Christmas period and once again it all happens with ease. Two backpacker lodges booked, and one bus journey with The Naked Bus Co. All the options I wish for are available. Soon, my backpacking first stopover is all in place. Leave Christchurch 10a.m. on 20th Dec. (Bus stop is opposite the Holy Grail Sports Bar). Ticket cost $27. Arrive Queenstown 6.30p.m. Stay 20-23 Dec. at *Southern Laughter Lodge* in 4-bed self-contained unit with balcony and kitchen for $23 a night. On 24th Dec. move to *Deco Backpackers* until 27th Dec for $24 a night. Second hostel has view of lake.

CHAPTER 19

I'm driving! I'm on a trial run into Christchurch, getting used to this automatic gear stuff so I can drive Lovejoy to her school Christmas play. I get a bit lost and confused on the American style crisscross roads but it doesn't seem to faze me, (getting lost) like it used to. No fear – just logic and a bit of faith. *Check the map, girl. Keep calm. Ask the Universe for a little help.* I stay on at the school to watch Lovejoy in her play and it's amazing. The story of how a little Paua shell finds her inner beauty after believing she was plain and ugly. The songs, the energy and the costumes are brilliant. The theme of the show moves me to tears as I feel the Universe speaking to me of the need to search for my own inner beauty. To let go of all the conditioned thoughts that physical ageing creates (around still being attractive) - which I see 'played out' in my own thoughts.

The next day I'm driving again and the automatic car is getting easier and fun! The day after, I'm back on the beach relaxing in the sun. I'm watching seagulls dip and soar, dip and soar in timeless wonder, when all of a sudden the sound of a text coming in on my mobile phone jolts me back into the real world. I stare at my phone. I don't recognise the number straight away and it's quite a shock when I realise that it's from an ex-boyfriend.

There's been four exes' now since my divorce seven years ago, but this was the guy I was most in love with. He felt the same, but ironically, the intensity of our love seemed to trigger an inner insecurity in him, that brought forth such emotionally destructive and controlling behaviours; that I could neither understand nor deal with. This relationship took me a long time to 'get over.' Its damage to my belief and trust in love had gone deep.

Carl's text informs me of the success of his holistic healing project and thanks me for past support with ideas around its initial development. (It's about one and half years now, since our last meeting or contact) Strangely (or not) I'd only been reflecting a few hours previously on past relationships and musing over how long it had been since my relationship with Carl had ended. Had I drawn him to me through the Law of Attraction, I ask myself?

It's a pretty awesome coincidence...

The Universe has given me a set of Anthony Robbins tapes to learn from (found hidden on a book shelf in my bedroom). I listen to them when the family are out. The biggest insight today is that I'm not really open to experience relationships because I have 'loaded' the pain aspect of them greater than the 'pleasure' aspect in my mind – due to memories triggered by past experiences. Ouch! There's definitely work to do there, I feel.

I cook a meal for the family tonight. It's fun and I buy a bottle of wine to toast 'new beginnings,' as today Gordon and Dorota have sold the family business; but are not sure what next? It's such a sweet balmy evening that I decide to take the bike out and soon I'm cycling along a river path, past teams of punters gliding gently along. Their coaches shout words of instruction and encouragement, as punts are driven deep into the water, in time with each other. This gentle rhythm and call is soothing to the mind, and I relax even further into my little world of 'no time.'

Strolling along the beach I come across a sand artist sketching on a sandy canvas. People throw money down from the pier onto his jacket in appreciation of his creative gift. On the beach there's hardly a soul around. I walk from North to South with an ever increasing pace, my mind becoming more and more restless; due to the unsettling effect that Carl's text has had. I converse with the Universe. I accept responsibility for any way I've been sabotaging relationships or attracting unavailable males in one way or another. I begin to see more clearly how I've acted from fear of pain, on many past occasions in relationships and attracted men who did the same (as a mirror of my own issue). I verbalise this out loud, but my words are masked by the boom of the ocean and carried away on strong winds. I give over any need to protect myself from fear of pain, as I acknowledge this transition. And then, I just walk and walk. A few tears come up, and there is a feeling of intense communion with God. I recognise my state of loneliness as a type of self-protection, and that a part of me has come to accept it, as a necessary protection, against pain and loss. I reflect again on my relationship with Carl and ask myself, *am I still in love with him?* I search deep within, for the answer. It comes back, *No, I don't think I am...*

CHAPTER 20

The next day is an adventure day. I'm off to Akaroa, a French settlement town on the other side of the island. Dorota and Lovejoy drop me off in Christchurch on their way to school and work, and I catch a tour bus from the city square. It's a lovely drive to Akaroa and the day starts sweet and warm. The mountain route is stunning and I take lots of pictures. We stop on the way first, at a rugged, shingle beach and later at a sleepy hillside outpost for drinks, pees and ice cream. This is my first real trip out (alone) since I've been here and it feels a bit strange.

In Akaroa I eat blue cod, chips and peas. I buy a local map and hike up to an original settler's cemetery: nestled out in the bush. Sitting in the sun, I reflect on those brave pioneers who came to this faraway place, to make a new life for themselves. Their spirits are definitely around these cemetery grounds. I feel their presence. Later, I sit in the sun drinking beer at a harbour front bar, soaking in its sweet seaside view.

On the way back there's a short stop at a cheese farm that allows me to treat myself to a nutty flavoured local cheese. In Akaroa I reflected (once again) on my limiting attitude to spending money. I wish I could become more relaxed and not check prices so closely. I try to make a shift by not buying the cheapest cheese (as I would have done). Oh well, it's a start... In the seat next to me is a young American girl, she chats away, about her own travels and adventures. Like many of the young, she's interested in the extreme sport aspect of New Zealand and ticking *done it* boxes (in her virtual travel log) as she goes.

<u>The next day</u> I'm whizzing along bike tracks amongst sand dunes with the wind in my face and the smell of wild lupines that grow abundantly and intermittently along these coastal paths. Bathing my senses in a melody of sound, smell and feelings, I hear the surf crashing and see it glisten as my bike rises and falls along the track. Occasionally I dismount; when sand blows into such solid heaps, it masks the grit that lines the track and clogs up the wheels. Breathless, I fall on top of a nearby dune; I can pedal no more! A wind gently blows through the tall Egyptian grasses. Silence envelopes me and the only sound is that of my pounding heart. I watch a seagull rise and fall. Down he goes, then high, high up above the sea. Again and again, I watch his dance of altitudes. At first I think he's fishing but on closer examination I see that as he reaches full flight, he

releases something from his beak. Then, he follows it down as it cascades onto the beach, before swooping to retrieve it again. Time after time he repeats this process. I finally realise that some poor scallop or mussel is having its head bashed open in this torturous dance of nature!

As I cycle home, a tiny flock of grey, fairy fluff cygnets huddle close by the river bank; under the safety of their mother's wing. Brand new and puffed up, like little coconut snowballs! A small water creature scurries across my path, in front of the moving bike as he dashes towards the water's edge. A boat full of punters glides swiftly and effortlessly past as the sun lights up their path on the glistening water. The (now familiar) dull and rhythmical sound of the coach calls out from his bicycle on the other side of the river. The punts cut their way through the water with such harmonious movements, in the sweet evening sun. How I love this place!

CHAPTER 21

The next day I'm coursing along the coastline on my bike again. How far can I go? On and on, mile after mile I travel. Lost in thought and not looking where I'm going, I suddenly run into the bumper of a parked car and the impact is so great it jolts me off the bike, causing sharp pains in my knee. I'm in shock! I look around and take a quick glance at the car; an older type. Have I damaged it? Oh my God what do I do? Fear grips me and I cycle hurriedly away. Travelling further and further from the 'scene of the crime', a nagging voice inside says that I must go back to the house and tell the owner of the car what's happened. Another voice says, *No! Embarrassment!* What to say and the question of what if it costs me something to repair? (Fear of lack, fear of lack, you are back!). I carry on cycling and try to get the 'go back' feeling to go away. But it won't. The overriding feeling is still, turn back. Be honest and take responsibility for what happened. So I turn around. Half reluctant, not knowing what on earth I'm going to say as I knock on that door.

Back I go, my leg bleeding and swollen now. I look for the road it happened on and the actual car. I'm half wanting to abandon this scary idea, when eventually, I locate the road. Yes, this is the one. I take a deep breath and peer down to where the car was parked. It's gone! I'm surprised. I turn back and go on my way, but with a 'knowing' now that I definitely would have gone to the house and spoke to the owner – even though it would have been hard to do.

Maybe it was enough for the Universe to know that I had the intention to be open and honest and take the consequences, whatever the cost? Well, I may have been let off that part of the lesson, but I'm left with a very angry looking, black and swollen knee for the next few days, as a reminder of this lesson!

December 10<u>th</u> Now I'm well and truly alone in this strange and wonderful land – in a human sense anyway! This morning I took the Catch family to the airport to catch a plane to their Australian holiday. My job, for the next week, is to house-sit their home, garden and cat. It feels strange arriving back at the empty house and a new, restless phase begins. I phone my sister Janet with the need to hear a familiar voice, but her voice sounds tired and a bit fed up. We chat for a while but even though its weeks since we've spoken, the conversation turns to the same old stuff. My sister doesn't seem to be able to catch my enthusiasm about my trip. Perhaps she can't comprehend it? I can sort of understand that feeling...

I'm sat in the sun reading, and recognising that I still have things I want to change. Out shopping in the afternoon, I try again, to let go of the 'purse strings' a little. The old familiar fear of lack keeps coming up. Or is it the: *'I'm not worth expensive things'* programme? I really don't know, but the resistance is still there for sure – as whenever I purchase something, I catch my mind busy working out the exchange rate to find out if it's a good deal! Oh dear! I'm also becoming aware that I've let a lot of things go in these last few years, since that failed relationship with Carl. One of these is my appearance. Many of my possessions need discarding, jazzing up or replacing. Like a good quality pair of high UVB protection sunglasses for starters – definitely essential, here! (Not the cheap kind like I have).

I start to think how nice it would be to have some classy clothes, makeup and accessories. Perhaps a set of pretty underwear? I did buy a fairly nice bra today (but still, more practical than pretty). And I got a blouse that will be good for work, so that's a token gesture towards the *New Me* project! I muse on my desire to have a smarter image. My hair is now informing me that it wants a new style. Yet another thing I've sort of stopped bothering with. And my diet could definitely do with getting rid of the junk food in it! I conclude that I need a complete make-over – not just the outside me, but the inside too!

The onset of middle years is such a challenge! Still single, I realise its harder now for me to look in the mirror at the droopy bits, the missing bits, the grey bits, and still think I'm attractive. A song plays over the car radio on my way home from the mall, it breaks into my negative thinking to remind me, *'Everybody's beautiful, in their own way'*. Thanks for that Universe!

By evening, I'm tired and a very strange feeling comes over me about being in the house alone. At first I try to push it out. Then decide that I'll just allow myself to feel it. It's okay. It will start to settle down and feel easier as I adjust to being in the house, alone. Then I remind myself that I'm not alone. That the Universe is caring for me, I know it is. It gives me signs all the time...

I've bought fresh green giant mussels today and so I busy myself cooking them, in a touch of garlic. Wow! They're big beasts, but so tasty! I sleep well and awake to another brand new day, feeling a little more settled in my aloneness. Actually, I have Sushi the family cat for company too, and she does try to talk to me, I'm sure! When I'm meditating, early in the morning, she comes to lie on my bed. I think of dear little Peaches my daughter's cat who lived with us back home and how I didn't really get to say goodbye, before he went on his own 'holiday'. These thoughts bring up sadness. I miss him.

CHAPTER 22

Sitting in the garden on the swing hammock, listening to a melody of wind chimes tinkling gently in the breeze, I feel the searing heat of mid-day sun. I'm so relaxed. I realise that I am now moving into a new phase of life; learning about my gifts and my life purpose. Things are getting clearer. Insights are happening daily. I begin to devise a daily plan for health and wellbeing and put my focus on what to include. I decide I want to smile more!!

By day two on my own, I feel fully relaxed and okay with it. I take a bus into the City and enjoy wandering around, watching street entertainers and enjoying Starbucks coffee and sunshine. Timelessly, I meander through craft markets and into a botanical garden to sit by the river. It feels great, not needing to watch the time or be back for a fixed time.

I let myself flow with whatever I feel like doing, and make a conscious effort not to check the time at all. Wandering slowly back to the bus station, one of the living statue street artists catches my eye. It's a blistering hot day and he's dressed in a full 'cracked' purple suit and top hat.. From time to time he touches up his melting make up and repairs its rapid erosion from perspiration. He is playfulness in motion, switching between sudden movement and total stillness. From time to time he pulls sweets from a pocket – to entice passing kids to stop. Then, suddenly he jerks into serious facial expressions and dynamic action postures for a bunch of Japanese tourists that stop to take a picture. The crowd laugh. I laugh. It feels good to laugh. Today has been full of smiles, laughter and sunshine. Life is very good. I place a paper note in his money box (resisting the second thought to give only a coin) and he acknowledges it with a jerky bow of the hat. We smile at each other. I walk slowly away, almost reluctant for the day to end. But evening is coming and it's time to head home.

Later, I decide to make a long distance call to my favourite and sweetest old lady friend, Pat. She is in a rehabilitation home recovering from a broken hip. It is early morning in the UK and Pat is both surprised and delighted to hear my voice. We chat for a while, but she's so shocked to be having a conversation with me, she can't think of anything to say! I send love and encouragement for her to get well. I have the opportunity to make cheap calls this weekend, (the Catch's told me about this before they left) some sort of NZ phone company Christmas special. Frustratingly, neither of my daughters can get their act together to be near a landline at a time frame that works for us to be awake, in both countries!

I consider phoning a friend or two, but on reflection, I decide not to. It's all good. Tired and happy I hit the sack.

CHAPTER 23

Another new day begins with another gentle start spent reading, pottering around and sitting in the garden. How I love these mellow, no agenda stress free days. Days like this grow themselves as I find a certain idea or mood settles and then I make my decision, as to what I feel like doing – much more fun than forward planning! After lunch I decide to cycle to the local QE2 Olympic stadium pool to do indoor swimming. The pool is still sectioned off into the lanes that were designed for its original use as an Olympic pool. I enjoy an hour or so of lane swimming and try to sense how this place would have been, full of competitors and spectators from around the world. As well as the competitor pools there's a fun pool with waves, flumes and rapids. I spend time hanging out in this part of the complex too, soaking in the fun. Loads of kids are bouncing around enjoying themselves and I join in by riding flumes in a rubber ring, around circular little whirlpools.

After coffee in the café, I decided to cycle home via the coastline route to watch the surfers. A surfing class is taking place, and an instructor calls out her instructions across the noise of the surf, underneath the strong afternoon sun. I muse over a question that's come up: *Would I like to take a surfing lesson?* Hmm. Good question.

I can't find the answer right now, so I shelve it. Hours roll by and the calming influence of the sea becomes a meditation of the mind itself. My senses rest as sun soaks its healing balm into my skin.

<u>The next day</u> I awake, still undecided about the surfing lesson. It's clear that I have an interest in trying it, but I'm now thinking about the effect it may have on an old knee injury I still have; which has already given me a couple of warning twinges since my arrival in NZ. Although it's true, I've made good recovery through intensive physio a year ago, my knee still reminds me occasionally of its limitations.

In recent years I've tried to listen to my body or ignore it at my peril! Now, I consider the possibility that a further injury may occur if my knee gets into an awkward position when surfing, and the potential impact this could have on other activities I want to do on this trip. Along with this, I remind myself that I'm not travelling with anyone to look after me, if I get hurt. I try to 'weigh up' how much I want a surf lesson. I'm still not sure, so decide to defer the decision until I really 'know'.

In past times, when I wasn't sure on a decision, I've wasted a lot of energy turning it over and over in my mind, worrying it to death! Putting pressure on myself, with the belief that I need to know and know immediately. Now I find myself being much easier and gentle with it; giving time and space for the right answer to unfold, when the time's right.

CHAPTER 24

The UVA indicator today is 11+ (the highest level!) I change my idea about going to the beach and decide to drive into Christchurch and go to the cinema instead. It's a blistering hot afternoon and I sweat profusely trying to find the place, after parking my car two blocks from where I estimate it to be. I choose the movie *Once*. The film is so very sweet and tender, a gentle love story but with such a sad ending. I emerge into brilliant sunshine one hundred minutes later and head straight to a coffee bar to contemplate its message.

As I sip my chai latté, a piano plays softly in the background. Suddenly I'm moved to tears. It connects me to the piano in the film and its story of two talented young musicians who meet as buskers on the street. Both are fresh out of failed relationships, but still carrying old emotional wounds. The girl is direct and open. No pretentious chat up lines for her. She says what she feels and doesn't fear the man's reaction. He finds this attractive. They slip into a friendship and begin to make music together with ease, little complication or effort. Their lives come together for a short while and it is good. But neither of them are over their ex's and the girl decides to return to her 'other'. The guy gifts a piano, as his goodbye present to her, and the film ends. It's a simple yet powerfully moving tale.

33

I muse on it, over the sweetness of my tea, and find I'm unsure of the film's main message. A few thoughts come up:

1 Just be yourself. Be authentic. Speak your truth

2 Will someone special come into my life, for just a short while, too?

3 Was it speaking of Carl and I getting back together again? The answer inside feels *No*.

I drive home and the air is intensely muggy and warm. I eat, and get my bike out with the idea of a little exercise before bed. The path is beautifully draped in dappled evening sunlight. I've not travelled it at this late time of day before, but the river is still full of rowing teams, and we overtake and pass each other, as they move up and down the water.. Tall bamboo grass majestically bows their greetings to me. Soft mountain ranges adorn the horizon, with dark hues of evening shadows falling across mellow peaks and falls.

It's heavenly here! I feel so blessed. So relaxed, and so at peace with myself. I decide to cycle along the dunes from south to north – just for a change. Two streets away from the ocean, I can already hear its boom, masked from my view but not my ears. I listen joyously, as I imagine its pounding surf and energy. Then suddenly, my view of the beach opens up, and to my utter amazement, and despite the lateness of the day – the beach is littered with people! Some are walking, some sitting, others are surfing or fishing from the peer. This unexpected sight is magical!

There's a haze across the coastline that I can't make out if it's spray or heat. I watch as it spread from one side of the land to the other and leaves an opening; a perfect clearing without any haze at all. I park my bike and step onto the beach captured by the energy of all the evening people. The beach is pulsing and vibrant. *The Salt of the Sea* roof café is alive with people, eating, drinking and chatting as they soak in the delicious view. I look back, and drink in a vista of mountains, a smattering of houses and more mountains, another smattering of houses then yet more mountains! Sweeping stretches of clouds; enormous and billowing, intense blue skies.

I walk out onto the pier and it feels like I'm down with the surfers. Deep in the water, out amongst the high waves I ride alongside them. I feel their energy in flight as they bounce and skim the milky surf. Jumping smaller waves and ducking larger ones, they skilfully anticipate the breaking surf. I see the enormous and powerful waves, not from the front (as viewed from the beach) but from both sides and behind, as they break and roll into the shore. A truly different sight altogether! Rolling and curling. Yes, curling (like butter curls made by a metal curler) they coil in beautiful ornate circles. I'm captivated, with a feeling of such blessedness that I'm in such a place of peace and beauty. I so like it here! I imagine owning one of the quaint little wooden seaside batches with verandas. I imagine the energy that could be in such a seaside home.

Even though it's very late, the 'evening people' linger on. Reluctant as I am to step out of the magic that's here. It feels like a story book adventure I'm in. Like nothing I've experienced before. Cycling slowly back, I watch the sun disappearing out of the sky as dusky clouds of night roll in. I love this ride. It brings me so much pleasure.

Once more I find the feeling of being blessed. *Know what gives you pleasure...* That's it! I thank God and the Universe for the beauty, majesty and joy of hills and sea, and life itself.

CHAPTER 25

The next day is a wet start. I'm considering driving out to a place called Hamner Springs for the day. I take a slow start to reflect on whether this feels a good idea. *Feel it out. Take your time, Lynette, don't rush, you'll know when you know. Maybe it would be a better idea to go tomorrow instead, when the weather might be better?* I meditate and visualise an amazing day then decide to pack up a lunch and *'just do it!'* It rains for almost the entire one and half hour drive. Slowly, the scenery changes from flat green plains to gentle undulations, to dramatic mountain ranges topped with peaks of snow. For miles and miles there's nothing but God's beautiful hills and sky. The energy of this area is inspiring and my spirits are high. I'm pleased with myself for being brave enough to take this long drive to an unknown place, alone. There's no trace of the *fear* or *worry monsters* today! I find Hamner with little effort, park up and buy a map that will take me on a walk up Conisen Hill.

The air is humid, but the rain has stopped and my walk zigzags its way pleasantly up a hill and through forest pines. I resist stopping at a few seating areas on the way up, as the view isn't high enough for me. Once at the top, a six point look out boasts it's amazing panoramic views; right across the Canterbury Basin. This is what I want as a view! Well worth the wait. My sandwiches come out and a very welcome lunch break is had. It's only then that I discover I've left my camera in the car! *Oh well, does it really matter? Why worry? It's done. I left it. Let it go. It really doesn't matter.* Small things fall away so easily these days. And, I'm being much kinder to myself; rather than beating myself up.

Lunch over; I walk back via a detour across Mujabi Walk. The path winds slowly down through forest lowlands towards the village. Past wetlands and newly planted shoots I go, enjoying this new adventure. The fragrant smell of pine is very pleasant. The walk seems to wander away from the village, and so I decide to take my own route; chosen more from instinct than anything else. At first it appears I'm getting more and more lost and I can't make sense at all of where I am on my little map. Eventually after what seems like ages, I come out of the forest area and see a road ahead. It's a huge relief if I'm honest! I check the map again to try and find my location. Not sure… I never was much of a map reader (always left it to the guy). Again, using a bit of logic combined with instinct, I head in the direction I sense is right.

As houses and streets start to come into view I feel more reassured and then it begins to look like Hamner. Turning the next corner, I find a café with people sat out, enjoying refreshments and think, *yes, this is right*. As I walk (wearily now) towards an outdoor seating area, a woman's face comes sharply into focus and looks vaguely familiar. One second later, we both fix on each other with a quizzical look and she says, "Its Lynette isn't it?" My goodness! It's Jill a fellow charity trustee from back home. Jill had told me she planned to come to New Zealand for a few weeks before Christmas (back in July) and had suggested we pre-arrange a meet up, but I'd resisted. Instead I'd commented that, "If it's meant to be that we meet, it will happen, wherever, whenever." And here we are. My goodness! The amazing synchronicity of the Law of Attraction is at work again!

Those unintentional wrong turns at the end of my walk have brought me to this street; one I wouldn't have walked down if I'd taken my original route back down the hills. I marvel at the synchronicity of the Universe; connecting us in time and place. It's truly amazing. Furthermore so, when I recall that I chose to come today and not tomorrow as I'd briefly considered. We chat for a while and drink coffee. It's raining now, but by the time I'm rested and ready to leave, the rain has stopped again – almost to order. Jill and I say goodbye and I move on to spend the next hour in heavenly relaxation at Hammer's Thermal Spa; nestling amongst the tall lush pine trees, complete with stunning mountain views. As I soak in a 34% sulphur and mineral pool, I feel pretty chilled out and blissful. Lying back on the water, a guy smiles across and I smile back. My energy is soft and open. I guess it's attractive...

After dressing I check out the little café bar and decide on pumpkin soup, chunky bread and a glass of chardonnay wine before starting out on the drive home. It begins to rain hard again and continues most of the way back. I get a nagging headache and think it's the alcohol; as I've not had any (nor felt the desire to) for the last 5 days. Once back I take a Jacuzzi bath as a pleasurable end to a perfect day, before sleeping soundly.

CHAPTER 26

I'm so glad I went to Hamner yesterday as today it rained and rained and rained! I have a slow start to my morning with a few cups of nicely ground coffee; taken in bed. I read the newspaper that a paper boy throws into our garden, wrapped tightly in a plastic roll each morning. I spend the day in a slow laid back way, getting things ready for my departure, next week. I email and copy up notes made from all the ideas and creativity that have been coming up. I do a little more personal development work on values and beliefs and then drive out to the shopping mall to buy makeup. I'm creating a new look for myself. A smarter, stylish look and I think by the time I return, I'll have all the ideas in place for it! I keep getting 'nuggets' from magazines and making a note of them.

I check out a couple of hairdressers in the area and plan to get a new hair style. Later in the day I find my hairdresser's. It's a cute little wooden salon painted sailor blue, near the sand dunes at South New Brighton. It's called *Ocean Blades*. The appointment is booked for Tuesday at 11a.m. After lunch at *The Salt on the Pier*, I cycle around the estuary of Heathcote and Avon and almost out to Redcliff's! It's a great feeling seeing how far I can go on my bike. Trying to decide which forest track or river path to choose that will take me on a new route – towards no-where in particular.

The days are whizzing by now and I'm more than ready to begin the next stage of my adventure. I start packing and research various areas. Today I'm thinking about what might be different when I backpack, instead of being in the same place. After checking my bank account online I'm surprised (and a little shocked) to see that less amount has been credited from my final wage than I had hoped. The old fear of lack begins to creep up, but then I catch it and let it go. It will be fine. Just let go and trust.

There's an article in the newspaper about Oxfam and a new way of giving. I decide to give my girls their Xmas presents in this way. To give something practical, like a cow or supply of drinking water, to those less fortunate. I want to change the focus of fear of lack to abundance and gratitude as I enter a no-wage phase of my trip. My last salary has now been paid, so no more income from that source. I give thanks for my money, my blessings and my freedom.

<u>16th December</u> A beautiful sunny day! I drive into Christchurch and take a walk around the Botanical Gardens and Arts Centre. There are not many people out simply enjoying themselves today, like me. It's too near Christmas, I guess. Most of them are busy shopping, just like I normally am at this time of the year, but not this year! It's time to say goodbye to dear old Christchurch. I have loved living in your suburbs and visiting your magical centre but now it's time for me to go. I suddenly realise I won't be in the City centre again until I catch the bus to Queenstown.

<u>18th December</u> Today I have my hair cut – back to a style similar to one I used to have years ago. The stylist takes her time and cuts skilfully, using a razor. The young girl who blow-dries it, tells me she's the hairdresser's daughter and that she's 19. When I tell her I have a daughter her age, she says, "Gosh! You must have been young when you had her."

'No," I reply, "28." She informs me that I don't look 47 (when I tell her my age) "More like 40!" That was a nice mid-life boost I must say. Thank you, Universe.

It rains all morning and the sky is pretty dull. I settle down to watch *Free Willy 2* on TV. It's such a moving story, it makes me cry. After lunch I check emails. A few days ago I placed a message on a website's notice board, that's mainly for travellers looking for work, or other travellers to hook up and travel with. I wrote: *If anyone is in Queenstown over the Christmas week and wants to meet up for walking or maybe white-water rafting. I'll be staying in the area and interested to meet up with likeminded travellers.*

So now, in my inbox is a response from a guy called Ian. It tells me he's just back from Chile and in Nelson at the moment but heading back to his cabin on the Shotover River above Queenstown, where he mines for gold! He's suggesting we meet up for coffee in Queenstown and tells me there are great hiking paths where he lives. He invites me to stay a few days and says it *would be nice to have some company over Christmas.* (!) To tell you the truth I was expecting to hear from fellow travellers staying in backpackers hostels around the area, not locals! And yet, this unusual offer does sound rather intriguing – if not a little crazy. And, (also) I *have* made a promise to myself to be open to explore whatever the Universe sends my way...

I type a response that suggests we exchange phone numbers and that I'll be in touch when I arrive. Ian replies again. This time, offering me a lift down to Queenstown from Christchurch; as he says it's on his way, back from Nelson. Tempting... But I decide to take the bus down, to reflect a little more on this most unusual invitation.

So Lynette... Be careful what you ask for...

I remind myself this, as a few weeks ago I'd sent out a request to the Universe to have some company for over Christmas, and had also been repeating the affirmation: *I am meeting some amazing new friends in Queenstown.*

CHAPTER 27

19th December. Yesterday I collected the Catch family from their night flight back from Australia, and relinquish my house-sitting role. I have left little gifts (from England) under the Christmas tree as tokens of my thanks for their kindness during my stay. Early this morning Dorota drops me off outside The Holy Grail Café, (very appropriate!) at my bus stop. I join a growing number of travellers and backpackers that are beginning to gather, with different shapes and sizes of luggage. In varying degrees of anxiousness, joviality and impatience we await our buses. It feels exciting. It feels fun. It feels so right to be here, at this next stage of my adventure, setting off into the unknown. Awesome!!

I'm relaxed and feeling great. A reassuring presence is calming the 'mind chatter' in my head that would (in the past) have become anxious by now, about getting on the right bus, about being on my own; and generally anticipating a whole range of problems that could appear. My bus is here and it's goodbye dear Christchurch. As I watch the city outline disappear from the window, I send out a wave of gratitude. How I have enjoyed your gentle creative energy and sweetness. I reflect on a few new things I've experienced here. Pineapple lumps (yummy) Chai latté, liquorice tea, sushi, hungi and hoki.

Our long journey down to Queenstown is a scenic feast of stunning lakes, turquoise waters, snow-capped mountains and fields of wild lupines. Such a profusion of colour is a banquet to my spirit, indeed! We stop for lunch by Lake Tekapo and the tip of Mount Cooke peeps at me through clouds in the distance. The bus driver informs his cargo that Cooke's peak is the highest point on this side of the world; he then pulls the bus over to take a rest stop. The miracle of nature is all around and I can hardly spare time to eat, for wanting to capture the beauty of this place on camera. This aim seems equally shared with another traveller, Mark, who tells me he's a photographer from Lancashire.

Together we make our way through a sea of pink, yellow and blue lupines, trying to get as near to the presence of Mount Cook as we can. Mark takes a shot of me alongside Lake Tekapo walking through lupines and promises to email it. He and I enjoy gentle conversations throughout the rest of the journey. As we draw nearer to Queenstown I watch, as a more nervous side comes out in him. Mark dithers and stutters on his cell phone; as he tries to make a decision over accommodation when discovering the hostel he's booked at is further out of town than he thought. As our bus pulls into Mark's hostel, we exchange phone numbers and he says maybe we'll get together for a beer? He's a nice guy but I don't get a sense of strong energy, so I know already that I'm not really bothered if we do or we don't.

It looks like my hostel stop is the last one; as there's no one left on the bus now. I sit up front, getting ready for my stop and fall into conversation with the friendly driver, Steve. He offers to show me where to buy food at non-tourist prices and even stops off there, before my hostel, so I can get some food in. We both pop into *Alpine Stores* and arrange to meet outside 20 minutes later. Steve is waiting and grins as he hands me half a roast chicken that he's bought. When I protest he insists, saying that it's way too much for him to eat himself. Steve's final act of kindness is to drop me off right outside the hostel door – so I walk straight into the reception, with my heavy bag. Such a luxury!

Once more it's thank you Universe! I'm well cared for, I feel it strongly. It's like I'm wrapped in a blanket of inner knowing that I'll be guided and helped, during this next period of travelling, alone.

CHAPTER 28

I heave my holdall and backpack up to the front desk and check-in to *Southern Laughter BBH* (Budget Backpackers Hostel) in Queenstown. I quickly discover that Southern Laughter is a chilled out place. My gratitude continues when I find that the four bedded dorm I'm booked into has only me in tonight, as the other three arrive tomorrow. So I get a chance to unwind, relax and adjust to my new surroundings in a slow gentle way; without having new people to adjust to as well. This is such a gift. I say a silent thank you for it. Looking around my new 'home' I see that the sleeping room is quite small and I wonder how on earth I'll get used to sharing such a small space with three other people! Oh well, all part of the experience I guess.

I relax and decide to go out and take a look at the view of Queenstown's famous mountain range called The Remarkables. With their snow-capped tops in the distance, I conclude they sure are remarkable!! As I walk around in the balmy evening air I get my first taste of Queenstown, home of bungee jumping and extreme sports. The town seems full of bars, eating places and lots of young people. It all feels very modern and extremely commercialised, with loads of trendy fashion shops and Internet cafés. Hmm.. Not quite what I'd imagined. I wonder how Christmas will be in a place like this. Still, I remind myself that my hostel is nice and that it's set back from the noise and hub of the main town.

I sleep well that first night, and during the next day a variety of texts come in from Ian, who's still keen to meet for coffee. Half excited, half unsure (well more than half unsure if I'm honest!) I try to think what to do. My mind starts a chain of worry thoughts, *Will he'll be young? Will he expect me to be? What are his real motives?* Of course I have no idea, so I decide to suspend any judgement or expectations and just be open to meet him and see.

<u>Friday 21st December</u> Well what an extraordinary day! The day I meet Ian Leadley a gold miner who lives in the mountains. We meet up outside a coffee shop on the river front, shake hands quite formally and very soon we've passed the initial awkward stage and are chatting with ease. He's about 50, I guess. Over 6ft tall, fit and tanned. Deeply weathered strong features, and dressed in shorts, a navy t-shirt and wearing enormous tan coloured rigger boots.

Ian Leadley is a most unusual man…

I'm engaging all my senses as I talk and listen to try and get a real feel for him and see if I can pick up any uneasy vibes (but I'm not getting any). He tells me lots of stuff about himself and asks about me. Surprisingly, we discover many threads and themes of conversation that interest us both. Interspersed between mutually interesting topics he tells me more about his 'alternative' lifestyle, in an off the grid wood cabin, in the hills. Ian speaks about the way he makes his living, mining for gold in the summer and shooting possums for fur, throughout the winter. I hear of his joy of living off the land and the simple life he's created. It sounds a fascinating world, far beyond what my imagination can comprehend and very attractive. Ian is inviting me to be his guest for a few days over Christmas, to see his world. It's such an off- the-card invite! So I share honestly with him about my difficulties around making my decision.

Before we say goodbye, Ian invites me to ride with him on Sunday, to a town called Alexandra (an hour and a half's drive away) where he'll collect iron from a friend. That way, he suggests, I can hang out with him for a while before making my mind up whether to go back with him ,at the end of the day or not. It's all so sudden, but pretty obvious that Ian's not going to be popping back and forth into Queenstown (a two hour journey) to keep meeting up – for me to get to know him gradually. Christmas is but a few days away, and it looks like I'm going to have to make my decision, in a short amount of time. I feel a bit panicky.

CHAPTER 29

Stalling for time, I thank Ian for his kind invite and say that I will have to think about it and will text him, if I decide to come to Alexandra. This way, he'll know whether to divert into Queenstown first to pick me up or not. Ian's energy is relaxed and open as I speak of my indecision. There feels no pressure at all from him either way, just a simple invitation that he seems happy to extend and that he's fine with whatever I decide. We shake hands again, smile at each other and say goodbye. Then he disappears into the crowd, taking long purposeful strides with his large muscular legs. In a bit of a daze, at this almost storybook event I try to gather my thoughts on what I've learnt, so far about this rather unusual, but seemingly gentle giant:

1   Says he originates from Nelson and still has family and friends there

2   Has grown up sons

3   He's a man who lives close to nature

4   Says he uses his senses and gut feelings to guide his decision making

5   Reads a lot. Current book *The Secret*! Talks of the importance of personal responsibility.

6   Has similar ideas and beliefs around the Law of Attraction. (All in all seems a spiritual guy)

7   Says he hardly ever drinks

8   Has a cabin with no electric power to and lives a self-sufficient life

9   Hunts wild goats for him and his dog to eat (their main source of meat)

10   Keeps a diary and likes to end each day with the affirmation *It's all good*

11   Says he's learnt more about himself since living alone – but sometimes wonders what on earth he's doing up there!

12   Says he sometimes misses having someone to talk to. Had a girlfriend who used to live with him.

13   His cabin is a two hour drive from Queenstown

I spend most of the afternoon alone trying to collate and mull over all this information and decide what to do with my extraordinary invitation!

CHAPTER 30

That afternoon I walk in blistering heat up to The Gondola, an oriental feature high above the town. It's a hard walk through forest pines and over dirt tracks. Sitting for a long while, I ponder my decision as I look out onto an amazing view. I listen to the distant wail of bungee jumpers falling to their chosen fate and take in the deep rich colours of The Remarkables. I'm also thinking what to do about another idea I have, of booking a 'white-water rafting experience'; as a Christmas present to myself...

That decision comes easier. I decide I'll go straight away and book it for tomorrow; whilst I still have the courage! I'm pleased I've made a decision about something but what to do about the other decision? It still lays undecided, like a heavy unsolvable weight in my mind. Walking back down, in the late afternoon heat I listen to a fierce inner debate, that's taking place in my head. One voice says, *you must be completely mad to be even considering going up into the mountains with a stranger, hillbilly miner!! He lives two hours from civilisation and has no communication up there, either!* Danger! Danger! Danger, it wants to say. The opposition in this debate reminds me, *You're supposed to be open to experience what the Universe brings and then you did ask for some amazing new friends for your stay in Queenstown, I mean, how much more amazing do you want them to be?*

I'm also reminded of the fact that whilst using my senses and intuition I didn't pick up any negative vibes from Ian, and that I was given lots of (un-prompted) clues and information about his spirituality. I was even given the link of *The Secret*. I mean, come on! How many gold miners read stuff like that? There's a lot to indicate that this could be an amazing experience. And what a truly alternative way to spend Christmas!! Even so, it would take a massive leap of faith and trust in the Universe for me to say yes, to this offer...

Still turning all this over, I return (much later) to the backpackers lodge. My three roommates have arrived and it looks like my first dormitory experience is to be a mixed sex one! There's two young guys in their 20s from Lancaster sat chatting in the lounge area. They seem friendly. We say hi. And then, there's Fiona...

Well, thank goodness for Fiona!

Fiona Jake is 31, also travelling alone and English, too. I'm surprised to hear Fiona is a C.I.D Inspector, but we hit it off straight away. Fiona is

43

bubbly with a positive, down to earth energy. She's single, never married. We share our stories well into the evening, giving each other our 'potted' life history. That evening, after thinking through all the issues around *the decision*, (and almost giving myself a migraine in the process) I share my unusual invitation with Fiona. I had sort of anticipated that as a police officer, she'd say *don't even consider doing it*, flat out (and maybe a part of me hoped that she would, to make the decision for me). But instead, Fiona is intrigued, and we find ourselves discussing ways that I can verify Ian is, who he says he is.

The idea of figuring out some sort of verification process had come up in my own explorative thoughts earlier, but as I talk it out further with Fiona, we see how difficult it might be, to find a way to do this. We conclude this is because:

a) He lives so far away from town and has no neighbours around him

b) Queenstown is such a backpacking, transient and 'young' population there's probably no 'oldies' who know him. Even the idea of asking at a post office seemed a poor alternative; as we don't have his address or even know if Queenstown is the post office he uses.

I concluded that any verification would need to be given in some sort of a 'sign' from the Universe – if it wants me to be reassured enough to undertake this wacky adventure it's presented me with! So I send out a request for a verification sign and decide I just have to leave it at that – even though I have absolutely no idea what such a sign could look like...

CHAPTER 31

<u>Next morning</u> It's 8.15a.m. Fiona and I head downtown, chattering excitedly and somewhat nervously. We're both booked (separately) on white water rafting experiences and Fiona amusingly reports to me that she is (in her words), "kacking herself!" I feel pretty much the same, and talk about the need to stay focused on what we want to achieve, to try to keep our spirits up. "Let's tell ourselves we can do it!" I say. We laugh, as we know we're scared, but that's okay, as we're both determined to push out comfort zones today and experience something new. Fiona and I exchange a goodbye hug, and a good luck wish, before heading off in separate directions to join our rafting teams.

The ride out is by minibus. It takes us high up, to a place on the Shotover River that my group will start their rafting from. The long, windy road is an old dirt track cut by ancient gold miners of long ago. Our tour guide Dan is fun and energetic. He clearly loves his job and keeps cracking jokes as the bus coils slowly around tight bends, with many sheer drops below. Dan keeps reminding us how dangerous this road is, and informs us of all the risks associated with white water rafting. A disclaimer form is passed round for us to sign – it says 'they' are not responsible for any injuries. We all know it's true. There is risk in this stuff. I feel some nerves coming up and a little *fear monkey* in my head asks if I should be taking this risk. I remember my advice to Fiona, and keep focused.

I stare out of the window at the beautiful day. The monkey chatter subsides and before it has time to reconnect, we're being directed off the bus and kitted with wetsuits, life jackets, helmets and rubber shoes. I put on my damp and clammy suit and shoes, still wet from their last occupant and waddle down to the water's edge. A small cluster of huge yellow and black rafts are bobbing about, their oars glistening in the bright summer sun. We're divided into groups and each raft is allocated a team leader. There's a huge vibe of nervous energy in the air as we wait impatiently for this long procedure to be completed.

I make small talk with a young girl from Holland. We encourage each other, and then get assigned to the same boat – it's good to have a friend along, as well as *Mr Fear*. Our guide is a magnificent, dark skinned, waxen haired Maori called *The Chief*. He appears to be the leader of all raft leaders and it's reassuring to know we have such an experienced rafter leading our boat. Soon the river is littered with yellow and black dots being launched into the crystal clear, still water. What a beautiful day! The hot sun follows as we heave our raft onto the river and jump right in.

The first half hour is spent practicing paddle strokes. It seems to be all about working together. We learn team techniques for keeping safe – if we hit a big rapid. All of us listen intently (ears straining against the thundering river) to instructions, guidance and river wisdom that *The Chief* imparts. He coaches us on how to respond fast, to his commands. Tells us it's of upmost importance to work as a team to have a safe and successful trip through the rapids. There's a real feeling of comradeship growing as we quickly realise how dependant we all are, on each of us doing our bit. With the training part over, *The Chief* announces that in just a few short minutes we will hit the first rapid.

CHAPTER 32

A moment of silence descends on the group. A flutter of excitement and fear fills my body. It's a strange feeling as we float along awaiting sighting of that first rising current, on the river ahead. Instinctively I want to hold onto something, but there's nothing to hold. And anyway, both hands are needed to drive the single paddle that I'm gripping nervously. Our leader points to the thin guide rope running along the floor of the boat, as my only anchor. I drive both feet deep under it, trying to find security and anchoring. But the rope is so loose and thin it fails to offer the reassurance I seek. A shout from *The Chief* signals a rapid is approaching, and then his deep reassuring and rhythmic command tells us to paddle, in unison and strength.

It's hard to re-create or capture in words what I'm feeling! The word *exhilarating* feels a good one along with *intense*, *exciting* and such, such fun! Our raft surges along at amazing speeds. We pass other rafts with crew members falling off, rafts getting capsized and rafts stuck in passing crevices! Our team work so well together that no one is lost from our raft, and this gives us a sense of superiority and glee! A cheer goes out from our boat, as we make it through the first section of rapids, intact. Confidence and reassurance in *The Chief* soars as he shouts words of praise and encouragement to us for our brilliant team effort.

The magnificent scenery that sails past is stunning! Tall rocks and crevices tower high above the river then suddenly, we disappear into a tunnel of solid stone, and out again. It's so beautiful, rugged, and raw; an untouched part of the landscape. Further down river we enter a section that man has 'claimed' as we raft under a bungee tower, just as one guy launches into the air.

What an awesome sight!

Water drives over the sides and roars into the raft, covering our feet. Time after time we're buffeted against rocks and it's really scary, but great fun! My legs ache with the tension I've created by pushing down onto the floor – trying to keep my balance, whilst perching on a wing of the raft.

Then, (what seems like only minutes) it's over. Phew! Such an adrenaline rush...

Chattering excitedly we fall out of the rafts and take hot showers, complimentary sausage rolls and coffee, amidst lots of animated conversation. I talk with an English couple. We share our feelings and pride in overcoming our apprehension and completing the trip. What an achievement this feels. I say quietly to myself, *Merry Christmas Lynette; you amazing woman you!*

CHAPTER 33

In the evening Fiona and I meet up to exchange 'fear stories' then go into town to share a farewell drink. She leaves tomorrow to spend Christmas in Australia with friends. Fiona and I chat about our tremendous achievement today, about life, about relationships and self-confidence. She speaks of her difficulty in relationships, and of the need to appear overly assertive and strong to survive in her man's world at work (yet not feeling this inside). I talk about the challenge strong women have, to balance both their masculine and feminine energies. Fiona thanks me and says our friendship has given her a lot. We exchange email addresses and in the morning say goodbye.

I have decided to take the trip with Ian into Alexandra today. I have also made the decision to check-out of my current hostel, in case I decide to go with him after our day out. I will make my *final decision* later today, when I feel I have more information. So I text Ian and tell him I'll meet him to go on the Alexandra trip. Putting my large holdall in the hostel's storage facility, I pack my rucksack with a few clothes and essentials to take with me (in case I decide to go). Ian will be heading back to his cabin later today, for the last time before Christmas. If I decide not to go then Plan B is to move on to my next hostel, as previously arranged and spend Christmas there…

Ian's text comes back late morning, to tell me he's on his way into Queenstown. He gives an estimated pick up time and meet-up place, but when I arrive, he's not there. Where is he? I go buy something to eat but feel so nervous it's hard to swallow. Ian's still not at the meet up place when I return, so I decide to check out an Internet café he'd told me was the best one to use.

I find him there, amongst loads of young people music and computers – seemingly oblivious to it all. Lost in deep concentration and reading his emails. I approach and he seems surprised, but totally chilled when I inform him of the time (it's almost an hour after our arranged time). For a minute, I'm not sure if he's just *'taking the piss'* or has genuinely lost track of the time. My already apprehensive and nervous state is heightened. I start to feel annoyed that Ian's kept me hanging around and this is communicated in my tone. He glances up, looks unsure, then apologises for the delay and says he had trouble getting his tractor started, that morning. That this had thrown him out (time wise) and now, he'd received an important email that needed replying to. I'm not at all sure what to believe or what not to. I'm almost talking myself out of the whole thing but then I decide I may as well go to Alexandra, at least. But at this point it really does not feel like there will be any trip, up any mountain!

Pretty soon however, the awkward vibe between us passes as we walk side by side, or rather he strides (great strides) and I try to keep up! Through the streets that Ian calls *Mickey Mouse Town* we walk and out towards a car park where his truck is parked. I'm still feeling unsure about the whole thing and pretty annoyed with the Universe for getting me to even consider such an absurd thing as going to stay with a stranger in a stupid cabin up a stupid mountain. Then the verification I asked for comes in, loud and clear...

CHAPTER 34

Just before we reach Ian's truck, I see a woman walking away from a parked car and heading towards us. She seems to recognise Ian, as she smiles and then stops to say, "Hi." Ian beams with delight and says, "Howdy, Susan!" And then I get to watch and observe as they exchange a very healthy and mutually respectful conversation together. I hear lots of information that indicate this is a longstanding friendship. Another sign is given when Ian introduces Susan to me and she says she's English and married to a Kiwi helicopter pilot. I smile and say, "Hi," but I'm more interested in the body language between them than anything, as it confirms to me that this guy is who he says he is, with every sentence they exchange.

Ian is relaxed and sociable. Susan is obviously pleased to see him, to hear his news and give him her own, just like old friends. Before heading off, Susan gives Ian an open invitation to visit over Christmas. It feels very much like I have received verification not only that Ian is who he says he is but that he is also (reassuringly) not a loner and has friends in the area. I begin to relax and smirk to myself, when I realise what's just happened. But the Universe (with its quirky sense of humour) isn't done yet. There's yet another challenge of trust, as I prepare to climb into the passenger side of Ian's battered old truck. With shock, I watch as Ian casually stretches across the driver's seat and, without batting an eyelid, nudges a hunting knife (in a sheaf) under the passenger seat and out of sight. As he does so, he mutters something about needing to remember he "Doesn't need to wear that thing when coming down into town." I blink in amazement as I look from Ian's face to that of a 6 inch blade, as it disappears from out of view.

Well I can tell you, it was one very strange reaction that I find myself experiencing next! My mind kicks into automatic red alert. *Fear warning! Warning!* It wants to link the knife to some hidden and sinister, dark intention, but just in time *Wise Mind* arrives to remind me of all the information given by the Universe and my own intuitive senses. *Wise Mind tells me that: of course this man will probably have a hunting knife on his belt holster, because his main place of residence is in the mountains... He's already told you that he hunts for wild goats and possums and so it makes perfect sense that he'll own a hunting knife...*

Fear Mind is not done yet though and tries again to set alarm bells going by asking: *Why would he have the knife in the truck?* But *Wise Mind* is having none of it and comes back with the logical answer, *maybe he has it on him so much, he forgets to take it off on his rare visits into town?* It feels almost ludicrous to think anything dark or sinister, as I feel such a lot of solid vibes around Ian. So I decide to use this short trip to get to know him more and make my stay-over decision based on Universal Guidance – not fear.

Yes, yes, reader, of course I realise this may seem a totally crazy and unconventional thing that I'm doing but hey, these are new times for me and the desire to explore another reality is greater than the fear. I now get to practice what I once read in a self-help book called, *Feel the fear and do it anyway!* As I remind myself of its useful acronym of fear: *False Evidence Appearing Real.* So I make no outward remark about the stowaway knife, as Ian chats on, in his rich Kiwi accent. The battered truck starts up with a rattle and a chug, and off we go to Alexandria.

CHAPTER 35

Once again, the conversation flows easy without any awkward silences. We drive away from the hustle and bustle of *Toy Town* and out onto beautiful open country roads. Ian seems genuinely interested to show me the region and tells me that the route we're taking is through old gold mining villages. He continues giving lots of local history and facts as we go. We stop off in the next village to buy home-made ice-cream that Ian recommends as being particularly good. He announces it's his treat! I smile, and let Ian recommend my flavour from the huge variety on display. Ian's favourite is boysenberry, a fruit that's a cross between a raspberry and blackberry. On we go to Alexandria sharing ice cream and chat; almost like old friends. I'm taking in information on many levels and sensing good energy around this unusual, interesting and fun guy.

One other thing I can't help noticing is his legs! They are tremendous in size and stature, deeply tanned and toned, and on full show right alongside me, in all their glory. Ian is wearing very short navy shorts. His legs are like a work of art! So aesthetically pleasing to the eye and so powerful looking. Pulling my attention back from the local 'artworks,' I hear Ian telling me I have an option of being dropped off in the centre of

Alexandria, while he does his business – or staying with him. I take the first option and we make a pick-up arrangement for two hours' time. I'm looking forward to a little space and free time to make my *final decision*. Deep down, there's a growing feeling that I'll choose to go with him and will be spending this Christmas in a log cabin in the mountains!

Walking away from the town centre, I head towards a clock face set into a hill that looked down over Alexandria. To get there, I cross a rickety shaky wooden bridge. Finding a comfortable rock, I sit down and call the backpacker hostel I'm booked in tonight. I cancel my bed with them until the 26 December and say that I'll confirm the rest of my dates as soon as I can. A friendly voice at the other end of the phone says: "That's all good, you have an awesome Christmas and we'll see you sometime soon." That was easier than I'd anticipated! So now it's definite. I'm making plans to go. Wow! *How does it feel?* I check inside. All is calm. It feels the right decision.

I walk up to the clock face in the rock and look down across the valley. All I can see for miles are open flat plains, fields and sprawling simple shack-type houses, interspersed with the odd tree. Today is hot and the earth looks parched. Making my way back to our pick-up point, a few nerves wiggle up inside. I start to think about how to tell Ian my decision and how to establish some 'ground rules' about personal space in his cabin. A niggling feeling is worried that he may think I'm coming on an unspoken agreement that our time together will include some sort of a physical relationship. I want to communicate to him that this is certainly not the case.

A little voice echoes somewhere inside me: *Of course that's what he's thinking, that's what most single men's (and some married ones too) would think…*

CHAPTER 36

As the truck rumbles off on our return journey home I tell Ian that I've decided to accept his kind invitation. Nervously, and not at all sure how to communicate my privacy needs, further words tumble out, ending with a kind of defensive sounding comment something like: "Well, Ian, I guess I know what it gives me to have this amazing opportunity to experience an 'alternative' Christmas, but what's in it for you – I ask myself?" There's complete silence. I glance nervously across at him. A long pause, before he answers. There's a hurt look right across his face as he replies, his own voice defensive and somewhat uncertain…

Ian's clearly uncomfortable and unsure of his words as he states that he'd simply thought it would be nice for me to see a bit of New Zealand that was off the tourist map, unspoilt and not commercialised, like Queenstown. Another awkward pause, then he goes on to explain that as he's just got back from enjoying a few weeks around folks in Chile, he sort of thought it might be nice to have a bit of company over Christmas, at the cabin... His words trail off. He looks a bit like a little boy now, explaining dubious motives to a teacher or parent. And yet, the manner he communicates in, and what he says, feels absolutely genuine. Suddenly, I feel awful that I've said such an unfriendly thing. Like saying there's a trust issue, from the outset. I've not been given one ounce of real evidence or information that says I can't trust this man, but instead I've used memories of past relationships with men, to inform my judgement. Ian Leadley seems a genuinely nice guy – just a simple living kind of bloke.

An awkward silence falls between us and I wonder if the damage can be repaired or if this will create a rift now, in the early stage of our friendship. Ian is thinking. His face shows he's still nursing the hurt. When words finally come, they reveal a confused but sensitive spirit, "What is it with you English?" He asks, "You don't seem to trust anyone!" I look at him in surprise. I'm a bit shocked. I'd never thought much about this but I guess it's true. We do seem to have a big level of mistrust, back home. I've been in New Zealand only a short time and already, I've stayed with professionals I've never met. Then the Catch's (who, after only a short while) entrusted their house and car into my care. A bus driver shared his chicken with me - a complete stranger. And now here is Ian, making this deep gesture of hospitality. Inviting me to share his world for a few days and here I am, mistrusting his underlying intentions.

This cold and sobering truth hits me right between the eyes. I try to make some sort of justification for it, but on an enlightened level there is none. I have no information to make this decision or validate this fear at all. Now it's my turn to hang my head, as Ian goes on to say, "And anyway, don't you think it's a big trust thing for me too? Taking *you* into *my* world, and trusting that *you're* not some sort of a mad woman, who'll freak out on *me* up there!"

This thought had not entered my head at all but when I think about it, I see it's true. Ian's all fired up now the passion rising in his voice as he goes on to tell me a story about a work-trade woman who had come to work for him and how she freaked out. Staying only a matter of days – she could never relax. In the end, Ian drove her back into Queenstown, as, "It's not very nice to be around someone with that kind of energy." His final comment to me on this subject is, "Look, if you find you don't like it, then I'll bring you straight back down and that's all I can say on the matter." I thank him for this and try to put the difficult conversation behind us, and change the subject.

Ian has told me we'll be stopping at a local supermarket on the way back, to pick up extra food for Christmas. I try telling him that I'd like to contribute to the shopping bill, but he shrugs his shoulders as he says (still with a wounded tongue) that it's up to me what I get; he'll get what provisions he thinks are necessary. The energy that was flowing so easily between us has been interrupted. Once in the store we separate and I go in search of peace offerings, with the intention of finding nice extras to make Christmas special. In the fruit department I buy fresh boysenberries (Ian's favourite ice cream flavour). I pick out homemade chocolate biscuits, a cake and fresh fruits, to make a fruit salad dessert with. A six pack of New Zealand malt lagers and a nice bottle of sparkling wine. When we meet back at the truck, I tell Ian about the treats and Christmas wine. He can't help chuckling and makes a comment about me getting him pissed!

The 'ice' is now broken and the thaw really begins when Ian pulls out two chocolate bars (a rare treat for him) and tells me there's one for each of us. I feel kind of embarrassed to take it as he'd bought my ice cream earlier and now a chocolate bar. What is this feeling? I recognise it as a conditioned-in reaction of not wanting to accept gifts in case there's expectations attached to them. Well, well, *Mr Mistrust* is here again (in a different disguise) and my discovery of him is not nice at all. I thank Ian for the chocolate bar, and tuck it into a storage area in the front of the truck, saying I'm still full from the ice cream and I'll have it later. Ian is completely oblivious of my reservations and gobbles down his own bar in two giant bites. We continue the short drive back to the hostel, to pick up my rucksack and put my larger bag in storage. The hostel is kindly letting me store it, free of charge. I tell a smiling girl behind reception that I'll probably be back for it on the 26th. The reply is simply, "No worries and have fun wherever it is you're going."

CHAPTER 37

My mountain adventure is starting to feel very real and exciting now. I head out of reception with walking boots strung across each side of a bulging backpack. Ian takes the bag and, as he throws it onto the back of his truck, the sturdy leather boots clunk noisily together. He eyes them with obvious approval. (This English woman does at least take her walking seriously!). There's a soft holiday kind of mood settling between us. We have our Christmas food and drink and I have my bags. The journey to his cabin can now begin.

Leaving the town behind, I soon recognise the dirt track road we're on. It's the same one the white water rafting bus had taken. But this time, we're going much, much higher. As it climbs, the truck bumps, groans and bangs around tight hairpin bends with barely enough width for its huge, chunky tyres. Ian grinds into first gear and slows the speed right down, as he negotiates the hazardous road, ahead. Well, I had said I wanted an adventure...

The journey takes a little under two hours. I focus on keeping calm and composed as I glance out the window and peer down sheer cliff sides into deep ravines, I see a pin prick of a gorge, way below. Ian's full attention is on the crude track ahead. Suddenly he announces, in an almost matter of fact way, (like he's making some sort of a casual suggestion) "This part of the journey will be the only time I suggest that you might want to *not* wear your seat belt for." I look across at him with confusion. Without taking his eyes off the narrowing bend Ian adds, "Because if something were to go wrong and we headed down that there gully, being free of a strap will give us our only chance of surviving, by jumping out of the truck." My mind does a double take. *Did he just say what I thought he did? Yes.* Gulp!

Ian chats on in his laid back way, informing me that although he's driven this road many times, he can never account for the effects of nature and its impact on the road – which is merely a cliff edge. (Second gulp) Trying to appear unfazed, I deftly unclick my seatbelt buckle and contemplate my exit route. *Fear Mind* conjures up a wonderful picture of the truck suddenly lurching off the edge and my body cascading down the ravine, into icy water below. Or maybe I'll get bounced and battered to death by every jutting rock on the way down. Thanks again Universe! Is this another little test?

I'm doing really well. It sort of feels it's been made easier by the fact that I've already stretched this comfort zone once, through coming this way with the rafting crew. Having the knowledge that their bus regularly make this journey (well, the first part of the track, anyway) is kind of reassuring to *rational mind*. Building on this knowledge, I manage to sooth my fear into a place of realism. If it's going to happen (I tell myself) it's going to happen. And if it does, well worrying about it won't do any good. So again, feeling proud of myself for conquering the fear I sit back and enjoy the ride. I keep my eyes on the sky or road ahead, rather than the menacing. And, just for special effects, this is on my side of the truck! Thanks for that, Universe...

And so eventually, after what seems like an eternity in a dusty hell we arrive at a flattened area and begin driving through a series of locked gates. At the first gate, Ian jumps out to open it and I watch. At the next gate I jump out and negotiate the rest of the openings, largely to prove to Ian that I do have a practical side. (He knows this 'untrusting English woman' works in a public sector job and lives a pretty urban life). My tactic seems to work well. I notice Ian watching as I work out the different ways each gate opens. Then, as he drives the truck through (beaming away) I stand on sentry with an air of seriousness – in the hope of gaining some respect back from this intriguing man.

We have arrived at a sheep station in the middle of nowhere. I listen. Silence. There's no one here. Ian comments to me that the station manager lets him use their freezer space for food storage and allows him to store his tractor on their parking lot whilst he's in town. Disappearing into a wooden shed Ian deposits some food we've brought and returns with tiny packages of frozen meat.

CHAPTER 38

It looks like this is as far as we go by truck. As we begin the process of transferring our gear, Ian pulls out that famous knife and in one grand gesture swings the leather holster around his torso and belts it up. The armour of the mountain man is complete when he layers coarse jerkins over his 'civilian' t-shirt, followed by a fleece coverlet, stained with blood. Ian informs me that daylight is fading and there's a lot to do before dark. We work fast, transferring shopping, luggage and sheets of metal (from Alexandria) onto a trailer fixed to a battered tractor. A long steel piece of pipe acts as a huge funnel and a homemade platform creates a wooden perching 'skirt' on either side of the driver seat. There's a lot to transfer and Ian works fast, securing the long steel girders so they won't slip off into the fast flowing river.

Pausing for a moment, he screws up his eyes and points across the wide but shallow expanse of river, to a thicket of trees huddled like sheep half way up a hill, "There's my cabin!" he declares. I look in the direction his finger points but see nothing. I don't want to say this, so instead, I nod with approval. I guess I'll see it soon… With a smile and a twinkle of the eye (I come to know so well as his joy of sharing) Ian invites me to climb aboard the skirt. As the tractor jerks into the water I instinctively hold onto the nearest thing (his shoulder) to steady myself from falling off. I apologise politely, but Ian shrugs it off and says it's fine. It's obvious he loves driving through water. Like a big kid with a big toy! The chugging tractor makes it impossible to hear each other talk. Undeterred, Ian shouts out information about the river. About the best way to work out where to cross, gauge the change in tides, etc. I marvel at his knowledge and catch my first glimpse of his world. An (almost) reclusive life set deep into the heart of hills, ravines and mountain ranges with snow-capped peaks.

We're two thousand feet above sea level. The air is cold and evening is fast drawing in. Slowly we edge our way through the strong current and onto the other side of the river. As the trailer jostles and lurches, I try to reach over and steady my back pack to prevent it falling off the trailer's edge.

It's a relief to be across. I realise I must have been holding my muscles tight, as the relief I have when I step onto land again, is very noticeable! Jumping off the tractor, Ian disappears into a clearing and appears again, on a quad bike. We transfer everything (but the steel) onto our next means of transport. It's a bit of a balancing act (again) as I sit aside Ian on the quad, clutching shopping and my backpack as the bike bounces deftly up a valley. Suddenly, and after such a long and exciting journey, we are here! The engine cuts out and a vast silence engulfs us in the descending darkness.

It's kind of eerie and beautiful all rolled into one. I look around and one hundred yards in front of me is a little green wooden cabin complete with a quirky chimney. There's an old water barrel to the left and a wigwam shaped corrugated area away to my right. I walk towards the cabin and see a vast, expansive vista that opens to its front elevation. Dark shadows of evening cast their net over a mountain range before me. Ian is delighted to be back in his world and someone else is clearly delighted he's back. Out of the cabin lumbers a sleepy looking black Labrador. "Hey Zach, you lazy old bugger!" Ian shouts and introduces me to his faithful friend. Ducking his enormous frame, he leads me inside and starts an evening routine that involves preparing food and stoking up fires on a battered old range. Ian lights candles and prepares a place for us to eat before the last daylight is gone. He clears away objects from a small couch at the side of a well-worn cooking range and informs me this will be my bed and I can store my stuff by the side of it.

There's a relaxed homely feel about the tiny cabin and I feel instantly at ease here. I arrange my few belongings by the side of my little bed settee. It is tucked underneath a window that looks out onto an enormous mountain range. The cooking range sits at the foot of my bed. A long piece of string hangs across its hearth, with a grubby looking towel drying over it. Little by little I take in my new home in a discrete, 'not wanting to be obviously looking around' kind of way. It's dark before we eat.

Ian fixes on his head a single miner's light powered by battery that he uses for a main source of light, after natural light has faded. He moves skilfully around the cabin, making use of his head light and hunching his enormous shoulders he reaches into the tiny sink, and begins to wash dishes. I go out to use the outdoor loo and Ian loans me this head torch. Black mountain shadows shroud my path.

The toilet turns out to be behind the wigwam of corrugated iron sheets – a little distance away from the cabin. Bloody hell, it's dark out here! I quickly take a pee in the old earth closet that Ian says was here when he first came. Carved by gold miners long ago, its gnarled wooden seat is full of character and the hole underneath it is... full of the same! Although the corrugated sheets provide privacy to each side, the front of the toilet is open, allowing its occupant to enjoy the magnificent view in private. Night stars twinkle amongst the huge inky blackness and it's an exquisite moment when stillness and beauty merge into one.

I hurry back to the warmth of the cabin to find Ian's retired to bed, in the only other room, with Zach. I'm aware that I feel safe and completely trusting of this man's energy and integrity. There's not a single shadow of doubt or unease in my mind, as I snuggle down under the cosy flannelette sheet and blanket. I breathe in a clean, fresh smell that's both comforting and relaxing. Despite the darkness and the separateness of our proximity, we still find things we want to talk about. The conversation continues, with us calling back and forth to each other. Sharing various bits of information, we uncover shared interest until the wee small hours.

CHAPTER 39

24th December Christmas Eve. I awake and realise what a great night's sleep I just had! I can't explain the feeling of relaxation that floods my body as I try to get out of bed. The effort is enormous, as my body seems to be calling me back to sleep. Just before I drift off, I hear sounds of stirrings from the other room. Ian is up.

First he lets Zach out for a pee then comes back into the main room. He says a few words of morning greeting, kindles the fire, fills a huge black kettle with water, places it on the stove and returns back to bed. Eventually, the kettle starts to hum and the fire begins to warm up the cabin. This, I come to know as Ian's early morning routine during the days I am here. It's almost like I feel drugged with a deep sense of relaxation and wellbeing flooding my body. I snuggle back down under my warm blanket and look around. In the bright morning light I see the cabin in detail for the first time. I notice it's well equipped cupboards, little sink, cooking range and stove.

There's a hot water tank, a small wooden dresser (crammed with food) and a simple table with two small chairs. A battered car radio and CD player, (charged by car battery) serves as a stereo system. One brightly coloured African drum rests by my bed and a small bookcase leans against a dividing wall between the two rooms. That is pretty much it. Although the contents of Ian's cabin appear old and tired looking it's clean and organised, in the main.

Everything seems to have its place - I guess it needs to with so little space. Ian is so big he takes up most of it with his body mass!! He's like a giant, living in a hobbit house! I laugh to myself as I look around the room, trying to get a bigger picture of his world. Every wall of the cabin is covered with newspaper cuttings, some faded and yellowing, looking like they've been there for years. I'm intrigued at the story lines that have captured Ian's interest enough for him to cut out and pin them up. Turning my attention from the internal space, I raise myself up from under the covers and peep out the window. The sun is shining, the sky is clear and it looks a great day! I hurriedly pull on clothes and get up.

After a lazy start with a hearty bacon and egg breakfast, I laze around in the sunshine on the ground out front of the cabin, watching Ian go about his various morning chores. He's declined my offer of help (work seems a pleasure to this guy). He's in a happy mood and smiles as he invites me just to chill out and enjoy the energy of the mountains. So I do. And their majesty and beauty is really something to behold. We're so high up here that the air is very clear and pure. It's wonderful to feel the warm sun on my back and know I have such interesting company for the next few days. The extraordinary ease between us continues. There seems to be no awkwardness, just an excellent rapport and relaxed energy.

Ian loves showing me around. His simple delight and pleasure in sharing is obvious. Whether it's something to look at, to learn, to experience or to eat! After chores are done he invites me to join him on the quad bike. We bob up and down the valley, making our way to a river inlet on the terrace below.

Ian has a rifle with him slung over his shoulder. As he drives he tells me the purpose of this trip is to check the rifle, before he goes hunting later on. The gun's sights need to be lined up, as during his time away in Chile it hasn't been fired. Ian laughs, as he tells me how he tried to shoot a wild goat yesterday and missed. I listen with interest. He goes on to tell me he'll need to shoot one today, for Zach to have dinner tonight. Wild goat is the main protein for both of their diets. Hmm…I'm not so attracted to the thought of it becoming mine!

I ask about its taste as I know the *smell* of goat and can't stand goat's cheese, so wonder if goat meat has the same rancid odour! Ian says there's a lot of difference between the meat of a Billy goat and a female.

Billy goat meat is the stinky stuff, but (apparently) female goat's meat (when cooked slowly with herbs) is delicious. At this point, I have to accept this as Ian's opinion and not mine! He seems to get very enthusiastic and excited when talking about how he cooks goat meat and the fact that we'll be having it for Christmas dinner. Ian reassures me that any Billy goat he kills is Zach meat – and the sweeter 'she' goat meat is for us. This last bit of information does kind of reassure me that it might be okay... Whatever, I am certainly open to give it a try!

CHAPTER 40

Hours melt away. Ian shows me possum fur rugs that he crafts from hundreds of possum skins hanging in a skinning shed outback. Inside the shed is an old, blackened fire place. Ian's eyes dance with nostalgia as he talks of wintertime, when the earth is completely frozen for week upon week. How he lights the fire in his shed and sits for hours just skinning, drying, sorting and matching up skins from the hundreds of possums hanging in row upon row. The range of colours, hues and shades are amazing to behold. I'm being soaked in so much fascinating information and new experiences.

All the time, even when we are walking, we talk. Ian is constantly explaining or commenting on nature and wildlife as he takes me on a grand tour of his kingdom. He is so in love with his world! His knowledge about gold mining and old mining ways is extensive. Such a fascinating man to listen to and *so* spiritually aware! I find myself captivated.

Back at the cabin, Ian's long, strong legs command a 'man presence' in the cabin. I take great pleasure in sitting on my little bed, watching his huge stature stride mindfully around this tiny space. Tanned and giant-like, the mix of his gentle and giving ways combine with an attractive masculine energy of hunter-gatherer.

As our friendship deepens Ian talks a little of a past partner that lived with him a few years back. Open and honest in words and feelings, Ian shares more of his life and his outlook. We have many similar values and delight in exploring ideas together. Slowly, we build up a picture of each other's lives, past and present. The day moves on and it's not long before Ian is restless to be outside, again. Apparently it's hunting time!

Inviting me along, he adds words of caution about steep ravine tracks with sheer drops. I'm completely undeterred and want to experience as much of his world as I can, while I'm here. So once again, the rifle is slung over one shoulder. A belt of bullets and knife belt is draped around his waist and an old fleece thrown about shoulders. Calling to Zach as he goes, "Come on you lazy old bugger! Let's go and get some goat for supper."

As he strides off with giant strides, Ian seems to have 'gone' into his own little world and no longer aware of my presence. I try to keep up as best I can, as I track Ian and Zach's silent movements through foliage and rugged mountain terrain. All the while, Ian's hawk eyes are scanning foliage on both sides of the ravine. This is Ian the hunter. He senses and sees goats that I can't make out, with my naked eye. Occasionally he calls out softly, "There's one!" and points across the ravine. But my untrained eye is unable to make out anything that looks remotely like goat! Hours later and I'm beginning to wonder if wild goats actually exist. I navigate, negotiate and stumble through an area that seems to keep going deeper and deeper. I'm get pretty tired.

At last, it is time to begin our return route. Ian's mumbling something about, "The buggers are keeping well out of sight today" when suddenly he stops in his tracks. He's spotted one. Ian's eye scans and measures. He raises his gun and a loud explosion of gunfire echoes through the valley. It's brings a shock and a chill to my senses. Quick as a flash, he disappears down the gully followed closely by Zach (but not me!). I stay where I am, waiting in a safe place. My senses fully alert, activated and unsure as to what I'll see or hear next. Ian is looking for the goat.

I wait motionless at the top of the gully, so tired and aware that dusk is falling. I try to keep Ian and Zach in my focus. I don't want to get lost out here! After a while, he comes into view. Ian's hunched over something I assume is the goat. I'm too far away to see details, but he's working hard and fast. Zach is close by his side. I concentrate hard, trying to understand what's happening when suddenly I see it clearly. He's gutting and beheading it! Quickly and effortlessly, Ian throws the torso over his shoulders. With blood and entrails dripping down onto one arm and his jumper, he clambers back up the gully and beams triumphantly at me.

The sun is setting fast. Ian strides off in the direction of the cabin, with Zach trotting faithfully at his side. What a majestic and awesome sight it is! I capture the beautiful and magnificent silhouette of this twilight image on my camera. This is truly a man of the mountains!

I feel so drawn to his energy and his presence.

Back at the cabin we are busy again. There's the goat to 'see to' and fires to tend and there's a new job of getting water ready for our baths which needs to heat, whilst we eat tea. A few hundred yards away from the cabin, alongside the full length of a lightening-struck tree, sits an old ceramic bath, complete with strip of hosepipe coupled to a natural spring. Ian arranges logs and sticks of wood underneath and lights a fire. The bath already has water in, as he shows me how to skim and clean the surface of the water from insects and leaves, before topping it up with clean water from the pipe. It would appear that when the water is hot enough, I'm to take the first bath.

Ian explains, quite matter-of-factly, the procedure for taking an outdoor bath. I am instructed to bring my wash things. To drape clothing and towels over a fallen tree – whose intermittent flat surface also serves as a display shelf for tiny animal sculls just for decoration! Ian hands me a block of wood and tells me that I'll need to place this at the foot of the bath to rest my feet on. This is to protect them from the heat that will rise up, from underneath the bottom of my bath. I must check the water temperature before getting in. I may use the pipe to add cold water (to adjust the temperature) if it's too hot. The actual procedure of washing itself must be done whilst standing fully out of the bath on a wooden slat. Soaping and washing is then to be completed by throwing jugs of water over my body to rinse off suds, dirt or residue. After the washing part is over, I can then return to the tub for a relaxing soak, to take in the night air and vista before me.

And so it is, that after tea I find myself, on Christmas Eve, sat in the middle of nowhere beneath the shadow of an old gnarled tree, soaking my bits. The water is beautiful and warm and a gentle hissing and spitting noise from the fire beneath me is the only sound around, as I gaze out on a Christmas sky crammed with stars. What abundance. What bliss. What a rare and special Christmas gift! I almost need to keep reminding myself that I'm not dreaming. It's magical. Eventually, I drag myself out of the tub and dry off – only prompted by the consideration that Ian's still waiting for his bath! As I skip back to the cabin, every inch of my skin positively hums from my delicious outdoor bath.

Later on we plan our Christmas meal and I offer up the items I picked up at the store, yesterday. (Was it really only yesterday?) The menu is decided. Roasted goat, (not Billy type) slowly cooked with marjoram and mint. Boiled potatoes and a salad with Ian's special dressing served with boiled eggs and chopped sausage. This, to be followed by a fresh fruit salad, and the whole meal to be accompanied by a bottle of sparkling wine; which is currently round the back of the cabin, keeping cool.

In many ways an odd and plain Christmas fayre, yet Ian's so excited and enthusiastic about it all - you'd think it was a banquet! As I snuggle down to sleep, that Christmas Eve night in my little fireside bed, I listen with a joyful heart to the gentle sound of snoring. A simultaneous chorus of one man and his dog!

CHAPTER 42

I slowly come to my senses after another solid night of sleep. The sun is bursting through cabin windows and although I can still hear the vibrations of Ian's slumbering tones, I'm anxious to be up and un-wrapping my presents. The sun entices me, so silently I pull on trousers and a sweater over my pyjamas, pick up walking boots by the door and head out onto the hills. The morning air is stunningly pure and the mountain peaks are adorned with light dustings of fresh snow to make a perfect Christmas card for me, as I pick my way through brambles and foliage on the lower ridge. It's like drinking an intoxicating drink! I can understand why Ian loves this place. The magic and the energy vibrations of the mountains bring a tingle to my skin. Up I climb, the sun draping me in its warmth, so much so that I start to get hot – with pyjamas as undergarments. I keep forgetting its summer here!

When I'm elevated high enough to survey the little cabin below, I sit amongst a clearing of wild flowers and peel my top layers of clothing off and bask in the sun, for a while. The stillness is profound. I feel a desire to capture my feelings and gratitude for this gift that the Universe has given. Once again, it feels like I'm dreaming. I pull out a little notebook from my jacket pocket and begin to write the outpourings of my heart. This is what is born:

The Kings of the Mountains lay their gifts before my feet, as I gaze in adoration with a heart that bursts with gratitude for the beautiful symphony I behold.

Snow tipped peaks, mysterious shadows

Sun bursts, white billowing clouds and soft sweet sounds of early morning stirrings

I un-wrap these Christmas gifts with all my senses, breathing in cool, clear, air and shedding upper clothing to let the sun's deep rays caress my body

My arms, my back, my neck, my stomach and breasts

I close my eyes and drink it deeply in

Sitting here on the hillside I feel my mind, my body and spirit merge into one with

the beautiful spirits of the mountains

Peace,   Contentment, Harmony

Love, Bliss and Joy, all transfuse into one

All is one and I am all

Far below my throne, nestles the little cabin in which lies the gently snoring man
who opened up the gateway to this special place, for me

His own powerful presence and statute

is fittingly placed

Amongst this majestic mountain setting

A special place for this man has woven itself into my heart, in such a short time

I know we must have met before, sometime or place.

Increasingly my spirit recognises

his face, his heart and soul.

Lynette. Christmas Day, 2007

Back at the cabin I'm surprised to find that Ian's still not up. I creep around, trying to get the fire to light, but it's a pretty unsuccessful attempt as I fail my first 'woman of the mountain' task – given to myself! I've brought a single wild rose back from my walk, as a Christmas gift for Ian. I screw a scrap of silver paper around its stem to make it pretty. Soon he's awake and that huge presence starts lumbering around the little cabin. I sense his morning mood is pleasant as he wishes me   "Merry Christmas!" Ian is clearly touched when I gift him the rose and casts his eye around for somewhere to put it.

The fire's soon lit, the coffee and tea brewed and we sit around chatting and hugging our mugs of steaming Christmas morning brew.

CHAPTER 43

There's a gentle holiday vibe around the cabin. By lunch time I'm still in my fleecy pyjamas, still drinking coffee and relaxing on my little bed. Ian's sat up at the table on one of the tiny chairs, playing bird warbling music on his battered car radio/CD player, when suddenly he sits up alert and listens. I hear a voice and then in the next breath Ian announces, "We have visitors." And to our surprise, delight and slight embarrassment, (pyjamas) so we do!

A middle aged couple with backpacks and dog come into sight as we stand in the cabin doorway. They wave and call out a Christmas greeting to Ian, as they draw nearer. Soon it's clear these are 'neighbours' of Ian and are having a Christmas picnic lunch. Ian says; "They have a place an hour and a half's walk down the valley." He invites them in without any hesitation and is thrilled to have visitors to his cabin on Christmas Day.

The kettle's soon on and two seats are placed outside the cabin doorway, for the couple to rest and enjoy the morning sun. They try to accept my presence at the cabin as normal but are clearly surprised and intrigued to find a strange English woman with the reclusive man of the mountain – and one who is still in her pyjamas at that! I make my apologies and slip away to the corrugated toilet to change and take a pee.

On my return the waters boiling and I open the special chocolate biscuits as a Christmas treat. Once again you'd think we were giving out gold coins, the delight that Ian shows as he offers round the biscuits. How simple a life, this man leads. I think of my own reaction. Taking a pack of biscuits as normal and not really see those as a big treat. How much we take for granted these days in our modern world of plenty.

It's a very pleasant neighbourly chat that follows about mountain life and the various domestic challenges it brings. There's neighbourhood gossip and in particular it seems to be about an old guy called George who died under strange circumstances (last year) and whose clothes were found down river - but no body. I listen quietly and with interest as Ian's already told me a bit about 'Old George' when talking about spiritual stuff the other night. I recall how he'd told me about the night (not long after George had been declared dead) that Ian couldn't sleep and how he'd called out to the missing man: "What you gone and done now George?" And how, much later, in the early hours of the morning, Ian had woken up coughing and coughing with a terrible restrictive sensation in his throat, like drowning. And as he coughed and gasped for breath, he'd heard George's voice say, "I just fell in."

After a lot of general and light hearted banter with this neighbouring couple Ian decides to take them on the 'grand tour of the possum shed'. I go (again) too, but I'm trying to make myself a bit invisible really, as I feel a bit of an outsider here! The couple are full of questions and make lots of exclamations about the beautiful possum furs. The whole process and procedure is carefully gone over in various details, to his new and interested audience. Once again, it's Ian's delight and pleasure to share his world with anyone who's interested to listen and it fascinates me more, each time I hear him talk.

A few dark clouds roll in and the couple agree it's time to head back down the valley, as they have no overcoats with them and the sun is fast losing its warmth. Ian asks a few times if they'd like the loan of coats, but they decline and say they'll be fine. With a sideways glance and farewell to me, they're off. Pushing hiking sticks deep into the soil, they call out that we're welcome to call in at their house for a Christmas drink, if passing. (!) We wave and watch as they become smaller and smaller dots on the landscape and once more we're alone. Turning back to the cabin, Ian exclaims how nice it's been having visitors on Christmas Day! He then proceeds to gently tease me about being in my pyjamas and make little jokes about what his neighbours will think! I wonder if mountain gossip is as fast spreading as village kind. I try to apologise ahead of time in case I've caused him any embarrassment or awkwardness, but Ian throws it off with a laugh, "People will think what people will think and be done with it."

He's so funny!

CHAPTER 44

I realise that because of the isolation of this place, we are spending an unusual amount of time together. And with our many connections and interests, my attraction to Ian just keeps growing. I'm in awe at finding such a spiritual and caring, guy, in the mountains. We go back to sitting inside and 'hang out' some more. Ian gets out a strange tea that he's brought back from Chile, and offers to brew a little. It tastes rather insipid to me. The way to drink it appears to be to take turns to sip from an aluminium decorated straw in a little round aluminium cup that Ian tops with hot water. As the leafy type substance floats on top, we suck through the straw into the murky water beneath. Ian claims it made him a bit lightheaded and high when he drank it in Chile but it only gives me a headache! We laugh as I pull my face and conclude that I don't like this weird tasting Chilean delicacy!

After an hour of our tea ceremony, Ian is restless to be outdoors again. Hunching his shoulders he peers out of the tiny window and announces, "The weather's brightened up once again!" So while the wild goat, dressed in its marjoram and mint dinner jacket, simmers gently in the oven, we head outside. Riding the quad bike we bump bump our way down to the river and collect piles of previously cut wood. We work hard and mostly in silence with just the odd joke or shared comment. Slowly the trailer fills with logs. By the time it's ready to go, the air feels quite cold and I'm glad to be heading back to our cosy little cabin. We unload the wood by the bathing area and Ian starts to prepare the fire underneath the bath. He chuckles as he says, "It will get nice and hot then, to warm us from the chill."

Back in the cabin, I wait for my bath water to heat and make the fresh fruit salad for Christmas dessert. I help prepare our table with candles before opening the sparkling wine. It goes quickly to our heads and we both laugh. Ian tells me again, he rarely drinks and that it doesn't take much to get him drunk! The music is on again, as we busy ourselves, making the cabin cosy for our little Christmas dinner. Ian prepares carrots, onions, mint, lettuce and radishes for the salad. He carefully pours over a special homemade dressing made from brown sugar, mustard, vinegar and evaporated milk. It's delicious! The goat meat is cooked. Ian carefully tears off a piece and hands it over for me to sample, then beams with pride as I nod and smile with approval.

It's time for my bath, before tea. I hurry through the cold night air to the open air bathroom. Undress quickly and disappear underneath clouds of steaming hot water. The fire smokes and simmers underneath me. An overflow of water steams and hisses as I wiggle about, trying to anchor the wooden block to protect my feet from getting burnt. Once more I'm in heaven! I do my wooden trellis ritual and climb back in for a longer soak. The heat that's seeping into my bones is quite extraordinarily delicious! The magnificent view that spans right across the valley is stunningly vast and open. I sigh gently, as I gaze softly at the mountains and 'soak' in the warm welcoming glow of Ian's little cabin. Getting out to dry off in the open is such an exhilarating treat and once again, my skin glows from the heat of the water. I've brought a sachet of sandal wood with me to smooth into my skin. It smells good.

Back in the cabin, Christmas dinner is served. The plates are piled sky high and Ian's appreciating every little single thing! The wine goes down fast and the goat meat is quite delicious. So is the fruit salad... And well, you would think he'd struck gold when he discovers it had boysenberries in it! Soon, Ian has the music on (he loves his music). "What shall I play you now?" he keeps on asking. (I'm not entirely sure if he's saying it to himself, or to me!) As he rummages through a small collection of CDs, we discover a shared love of Enya. Ian had three of their discs. We listen to them all.

Their deep and sensuous sound swirls around the cabin like a velvet mist, and out across the silence of our surroundings.

CHAPTER 45

Ian's lying out on his bed, listening to the music. It's the only place that can accommodate him stretching out fully and I'm lying on my bed when suddenly I get the thought that it would be so nice to lie and listen with him. Before I can stop it, I hear a voice asking if I can join him. Ian welcomes me in and we both lay and listen for a while in the dark as he idly flicks his head torch on and off. Playfully, he casts the tiny light across beams above his head. We share a few words, but listen mostly in silence, before he goes off to have his own bath. As he leaves, Ian turns and says I can stay and listen on his bed if I like - but not to get too comfortable, as it's his bed! Once he's gone though, all of a sudden it feels like an intrusion to be in his room without him. I leave and go back in the room. The CD finishes and I sit on my bed in silence, reflecting over these extraordinary few days and my imminent departure tomorrow.

After a while, Ian returns and somehow, the conversation turns to me leaving. The thought that I'm leaving this beautiful, hidden world tomorrow (as planned) seems almost unthinkable.

"I guess tomorrow, it's time for me to go." I say.

"That was the plan." Ian replies.

A pause accompanied by a horrible feeling in the pit of my stomach. I scrabble around in my mind for a way that might work for me to stay here. I consider the thought of staying until the New Year. Or staying a few weeks? Or staying the entire period until my time at the spiritual retreat centre in February? Right now, it feels like I can experience nothing any more amazing and wonderful than this place. Besides, I know there's such a warmth and closeness growing between us, that it seems crazy to lose this lovely feeling so soon. Ian tries to ground our conversation in reality. He talks about starting up his gold mining work again soon and I suddenly realise that the three days I've been with him are far from typical. That his normal day is filled with hours of work (and long ones too) with lots of walking, hunting and building overnight camps. Ian's 'real' work takes him away for days at a time, trekking up river to find mining sites and setting up camps, to work from. I consider offering to stay and to help, then think about what attachments might form and how will I feel when I leave?

I tell Ian honestly, that I'm finding it hard to think about leaving and searching for ways to stay. He admits that he's enjoyed my company and has also wondered if there's a way for me to stay longer. He speaks of how he has already arranged for help (that arrives in February), for four months. As I move away from the storybook image I've had of Ian's world to the stark, reality of day to day living up here, it feels beyond my mind's comprehension. We both come to the conclusion it's not workable for me to stay and the conversation ends with Ian saying in a light hearted way, "I can always come and get you, from wherever you've got to on your travels if I need help and it doesn't work out for you in other ways." I think we both sort of know that isn't practical for either of us, but it feels a nicer way to end it rather than the finality of goodbye.

The mood's gone a bit low now with all this talk of leaving and the evening light has faded. Ian decides to retire to bed and asks if I'd like him to leave the music playing for a while. It feels sad and a little lonely as I listen, by candlelight and try to remember the Law of Non-Attachment. Remember all the good things about our time together and then let it go. Not hold on or suffer.

A little later, I turn the music off and lie in my cosy bed for one last time looking out of the little window. The night sky is pure black. For a long while I just lay there with my mind pretty much empty and a heavy feeling in my heart. Then slowly, slowly, the moon breaks through the dark sky and a beautiful, bright light fills my entire window. Once more, I know the Universe is signalling to me that its love and care is with me. I close my eyes and sleep soundly.

CHAPTER 46

When I awake I know instantly it's my last morning. I take an early morning peek at the mountains covered with fresh hats of fallen snow. Ian takes Zach out for his early morning pee then returns back to bed. I sense a lonely feeling wash over me, again. As I get back into bed, after my own morning pee, a thought comes in, "Just ask if you can go in for a cuddle." I try to push this absurd thought away but it refuses to go and keeps marching around my head. My heart starts to pound. It feels a crazy thing to do but being true to my instincts and body signals I head over to the bedroom door, clutching my pillow for courage. Ian looks up from under his bed covers and with surprise, warmly accepts my request.

Zach is laying on the bed alongside side him and Ian tries for a while to get the huge dog to move up and make room for me. After much laughter and pushing, he manages to push Zach over. Ian shuffles up to make room for me. I lay cradled under his enormous arm. It feels so good. I smell his slightly sweaty man body smell and feel the strong arm around me. Ever so lightly, I feel him gently caress my left arm.

I snuggle down, feeling content and happy. We both seem comfortable and after the occasional rubbing of toes, we fall back to sleep. Ian's snoring vibrates round the bedroom walls and lulls me into a relaxing slumber. On awaking, he asks me the time. Its 8.45a.m. Ian says he must get up soon, to light the fire, then comments on how hot it is. And it's true we seem to have generated a lot of energy (although I do have my beloved fleecy pyjamas on). I get up, leaving Ian to dress and return to my cold, empty bed. I leave in such a hurry that my pillow gets left behind.

But I wanted to stay. It felt so right, so nice and extremely tender and loving. Ian busies himself, lighting the fire and putting the billycan on to boil. Once more he returns to his bed and says to Zach (but I feel it's to me, really) "We're not stopping here long – it's getting late!" I should have left it at that, but I didn't. A thought kept pounding in my head and then the heart beat thing starts up, again. Its always been a cue for me, that says I need to express what I'm thinking: *how lovely to complete the many things you've shared, by making love together, before you leave each other.* This unconventional thought is shocking, and a part of me rebels against it. But another part says, *think of it as part of the 'non-attachment 'thing'.* It's a powerful feeling that's forming, and an immense attraction to this man, his spirit and strong, physical presence.

And so, (here the mad woman goes, again) I call out the suggestion to him, somewhat afraid, but with a courageous spirit. There is silence. Then Ian comes into the room, his large frame stands awkwardly, in the door way. He talks about not having thought this to be part of what we would share. Of how he's had three wonderful days with me and doesn't want anything to spoil what we've shared together. I feel disappointed and quickly realise that my brave words have probably taken things too far.

A little later, Ian brings up the subject again. This time he wants to acknowledge that he had also thoughts of how nice it might be for us to make love. But then adds that it'd been a long while since he'd "Gone there." Now he begins to speak of the fear that if he did *'it'* once, he'd want to do *it* again. Then I'd be gone, and he'd be alone again and it would be harder for him to come back from that place; than if he hadn't gone there at all. My spirit soars in delight that Ian too had thoughts about us coming together. I try to reason. "Could we not just experience it as a beautiful sharing of something special, and not fear its loss?" Ian shakes his enormous head and lowers his eyes.

Once more, he repeats that he's decided it's best not to and again, tells me that he doesn't want to spoil what we have. Disappointed, I accept. I respect his decision and understand his difficulties around it. Guess that we all have our visits from *Mr Fear* at different times…

That said, we brighten up and begin chatting and laughing again. The morning rolls along but it's clear that neither of us are in any hurry to go. I pack up my few things and waste a little more time, taking photos of this and that. Ian brings out his biggest nugget of solid gold. Placing it in his open palm, he poses for my camera. Then he shows me a book of his grandfather's war memoirs. It's obvious that Ian has his grandfather's spirit of courage and determination and applies it to his own life challenges. Ian talks of an idea about making a DVD of his experience in the mountains and of recording his gold mining knowledge. It's fascinating and we talk through ideas about how it might work. But, after a light lunch of Christmas leftovers we can delay my return journey no longer.

CHAPTER 47

On to the quad bike and down to the river we go. I'm fighting back tears and trying to focus on positives. Transferring to tractor, we chug noisily across the river with Ian's home-made funnel wobbling about all over the place and smoke pouring out! Half way across, Ian asks if I'd like to drive and so I take the wheel. What fun! We beam at each other; both sharing the pleasure. He's seated, (a little higher up) alongside me, on the apron over the wheels. His handsome legs are level with my shoulders. I joke about our role reversal and can't resist touching his leg briefly as I speak. Ian seems genuinely surprised that I find his legs so attractive and looks kind of bashful as he says now I'm embarrassing him, and tells me to stop it!

When we hit a dangerous bit of the river, Ian takes over the driving and now it's time for me to sit with my legs next to his shoulders. Playfully, he turns the 'leg' joke back on me as he briefly touches my leg. It feels like he's reaching out to connect with me. Has he changed his mind? I say nothing.

Now into the truck we go and through all the gates. Past the sheep station and out onto that windy, mountain pass. Further and further away from my beloved Christmas hideaway. Unexpectedly, Ian says he's not sure if he's made the right decision about us making love. Speaking honestly and openly of how he's been changing his mind, again and again, since I'd asked him. How he realised it's for selfish motives he's doing this; to protect himself. But also adds it's partly because I'd given him such a stern 'warning' at the beginning of our time together and told stories about men making unwelcome passes at me; that I didn't invite. He says these comments had made him unsure later, about making 'moves' towards me. Suddenly, I see how my earlier fears could have damaged a beautiful spontaneity that may have flowed between us both. But is this just about my fear, I ask myself...

It seems that Ian is now speaking of his own fear, too. A fear of loss, that's blocking the ability to be open to experience the 'moment'. So I guess we're a mirror of each other's fear. And now we'll never know... Ian goes on to share how he too had feelings that were growing and how he really enjoyed cuddling with me that morning. That it had crossed his mind about taking it further. I'm flabbergasted and amazed. Me and my stupid need to 'police' and pre-determine boundaries! We continue down the mountain road, intermingling jokes and ribbing each other, but without taking it seriously now. But as we make our way down the steep cavern road, it feels like there's the energy of urgency between us, as we both know time is running out fast. Like a proverbial basketball, we keep passing *the decision* backwards and forwards. Have we made the right decision? Haven't we? What would it have been like? As we verbalise our anticipation, the truck becomes filled with a huge ball of sexual energy that we've created. Phew! We decide to stop talking about it (delicious as it is) because of the frustration and restless energy it's creating.

Our next approach is to adopt the philosophy that if it's meant to be, it will be. That like a boomerang, if I'm meant to return I will. Ian tries to encourage me gently, by telling me that this is just the start of many adventures for me. He tries to move my focus towards future travels, but I'm not interested and dismiss it. How can he put this experience on the same scale as anything else? Ian falls silent when he realises it's not working.

We decide to stop off for a Christmas drink with the couple who called into the cabin yesterday (or was it a year ago?). They seem pleased to see us. We sit in the sunshine, drinking tea and eating cake. I enjoy looking at Ian as he makes discreet glances over at me – when he thinks I'm not looking. The conversation falls again to mountain gossip that I'm unable to contribute to, so I sit and listen. It's another reminder to me that Ian's in a world, in which I don't belong.

Before we know it it's 5.35p.m. and reluctantly, (once again) we press on to Queenstown, our final destination. As we pull up outside my new 'home' Ian keeps his truck engine running. There's an awful feeling of finality and Ian seems anxious to be gone. A group of young backpackers sit near the entrance. I want to kiss him goodbye, but it's so public here. Has he parked the truck here for this reason?

Ian unloads my bags and hands them to me. We exchange an informal farewell and look at each other. We hug and kiss briefly on the lips, then another hug and another. I don't want him to go, but he must. He walks slowly round to the driver's door. I dash to his side and try to share one more kiss; but it's like Ian's already left. I pull away, walk back round the other side and we joke about it. A few more farewell thanks, good wishes and a wave. And he's gone.

CHAPTER 48

I check in. I go to my room. I make tea and eat in a daze. I walk down into Queenstown and buy groceries. It's raining and I'm glad, so that my hood and the rain will hide the fact that I'm crying. Crying, a mixture of tears of joy and sadness all merged in one. I cannot comprehend what's happened these last few days; I'm struggling to make sense of it all. I miss Ian already and struggle with the awful thought that I may never see him again. Not ever. It's so very hard. And I don't know how to bear it. The tears keep flowing and yet I know I mustn't create an attachment to this wonderful experience that's been given. I send him a text of apology, in case I caused any discomfort over seeking that extra kiss. I thank him again, for such a special time.

His texts are initially silent. Then one comes in. It says *I'm happy to know that I've given joy to someone travelling.* He ends it, *Love from Ian and Zach. It's all good.'* I sense he's already distancing himself from me as he travels back, alone again. I feel a bit lost. How do I pick up and move on? I sit looking at the beautiful lake – not feeling at all grounded. I decide to take a shower and re-connect with my girls.

I'd told a few family and friends that I was spending Christmas, in a 'back to nature' cabin in the hills, without a telephone signal. (No mention of the gold miner bit though!). And that I would be in touch when I got back in an area, with a signal. Gemma's reply comes straight back and it's lovely to hear from her so soon. As I prepare for bed, another text comes in from Ian. It's a chatty one this time, telling me about somewhere to call at further up South Island, to see a friend of his (if I pass through). I'm pleased to hear from him, if not somewhat surprised.

I meet one of my new roommates. He's a young French guy. We chat a little about our travel paths and I tell him where I've just come from. He's curious! I show him pictures I've taken and he's fascinated! I know it's not a dream. I have these pictures. Only by these, do I know it wasn't a dream…

27th December I take a long, long sleep. I'm emotionally exhausted. Plus, the change in altitude seems to be making me tired. I speak to Gemma on the phone. She's pleased to hear from me and I'm happy to hear her sweet voice. We chat for a while about Christmas in the UK. I haven't had a reply from Melanie, yet. The news from Gemma is that the two of them fell out, over Christmas! I tell Gemma that I'm not going to get involved in the fallout - when she starts giving me her version of events. I sense that she'd like me to 'take sides'. But my girls are adults now and must learn to resolve conflict themselves. I know, (being their mother) that this is a big thing for me to say as I've always tried to be mediator and peacemaker between them. I hate it when they fall out and just want them to be friends again, as soon as possible. But it's not helpful keeping stepping in to 'rescue' them from each other...

The French guy's moving on after only one night. We have one more chat and again, he's curious to know more about the gold miner. He says, "Bravo!" to me for being open to have the experience. This is the first time I've shared my 'tale' with anyone. I begin to realise that what I did might seem quite a big thing to most people – coming from the rational mind. And yet at the time it felt so right for me, to follow my internal guidance system and go.

The day starts off bright so I do hand washing, and head into the town. Soon the weather turns to rain, but I don't really care what the weather does right now. I'm still feeling in a daze and wander around the shops, aimlessly. I find myself longing to make contact with Ian. After spending every waking moment for the last few days in his company, its absence leaves a huge energy void. I decide to send an email saying that if his 'help' doesn't arrive, that I am open to return and work with him for a month. I try to assure him that we could just be friends, however it works out. (Couldn't we?)

It's all good and perfect in the Universal Plan. *Just need to keep open and trusting Lynette and take some retail therapy*! I buy a fleecy jacket in the Kathmandu sale and a few souvenirs. I start to make phone calls to find a bed in my next location. My next stop will be Franz Joseph, a tiny town that has its own ice glacier! The evening is mostly spent packing for an early start tomorrow. I catch up on my journal and enjoy a beer. My thoughts turn to Ian, again. What is he thinking? What is he doing right now on his magical mountain?

CHAPTER 49

28th December 7.00a..m. Leave Queenstown. The morning air is cold and there's a sprinkling of snow across the Remarkables as I trundle my holdall along deserted streets to the bus stop. Well, Christmas in Queenstown has certainly been remarkable! I arrive at Franz Joseph around lunch-time, check in to my hostel and take a rest. A quick walk reveals that the ice glacier and a rain forest are pretty much all there is in this tiny little place and due to no public transport over the New Year break; I have to stay here until the 2nd of January. An idea comes in to, *try and find some sort of casual work over the New Year period*. That way I could pay for a (rather expensive) one day guided trek up the face of the ice glacier and also help fill some New year's eve 'party hours'. I'm not really into the excess drinking game... So as I stroll around town, I call in at two restaurants to enquire if there's any casual work going. To my amazement, the second place takes me on!

Jamie, the owner of *The Landing* comes out of the kitchen and peers at me over the bar, in an interested sort of way. I explain my aim to work to fund a glacier trek. He agrees right away to employ me and offers incredibly flexible hours and split shifts of 1 to 3 then 6 to 10. When I ask Jamie which days he wants me to work, he says "Oh, you just go and book your trips and stuff, then let me know when you can work." Wow! Once again I'm in gratitude to the Universe. So the schedule's mine to decide. Hmm. I return to the backpackers to plan my time here. I decide to walk through the rainforest that goes right up to the face of the ice glacier tomorrow and book a full day guided trek to go *up* the glacier on New Year's Day. So off I go and book my little trip, then head back to *The Landings* to tell Jamie I can work the 30th and 31st. He simply says, "Cool," hands me a black shirt with *The Landings* embroidered on it then adds, "See 'yah." We've agreed on a rate of $13 an hour (cash). I'm to clear and wait tables. What fun and such perfect hours (as I don't usually stay up late!) Well, it really is *all good* as they say in New Zealand!

Back at the hostel, I cook a tasty meal and begin chatting to two Irish women (about my age) who've just arrived. They're curious that I'm travelling alone and ask where I spent my Christmas. For the second time I retell my 'crazy' Christmas story. They listen in awe, with jaws agape and it's clear they don't know whether to believe me or not. So I fetch my camera and show the pictures again, to prove it – as it sound more far-fetched (to me too) every time I tell it! The women both comment over what a handsome man Ian is. And in her rich Irish twang Nell declares, "A real Rambo!" I smile to myself and agree.

Currently there are three young German girls sharing my room, but that can change any day (and usually does!). Two are sisters (about my daughter's age). The day is sunny and bright so I make a packed lunch and go in search of the path that leads into the rainforest. A three hour walk takes me along a fairly well-trodden path, to begin with. The rainforest is extremely lush and there's such an infusion of tropical plants in here. Some are like giant triffids, towering above me and there's green moss everywhere. It's strange that so close to a mass of ice, is something

73

as tropical as a rainforest! The track I take goes across a shaky bridge and underneath, a milky grey river, that raging past. I cross alone. (gulp)

As I go deeper there's boggy forest undergrowth to navigate through and my path becomes hidden and uncertain in places. Once again I'm stepping out and doing something alone that I'd never have dreamed of doing before. And once again, I feel that I'm not alone. (Even though I know I am in one sense). I find a pretty spot to eat lunch by the river and am fascinated by shiny stones that lie underneath the water. Sparkling flecks of fool's gold wink at me, and I collect a few for souvenirs. The sun streams through the creepers and warms my body. I could rest a long while by the sounds of this sweet, babbling river but time's moving on and I need to keep going.

I pass not a soul. Eventually my path breaks out onto a still and very beautiful serene pond surrounded by bulrushes. The Franz Joseph glacier is the back drop to this scene. I sit on a little wooden bench and just stare for a very long time, in utter wonderment. What beauty and majesty! It's so very moving. Another woman is also here, admiring the view. We share a few simple words of appreciation. Soon a party of younger people arrive and the woman slips quietly away. I stay on to 'meet' the group before resuming my walk, with new acquaintances I make from the group. Both are around their thirties, one is Chilean and the other German. We seem to get along really well, joking and chatting in turn as we walk. At the face of the glacier we help each other take photos of the stunning sight, trying to get as close as we can before *'closed off area'* signs block our path.

Walking away from the glacier my thoughts turn to the long walk back. Tour buses and cars are departing from viewing areas. We playfully decide to try and hitch a lift back. We're all surprised when a kind tour driver (doing a return journey back, after dropping a party off) stops to offer a ride in his empty bus. I think again, how relaxed and friendly it is here and how this sort of thing rarely happens back in the UK. How did we lose this laid back approach and simple acts of kindness to each other? Back in Franz Joseph we find a bar and share a few beers together, over lots of laughter. It's so good to laugh!! Two hours later we say goodbye, with hugs and kisses all around.

CHAPTER 50

Preparing my dinner in the hostel kitchen, I find Marie and Nell (the Irish pair) and we fall into conversation again. They're both hungry for more tales of the mountain! Marie comments that Ian "Looks just like George Clooney." Nell wants to look at the photos again and asks when will I see Ian again? It's a question that's very close to my heart, too. To return is what I want to experience more than anything else right now – all other things feel secondary.

The next morning Mr Chilean is here (but Mr German has left). We fall into conversation over breakfast and later decide to take a walk together. Our chosen track ends up outside a small dark cave. We hear the sound of running water inside. Mr Chilean is keen to go in and explore, so we venture into the first section, but without a torch it's difficult. The water on the floor is making it a bit treacherous and we're just about to turn back when we see tiny sparking lights on the roof. Are they glow worms? Well there sure are glow worm caves in these areas, so it's kind of likely they might be. This is fun! We make our way back out into the daylight and start the walk back to the hostel. Mr Chilean begins to talk a little of his life. He's a wine expert, currently working in Hawke's Bay at a vineyard and learning all about wine making. He tells me about Chile and it's kind of strange that the Chilean connection is here again (where Ian had returned, just before we met).

Soon I'm busy washing and ironing clothes in the hostel laundry, as I'm working later, plus it helps to take my mind off Ian and the longing to go back. Work turns out to be quite fun really. As I guessed, Jamie runs a relaxed and friendly ship with a lot of happy staff. When I finish at three, I spend a few hours in the sun on the veranda with a ginger beer and soak in the peace of this magical place. I check emails, eat and shower before going back to work. It's busier on my second shift, and hotter. My poor feet are definitely ready for a rest by the time I'm done at ten o'clock

Wearing a black shirt doesn't help. Half the restaurant area is terrace and the sun's still hot. Jamie is struggling to organise a 'mad chef' in the kitchen and some rather laid back younger staff, but it's clear the guy loves both the work and his gang. In between all this, he's been quietly watching me. Jamie can see I'm good with the customers and that they seem to like me. He tells me I can stay longer, (if I want) and work extra days. Again it's tempting to be offered more work, but to accept would tie me to a place. I re-remind myself that this trip isn't about work; it's about freedom.

Three Austrian guys are in my dorm when I get back but they're quiet sleepers and respectful guys. No bother at all. Just a few early morning lustful moans in their sleep! At breakfast, we chat over coffee on the terrace. They tell me they're off to a neighbouring ice glacier called Fox Glacier today, so we talk ice glaciers and adventure. I decide to check-out of this hostel and move to one called Glow-worm Cottage. The energy around this place is getting a bit weird. Food has been stolen from food boxes in the kitchen and communal fridges and I've noticed a lot of younger residents sit aimless about, watching TV or playing videos all day. It's not the vibe I want.

There's a totally different energy at Glow Worms. They have peaceful sun terraces with hammock seats and a free outdoor spa, to relax in. I get chatting to a girl from the Netherlands called Elsa, who's suffering miserably with a head cold. I offer one of my herbal fruit drinks to sooth her sniffles. We become friends.

CHAPTER 51

New Year's Eve So here we are at the eve of a New Year. I'm half way across the world, far away from everything and everyone I know and it all feels absolutely fine. The fact that its New Year's Eve is not such a big deal to me these days, as I now take the view that every day is a day to be celebrated! Still, there'll be music and a party atmosphere down at the restaurant and it's kind of nice to be around that vibe. Elsa tells me that the ATM machine in this little place is reputed to run out of money and she's predicting this before the night's out. The little supermarket has also been known to run out of food, so Elsa warns me to be sure to get provisions in too...

I love taking little walks around this place! It has such a mystical feel about it in the early morning. Low mist rises over the rainforest and obscures whole sections of the glacier, towering above me. When I finished work last night, the evening had such an air of magic about it. A soft night mist was floating eerily between trees and clouds, weaving a web of beauty across my path.

Phew, it's hot today! I sunbathe between work shifts but that makes me even hotter. Whilst relaxing in the sun, texts start to come in from Ian. I read with the hope of an invitation to return for New Year (but then I always was naive when it came to men and that fairy tale kind of dream). Ian's texts say:

Hi there! Hope u r having fun travels. Xmas with U was a very lovely few days. Was nice. When we travel things like that happen; I've had sum special times over the years.

Text 2 - *'It's what makes travelling so good. The more we get off the beaten track, the more encounters we have. Life is good and we must treasure good meetings and connections. Will keep in touch. It's all good. Don't 4 get to catch up on my friends in Ross at Empire Hotel? Ask if Grant Medley around. Get a moss farm tour. They'll have you on a bit. Great folk"*

I'm still trying to keep focused on the belief that *it's all good* as I try to let go of expectations and attachments. If it's meant to be it will return and if not – then there must be something better.

So back to New Year's Eve…

For many, this night's about drinking yourself silly. That's no longer of interest to me and so I kind of don't fit in, anymore. I go to work my evening shift and find I'm observing customers and their behaviour. Some are clearly focused on drinking as much as they can from early evening, whilst others are just relaxing, and appreciating good food in nice surroundings. A woman comes over half way through the evening and says, "I just wanted to say thank you for being so welcoming and friendly." I'm surprised as I've not really done anything much except offer her a jug of chilled water on a hot evening, as she sat down. But she makes a big thing of this and gives me lots of positive eye contact. Quite touching, that such a simple gesture had such a big effect

I walk slowly back from work and away from parties and people 'in drink.' Loud music grows fainter and fainter as I walk the (now familiar) road back to my hostel, in the last night air of an old year. It's true New Year's Eve is really no different than any other when you're living life from a place that beliefs every day is an amazing new day, full of adventure and new potential.

Back at Glow worm Cottage, Elsa and I find each other and crack open a malt beer. We share each other's companionship in a quiet, but gentle sort of way. As Elsa does mind puzzles, I catch up on my journal. I could become melancholy but decide against it. My intention is to end the old year with gratitude for the many blessings in my wonderful new life. I do believe *it's all good…*

So I thank the Universe again for the experience with Ian. If anything, it helps me now feel more sure than ever that there is a special man (somewhere) for me and that we have something wonderful to do and experience, together. It has also taught me to:

a) trust and be open more with myself and men

b) use my intuition and gut feeling wisely

c) realise that spiritual kind of guys are out there – even up mountains!

I don't want to be late to bed as I need a good night's sleep in preparation for my seven hour glacier hike tomorrow. The $150 I earned waitressing will pay for the hike and my accommodation tonight. *Happy New Year, Lynette, you're all good!*

CHAPTER 52

<u>New Years Day 2008</u> Wow, what a new year's gift! And what a challenging experience the glacier hike was! A long hard day, walking over ice with crampons attached to walking boots. A real opportunity to push out comfort zones! Small groups of fifteen or so hikers each have a personal guide who tests and clears the ice with a huge ice pick. Ours is Thomas. He's a young, tanned, hyperactive kind of dude. Thomas delights in urging his group to crawl into tight little ice tunnels, barely wide enough to take our bodies and filled with icy cold water. Then we must haul ourselves towards a tiny ice-hole ahead and towards the rope that's dangling through it. The keeper of the rope is laughing Thomas, who gleefully hauls each dazed wet body out, triumphantly!

As we climb higher the scenery changes dramatically from greys and murky whites, until a striking turquoise reflection of ice is all we can see. This glacier is a living, moving thing! It shifts backwards or forwards all the time, giving evidence of the powerful ability of nature. It marks the landscape in such a stunningly beautiful way.

Thomas hacks away, making ice steps for us to cautiously tread. With skill and expertise he bounds ahead, assessing crevices and gorges for safety and stability. He adores his job and never rests (not even for lunch) the whole time. With their backpacks of food, our small group of multi-national characters sit on the ice together and eat. The remoteness of our location is forcing us to bond in light-hearted and humorous ways. We laugh and chatter, making offers to take pictures of each other. When we finally make it to the summit Thomas takes a snapshot of the group together. It's a tremendous feeling to make it to the top and look down over vast expanses of glistening turquoise and white ice, right down to Franz Joseph below.

What an achievement. Quite a trek! The long descent proves wearisome and never ending. We're tired now – and having burned up masses of calories, we're also hungry! The repetitive downward stepping movements aggravate the old injury in my left knee and it starts to ache. Still, I'm feeling good and sense that I'm moving on from a need to be back with Ian. That energy feels like it's freeing up a bit and letting go now.

CHAPTER 53

Once back at Glow worms, I pull off my clothes, open a beer and head for the little outdoor spa. Ah, how sweet are small pleasures like this! A couple of older women from Essex join me in the hot bubbling water. As usually happens (these days) we fall into travel talk. One of them is clearly fascinated by the fact that I'm travelling alone. I can see from her face and hear from her comments that she'd like this experience herself.

After a shower, I buy fish, chips and ginger beer from a local fish shop. Then a random thought pops up: *Send a 'Happy 2008' text to Carl, to demonstrate to yourself that you're moving on from the past.* Other Happy New Year texts have been coming in from friends and family and once again I'm reminded how blessed I am with such dear friends and family and that *it's all good.* A text comes (almost straight back) from Carl thanking me and adding his own good wishes.

2nd January The buses start running again today and it's time to move on. My bus to Greymouth goes through a place called Ross, I recognise it as the one Ian mentioned in a text. After passing through, I get to thinking I could have stopped off and gone to find his moss farm friend. But by the time I've had this thought it's too late to get off.

The hostel I've chosen in Greymouth is called *Global Village.* There's a real ethnic and African feel to the whole place. Very tastefully furnished, fully made up beds and a cute little outdoor seating area. For the first time, I'm allocated a top bunk in a dorm. With paper thin and creaky floors above me, I soon find it's like Chinese torture!!

This is quite a noisy, but lively hostel with lots of comings and goings and a real mix of cultures, all living and cooking together. There are quite a large number of African travellers here, which is something I haven't encountered in other hostels. It's a friendly vibe with lots of action in the kitchen. We all cook up our traditional dishes; creating a cocktail of rich, aromatic and spicy smells. The energy is vibrant and alive. I like it.

The next night I take two of my herbal sleeping tablets in the hope of getting a better night's sleep. I'll see how it goes and maybe decide to move on earlier than planned if I don't get enough rest. It's as simple as that.

I'm sharing the bedroom with three young Japanese kids, one male and two female who have their gadgets and gear sprawled across the room. It doesn't feel quite me but again, I think *let's see what tomorrow brings.*

I do a food shop, check emails and go for a short walk down to the sea hoping to catch the sunset. By the time I reach the centre of Greymouth the sun's already set. I've been told they have lovely sunsets in this area...

Back at the hostel, I lie on my top bunk and feel each creak, groan and thud on the floor above my head. Definitely an ear plugs night tonight.

CHAPTER 54

It's a bright sunny morning and it looks like there's been rain last night. This hostel offers free kayaks. We are right on the riverside so I decide to take a kayak down the river and up to the mouth of the sea. This is to be my latest adventure and quite a lesson in trusting the Universe. I'm pushing old comfort zones again as I don't really know much about kayaking and will be going out alone. Putting on the lifejacket and tucking food and water into the hold, I launch my faded yellow, fibreglass kayak into the water without too much trouble. Paddling slowly through narrow, bulrush filled inlets; I eventually reach the mouth of the sea. I feel a big sense of achievement, confidence and happiness - then the real challenge begins...

As I turn the kayak around to head back, I realise that getting here is one thing and finding my way back is something else! The kayak drifts and wanders along the intricate, unmarked web of marshlands and I find myself getting more and more confused over which little inlet to take back. I'd not been aware, on the outward journey of how many off shoot routes from the main one there were!

It slowly dawns on me that there's a real chance I could get lost in this water maze and no one would know where to look for me – or even know I'm missing! My mind begins to whip up fear and panic. A strong parental 'voice' scolds me about my poor sense of direction and a history of getting lost that dates right back to being a little girl.

Racing ahead, it tries to imprint images of me drifting aimlessly for days; in a silent 'grave' – with no one knowing I'm here. Feeling a little sick, I pull back these thoughts from this unhelpful state and try to refocus. *Panicking is not going to help! Okay. Keep calm.* I take charge of a counter-conversation; *you found your way out here. You can find your way back. Use your senses, ask the Universe for guidance.*

Remember the times when you've been lost before (like in Hamner Springs) and it all worked out just fine. The Universe knows the way out. Just trust.

So I work on keeping focused and hold onto my affirmations. And I find that I'm doing a pretty good job at keeping *panicky mind* at bay. I look at the pretty scenery that drifts past. I see a heron, or maybe a stork. Make a mental note to find out which, when I get back. It's so peaceful and still as I glide along without paddling. I just let the silence wash over me and the sun tan my skin. Somehow (eventually) the familiar mooring sight of my hostel floats into view and I breathe an inner sigh of relief. Once again, I send up a silent thank you to my wonderful friend and guide the Universe.

I have requested a change of rooms. A quieter one and I am rewarded with a transfer to a six bedded dorm that has lots of personal space. I have an actual *bed* (not a bunk) and there's a sitting area and sun balcony tagged on at the end of the sleeping area. Wow! The furnishings of this hostel are bright and stylish. All the beds in my new room have matching duvet covers. And even the plates in our communal kitchen match mugs, in their rich black and red ethnic design. As I pass by a double room, I peek in and see matching cane furniture and a beautiful African printed duvet. The walls are full of artefacts that speak of jungles and Africa. I make a mental note that if I ever return to New Zealand (with my beloved) that we will enjoy one of the private rooms here, together.

CHAPTER 55

More and more I sense that a new partner is drawing nearer. I read again, the list of qualities that I wrote down in Christchurch:

A gentle warm and loving spirit. Passionate about love and life. Open to learn and grow. Shared family values. Strength of presence - physically and in personality and one who values the same in me. Secure in Self; not needing to control or have power over me. A relaxed attitude to money, abundance and giving to others and themselves. Open to grow deeper in levels of intimacy and experience a relationship that gives us freedom to become 'who we really are.'

I read the list over again and reflect on how I found much of this I found in Ian - and in such a short time. Yet again, I return to the belief that if our relationship was not to 'be' then a more perfect relationship must be out there. It's all good.

At breakfast this morning, a young German guy starts up a conversation with me. He's camping, busking and hitch hiking his way around New Zealand with no money, and no plan! He smiles as he tells me he sometimes lets the Universe choose his next destination by standing on the roadside with a sign that says *ANYWHERE* and just goes with the flow. He says he's done this enough now to trust that the place he gets taken to will have a gift, a message, a meaning, work or a person to meet. I laugh and think how different it might be if we could all live more in this way!

I take a walk into Greymouth today and have coffee at a local café. I share a table with a Canadian guy who tells me he's here for five weeks touring on his bike. We enjoy a pleasant and relaxed conversation as I learn there's a wife back home that's happy for him to take lone trips. How cool. On my return walk, back to the hostel, I pass a lovely ethnic kind of shop with beautiful snug cobweb lace cardigans on a rack outside. Even though the price seems a little high at $49 dollars, I decide to buy myself one when I remember that I'm working on freeing myself up from financial limitations and fear of lack. And of course, I'm also working on the intention to create a more stylish and quality wardrobe for my return! Later, I post another travel update to dad and decide that tomorrow I'll take the bus back to Ross.

After my walk I enjoy lunch and a cold beer with a young Japanese girl who's work-trading here. She's keen to speak and practice her English with me. I return to my room and soak up the sun on our private little terrace. There's no one around, so I pull a lounge chair from out the bedroom to sit on. I read and write up my journal. I drink coffee. Life is good. Life is simple and uncomplicated. I catch up on my washing and it's a perfect day for drying. The hostel is very quiet, before its next arrivals. I'm really enjoying the luxury and privacy of this dorm and sun terrace, knowing that by tonight it will be full again. Such a popular hostel!

CHAPTER 56

<u>Friday</u> I take the early bus back to Ross. It's the same friendly driver as before. She promises to pick me up on my return journey – if I need a ride back this afternoon. It's only 7.50 a.m. but this is the only bus, so it's this or nothing. Ross is still sleeping when I arrive and the Empire Hotel that Ian recommended I visit is shut up and silent. I take a walk around the village heritage trail area and there's still no one around. I tread the path of old gold miners and marked tourist signs that tell the gold rush story and how the biggest gold nugget in NZ was found in Ross! I take a peek in an old cemetery, trying to imagine the old characters that rest here and what kind of life they must have had. Thoughts of Ian keep popping up, as a modern day miner whose work now follows these ancient ones.

Back in the village I have a coffee and kill time, still waiting for the hotel to open up and ask about Ian's friend. At 10.30 a.m. the Empire Hotel slowly starts coming to life as deliveries begin arriving and doors swing open. I'm feeling a little shy now (as a stranger) asking about someone that knows Ian and realising they might be curious to know who I am, to him. There's a middle aged couple inside a dark gloomy interior and bar area, as I venture inside. They both look up, surprised to see a customer so early in the day. I smile, take a deep breath and ask if they know of a Grant Medley?

"Yes we know him but he's not about," the guy replies. The woman fixes her gaze on me and adds, "He's babysitting! Has his daughter and family staying over Christmas, so he's not been in much."

I'm not sure what to do. The man kindly suggests I leave a note. So I scribble briefly that a friend of Ian Leadley called to say hi. I write down my whereabouts for the next couple of days and cell phone number. Back outside after such a brief and unfruitful mission, it feels like my business in Ross is over.

This is such a small place with nothing to see or do. I wander about (a bit aimlessly) contemplating what to do next. I sit awhile by a lake and read my 7 Spiritual Laws. By lunch time, I've decided to have a go at getting back to Greymouth by some other means of transport. It is hours, before that one and only bus is due to come through...

I walk to a place where the road to Greymouth forks off and watch the traffic coming and going. I've never done any hitchhiking and I'm a bit uncertain as to how to go about it, in the safest way. After a while a campervan stops in a nearby lay-by and three middle-aged people get out. The woman dashes about, snapping photos and I make a quick decision to approach another member of the party, who are just standing about.

I ask the friendliest looking guy if there's any possibility of a lift to Greymouth with them. After checking in with his fellow travellers, he tells me okay, and I climb into the rear of the van, whilst the woman and the other guy get in the front.

And off we go. That was easy!

In no time at all, I'm back at the hostel, sitting on my personal little sun deck, eating lunch and enjoying a cold beer in mid-day sun. I jump suddenly, when my phone registers that a text is coming in. I'm surprised, as I still have my NZ Sim in (so either it's Grant Medley – or it's Ian).

I'm delighted to see its Ian! Guess I'm still half holding a hope that the text will say *Come back. Let me fetch you from where you are.* (You know, the knight in shining armour bit, we women all long for deep down). But it says *Hi. Howzit going? Have u got to Ross yet and caught up on any crazy locals. Hope u r having fun and happy travels.*

I marvel at the synchronicity of the Universe that brings this text here in such perfect timing and puts Ian somewhere that he has a phone signal to make this call today. I reply to let him know that I went to Ross this morning but that Grant wasn't there.

I tell him I miss him and let him know where I am, and where I'm heading next. For half an hour we text back and forth:

Ian - *Was a nice xmas. Think you o-deed on that buzzy energy we have up here. Really affects people. Worse in winter. Sum 1 like your maline wud c and feel allsorts.*

Me - *Yes, the place was one intense experience of energy, but my experience of your energy was another thing. I have not felt an attraction on such a level for years.*

Ian - *There's huge energy out in front of me hut. All those big valleys spilling out there. It really does affect people, I know 4 a fact. Been a quiet New Year, few beers down the valley.*

Me - *Yes, there is certainly a huge energy inside you and as well as out front of your cabin, and I know that for a fact, cos I've experienced it and also imagined it, many times!*

Ian - *I guess I can't live there and not take all that energy on board. Ha ha, 2day I was paying 4 sum thin in a shop. Girl got a wicked shock off me. Made a real crack! Ha.*

I sent a big hug to him and Zach and then I hear no more. Receiving his texts has unsettled me so I take a bike ride out through Greymouth, with our conversations turning over and over in my mind.

CHAPTER 57

I'm leaving tomorrow, so I sort out a taxi to take me to where the bus pick up is – to get to my next destination; as it's too far to walk to the stop with my heavy bag. Later, I run through the streets to try and catch the sun setting over the sea, for one last time. I chase the bright red ball as it falls lower and lower in this sky, hoping to see it set across the ocean. I don't make it in time but catch a brief glimpse of it setting whilst still en route. I walk slowly back to the hostel and eat a burger on the way, before heading to bed for one last night in Global Village.

The journey to Nelson is long, hot and stuffy. The bus is packed and a man in the seat in front of me is *so* loud. I finally arrive at my hostel and after dumping my bag in the dorm, I head down to the pool, in my bikini.

Yes. A hostel with a swimming pool - as well as an outside hot tub! My smugness at picking such a good hostel is soon short lived, as it's soon apparent that this is very much a young people's hostel. (gulp). The dorm is also very large and I end up with a top bunk, again. Rats!

I climb up into a stuffy loft that houses computers, to catch up with emails. Putting my dollars in the slot, I go online and am able to sort out bus and ferry crossing arrangements, in this way, too. I'm blessed with another 'nugget' of abundance from the Universe when I get a *Naked Bus* ticket for $1 that will take me to Picton, where I'll catch the crossing to

North Island in a few days. With all this sorted, I try to relax. But the hostel is so noisy and buzzy with the energy of youth, this proves difficult.

My dorm is crammed full of young girls, who don't seem to sleep much or respect the fact that others may want to! They're texting, phoning, eating, rustling bags and going in and out of the room all night long. I have the worst night's sleep of my entire trip and in the morning go to ask for a move. Paying a small extra amount, I manage to get a bunk in a four bedded mixed room in a quieter part of the hostel, with its own toilet and shower room. En-suite, I'm fast learning is a big treat, in the world of backpacking! I am first to arrive in the dorm, so I get to choose my bed, (no contest.) Lower bunk, furthest away from the door!

I take a walk into town after deciding to buy new ear plugs (seem to have left mine under the pillow, back in Greymouth). A necessity item when backpacking! I also want to buy a second pair of sunglasses. I invest in a medium priced pair (not cheap) as I want to care for my eyes. The rays and glare are so very strong here. Despite being here over a month, I'm still wearing factor 30 sun creams and feeling the sun's searing rays on my thin, English skin!

The day feels warm and muggy, as I wander among shops, getting groceries and treats. I can't resist buying ground coffee! The whiff of coffee beans as I pass by the counter is so divine - it reminds me that I spotted a rare item (a cafetiere) in the hostel kitchen, this morning. After labelling groceries with my name and date of departure, I place fresh food in the shared fridge and go out exploring again. Unexpectedly (and to my delight) I come across a Japanese garden and sit for a long while amidst its peace and tranquillity. I like the feel of Nelson. I love the colour of my hostel and its beautiful colonial looking, veranda type house. It's painted deep buttermilk with white windows and dark green window ledges. There's a white painted veranda, wooden lattices and a huge door with antique leaded glass panels. Just for fun, I sketch it in my journal, for future reference.

I text Ian to tell him I like Nelson. He'd told me how he used to live in Nelson and still spends time here, in the winter. I sense his energy now – I can't escape it! I tell him that I'm leaving for North Island in a few days. I guess I'm still hoping he'll ask me to return and come for me before I sail away from this Island, for good…

CHAPTER 58

Back at the hotel, I climb into an empty outdoor Jacuzzi and enjoy a good soak. I read my latest book. A guy gets in, also with a book. After a while he asks what I'm reading. Soon, we're chatting about books. My book is called *Strange Days*. It's about a woman's life with a guy (I've never heard of) called Jim Morrison. 'Jacuzzi guy' informs me that it was the anniversary of Jim Morrison's death, yesterday. Wow! We talk in amongst the bubbles and under the afternoon sun, for a long time about a variety of things. Our jobs (always a common subject) followed by psychology and then the subject of human behaviour. The conversation starts to get rather interesting, so I take a closer look at Jacuzzi guy. He looks about 40. Tells me his name is Will Fern and that he's a magician from New Jersey. Hearing him speak about his work is fascinating! We're in the tub a long time and I'm getting wrinkly from being in water so long. I need to get out soon, so I tell him I'm going. Will asks if I'm going out to eat. (Well, I guess I could be)! We arrange to meet in 45 minutes to eat somewhere together.

As I get ready, I suddenly find myself feeling nervous and a little self-conscious about what to wear and how I look. So I begin talking (reassuringly) to myself, like a good friend would. It's certainly a nice feeling to be going out to eat and also to have manifested (once again!) such an interesting new friend. Thanks Universe.

When we meet up in reception, Will has already enquired about where might be a good place to eat and asks, "Do you want to eat cheap, like a kebab, medium expensive or what?"

It's a bit of an odd type of a question and I'm a little taken aback. I say no to a kebab type meal and so we take a taxi to a seafood restaurant that the reception girl says has a good reputation. Will asks the taxi driver if it's expensive? I think, *that's a bit odd*. The vibe feels very money focused...

I sense that Will wants confirmation that I'll pay for myself so I say, "I have my credit card with me*"* and mention something about paying for our own food, to reassure him. As he pays the taxi driver, Will says to me "You can pay the return fare, eh?" I groan an inward groan as it dawns on me that I've attracted another guy that mirrors money limitations. Oh well, I guess I'll keep doing that until I move through this lesson in my own life!

Will Fern is nervous and seems uneasy in my company now that we're away from the safety of the hostel and in a 'date-like' situation. He's wearing glasses now, and I'm less attracted than when we were in the hot tub! Dress wise he looks a bit geeky in long sleeved t-shirt and shorts.

There's a distinct absence of aftershave (which I love smelling on a man!) Suddenly, I'm not finding his personality particularly attractive anymore, either. Will is quite good looking but *so* money focused! During our meal he spends a lot of time commenting on the cost of each dish – which takes a lot of the fun and pleasure out of eating them. Apart from this, his rather direct eating manner and comments on size of portions (when they finally arrive) is a real turn-off.

"Is this going to fill me up?" He asks a bewildered young waitress.

As the meal continues, we have quite an enjoyable time conversing about relationships (fast becoming my specialist subject!!). We discuss the difficulties of dating and from his conversation and mannerism, it seems Will struggles to 'read' women or understand how to relate to them on a closer level. Between mouthfuls of sea bass, he informs me that he's never married. That he lived with a girl for a while and was engaged, but they fell out. Will tells me that his job has become his 'wife, (I guess that could be a mirror too!).

He touches my hand a couple of times whilst talking, but I feel no connection or desire to respond back. At one time he tells me he realises he's quite good looking, and has no problem attracting dates, but the trouble seems to be getting timing right over moving things on to the next stage…

I would certainly agree with that one Will. At one point in our conversation completely out of the blue, he throws out a random comment about him having a fourteen inch penis! And, I'm not at all sure if he's making a joke or not. (I resist a mischievous thought that suggests I find out if it's true!).

Will Fern is certainly an unusual dinner companion, that's for sure! At one point he leans across the room and starts to entertain neighbouring diners with magic, whilst keeping our poor little waitress busy fulfilling his needs and gripes! I smile and try to silently reassure her, as it's clear she's not at all sure whether Will is joking or not, (either) with his bizarre and random, odd comments!

CHAPTER 59

I drink half a bottle of good wine, the evening softens and the sky darkens. This sweet little place has once been a boatyard, anchored half on land and half overhanging the sea. Sea gulls circle the inky sky, outside its large glass windows - probably catching left over scraps from seafood diners. Soon the meal is over, and we share up the bill and pay for our expensive, but delicious meal. Well, it is the most famous seafood restaurant in Nelson! We decide to walk back into town, as the night is still warm and Will says he wants to finish up at a bar. But he seems to have a restless energy about him now, and leaves me sat at the bar to go listen to a singer in an adjoining room. After a short while, I tell him I'm going and he decides to come too. We part at the door of the hostel, with him asking me what time I'll be up for breakfast. I say around 8 a.m. I guess, and he says maybe he'll catch me then? We bid each other a formal goodnight, and that's that. I hit the sack big style, after a most extraordinary evening!

The next morning, I don't get up until 8.30 a.m. Will's not in the kitchen when I get there, (thankfully) and soon I am chatting to a Dutch girl called Dana. Dana and I get on well, so we decide to pack a lunch and go hiking together. Our walk takes us out of the town, into the hills and through a forest area. Following the river, we look for a good track. Some bird is tooting his song from the treetops and it's another beautiful day in Nelson. Dana tells me she's from a farming family in Holland and that she speaks Friesian, Dutch and English. Never having been away from home before, it's a big thing for her to be abroad. I like Dana and learn a lot about her close-knit family. Dana is a very mature thinking, young and yet wise girl, in many ways. On our return journey, it suddenly starts to rain and the walk turns into a bit of a wet slog home.

Back at the hostel, I take off wet clothes and crawl under my duvet to doze myself warm again. I love the freedom to do what feels right, without needing to think about anyone else's needs or be distracted by obligations or responsibilities. I have such gratitude for this precious gift that my time away (alone) gives me. I am realising, more and more, how much I'm relaxing, after carrying the stress of feeling responsible for (what feels like almost a lifetime) of other people's needs.

Now it's my time to love and nurture my needs, without distractions. And ah, how delicious it feels! I catch up on reading and make fresh coffee. Later, I climb the wooden steps to the internet shack and book my next hostel, (in Wellington) then decide to go find the Nelson Meditation Centre; to attend a meditation session, that's advertised for tonight.

A fairly short walk into town and I find it - hidden inside a quirky shop-front, with lots of raggedy prayer flags draped gaily across its window. There's just one woman sitting inside the dark, incense smelling room as I enter. She seems friendly. Two others join us and then the teacher arrives. Apart from an opening and closing prayer, the meditation is made up of silence. I slip into a deep relaxed state as I open my mind to all possibilities. It's a simple, peaceful sharing of silent space. Then, a few brief words of greetings and farewells with strangers cum friends - and a walk back to the hostel.

I decide to treat myself to a ready cooked meal this evening, when I spot a little Thai fast-food van in the hostel car park. Choosing Thai Green Curry, I gobble it down right there and then. It tastes scrumptious and at $7, it's a great price too! (I just realised I sounded like Will then, or he sounded like me?) Mirror mirror. I catch sight of him later (in the spa again) complete with book, chatting away to a girl! Ha! His next victim, I wonder? I check emails; book my next bus passages and do some travel research. I resist replying to non-urgent emails – as I am really trying to disengage from the 'world back home', as much as possible.

CHAPTER 60

There's a young couple with huge back packs and an African guy in my room when I get back. Early next morning the couple leave and it's raining so hard, they have to cover up their heavy backpacks with plastic. Poor buggers! The black guy and I are left. He sleeps on and I feel no desire to get up either. It's a funny experience these mixed sex dorms, but a good one, I think. Certainly challenges conventional beliefs about right and wrong gender etiquette, etc. I mean, what the hell does it matter? We are all humans, in different skins, whether male or female and surely there is nothing to stop us sleeping in the same room, except our social conditioning!

I glance over at my roommate. He is sleeping peacefully in the early morning heat. I can see his ebony back and it looks beautifully smooth and shiny. Last night I caught a glimpse of him getting into his bed in skin tight undies (very nice butt!). He makes no sound as he sleeps and is a clean, sweet smelling guy.

I'm just dozing back off to sleep myself, when a text comes in from youngest daughter, Mel. I decide to give her a quick call and we chat for a while about driving lessons, her job and the difficulties she's having fitting in extra cleaning work she's doing for her elderly grandma. I hear myself slipping back into adviser/rescuer mode again. (Oh God! It's *so* easy to slip right back into it!). The call ends with words of love for each other and my task now, is to let it go, so that my daughter can live her own life without my interference, but with my love.

I have breakfast with Dana and we gripe about the grubby state of the hostel kitchen. It's true. The worst I've been in so far. Dana says it's the same for her too. I muse over the fact that I should have left here days ago really, as the owner has such a negative energy about her! I recall how fast I'd moved on in Franz Joseph, from that sort of vibe. People are complaining of things being stolen, out of fridges. I experience it later myself, when I go to get one of my cold beers. They were there last night, but have now gone. Bloody hell! It's all symptomatic of the negative energy this place has and it's not good. There's a 'pleading' sign on a notice board, asking for someone to return their camera and precious memories of their travels, that's been stolen. How sad.

To take my mind off all this, I decide to sort out clothes I'm not using anymore. My bag is getting *so* heavy - as I keep picking up little souvenirs on my way. I take some items to a charity shop and parcel up others and post them back home. What a release! But I'd still like to buy more quality clothes, and have the experience of buying without feeling the need to purchase low priced or sale stuff – which has always been a default position I've gravitated back to. I realise once more that whilst ever I resist paying expensive prices, I'll be attracting guys with money issues – as I still have these limitations myself. Oh well, until it finally shifts, I guess I'll just keep working on it, as best I can…

Back at the hostel I take a swim, and I'm the only one in the pool. An older German woman is reading by the poolside. We smile at each other as I swim by and again, it's nice to make connections. I realise that I'm starting to feel a little lonely for company and conversation, again. I'm also becoming aware that I'm a little too hesitant and reserved for my own good, when it comes to starting up conversations. After a shower and clean-up I walk in the mellow evening sunshine, and just keep going until I reach the Japanese garden.

It is so beautiful here. I sit for a while again, making little sketches of aspects I particularly like and hope to recreate one day in a garden of my own. There are couples in the gardens and I realise that I'm lonely to 'couple'. I comfort myself with thoughts that maybe I'll return to this area one day, with my own mate…

I go back to the hostel. I cook a meal and eat alone. This evening, I am acutely aware that everyone else around me seems to be with a mate. Back at my dorm everyone's in bed and its only 10p.m. The African guy's bunk now has an older Malaysian guy in it. He has a strange musty smell to his skin, and he snores. I push my earplugs in deep and go to sleep.

CHAPTER 61

9<u>th January</u> There's rain on awakening but soon it clears. I do a little hand washing then pack lunch and head out for the day. I aim to walk in the direction of the nearest beach. It takes me about an hour to get there and on the way (to my amusement) I pass the Boathouse Restaurant where Will and I had eaten. I take a photograph and chuckle to myself as I recall his penis comment. How on earth do I attract such guys?!

This day is beautiful clear and sunny. When I arrive at the seashore, I kick off heavy walking boots and enjoy the feel of cool, soft sand as I walk across the deserted beach.

Resting for a while I doze, relax and then think a little, intermittently. I read. I write in my journal. I watch the sea. I think some more. I come to the conclusion that I'd like to have a travel companion for the next part of my journey. A friend would be good right now. So I send out these thoughts and the intention to attract a travelling buddy. So much is being manifested on this trip that it's hard to ignore the power of Universal Laws and yet still, I often forget to apply them, as a first course of action. How strange! The Universe keeps offering amazing evidence that all I desire can be mine. I just need to believe it!

Tomorrow I cross to the North Island and move further and further way from Ian. On the way back from my afternoon at the beach I stop off at a beach café. I'm spending lot of hours with my own thoughts and company lately; whilst observing others in relationships. It's a strange experience. I order a Mac's Gold malt beer - the kind I bought before Christmas, to take up Ian's mountain. So I toast his memory again, as I continued my 'closure' around those special mountain times. It's a hot, hot day and it's too late, before I realise I've burnt my ankles. After I changed from walking boots to sandals, to walk the beach, I forgot to apply extra sun cream to protect my feet. Now, I need to squeeze angry red skin back into hot, leather boots before I can set off back. It's an uncomfortable walk, so I stop at The Boathouse to take a coffee stop. Sitting on a narrow, outdoor gallery bar, looking out to sea, I wonder when my own heart will know real love. I guess the answer lies within me and my own limitations...

What a frustrating thought!

Two young American girls and the Japanese guy are in the bedroom when I return to pack for my departure, tomorrow. We chat about our day and the man asks me about my own life back in the UK. He says he is a teacher and about to retire. It's his first time hostelling and informs us he didn't know about mixed-sex dorms. That must have been a shock to him!

CHAPTER 62

<u>10th January</u> Today I have been two months in NZ and now leaving South Island to sail to North Island. What an eventful two months it has been! I wonder what my second two months, will have in store.

I'm on the sun deck of the ferry as it pulls out of the harbour. *Goodbye beautiful South! I leave with many wonderful memories in my heart. Thank you Ian, for those you helped me create. I hope we meet again. x.* This is the text I send to Ian whilst the ferry toots and blows, as it forges its way out, into open sea. A well of emotion rises up from my stomach and into my eyes. It's cold on deck in the early morning air, but gradually sunshine breaks through. I watch the landscape getting smaller and experience our captain's careful navigation through the Sound and out onto the Tasmanian Sea.

I'm in Wellington! The ferry crossing cost $52 and now I need to take a taxi to where my hostel is located, in this big city. My taxi driver doesn't know where the street is (gulp)! I end up having to show him (on my map). Feeling annoyed, I hand over the $12 fare and can't help wondering if I paid extra for his incompetency! What a start to my time in the cosmopolitan city of Wellington. The backpackers I'm booked in is my second - not first choice. It's high on a hill looking down onto the city. I soon discover that *Rosemere Backpacker's Hostel* is a rather tired and worn out looking place.

It's clean though, and run by a fairly friendly, middle aged ex-backpacker called John who tells me he took a year out from work to travel and ended up here. My four-bedded dorm is shared with an Irish couple and a young Irish girl who are all living here, whilst working. I decide that this is an okay sort of base for now. Free Internet and breakfasts are two of its perks. Quiet location and quiet residents too! Lots of long term residents (I seem to find that in hostels in bigger locations).

It's my first night, so I amble down the hill and onto the water front. There's hardly a soul around. *It's pretty desolate for a city!* I think. Finally, I end up at a MacDonald's - just to get something that I know the taste of and that's a cheap, hot meal until I can find a supermarket tomorrow. I take my food tray upstairs in the hope of finding a window seat. There's only one other woman on the upper dining floor and we smile at each other and say hi. This is Jenny aged 38 from Germany. She tells me she's also travelling alone but doing a different route to me. In a few days she will take the ferry to South Island (reverse journey to my own). We both comment on how nice it is to have a like-minded person to talk to and both agree it'd be great to spend time together - before her ferry departs. Later, I realise that here is my latest manifestation...

Jen and I part company in a happy mood after sharing a few beers at an Irish Bar. It feels great to be around the pub's lively energy and have someone to share it with! My new friend and I are delighted with each other's company and agree to eat out together, tomorrow evening (as a treat) - we both haven't done much of this, whilst travelling alone. Oh, what fun!

I get a good night's sleep and there's a beautiful day waiting to greet me. Via the Internet, I've arranged to meet up with Mike Sykes (that first contact of mine in NZ) whose emails sparked my interest off back, in another life… Mike has offered to pick me up and take me for lunch to discuss professional practice and show me a little of Wellington. What's also amazing (if you remember) is that he'd previously told me, his wife is also called Lynette! And it's really not a common name, is it?

I shower and dress in a skirt, cream camisole and the cropped lacy cardigan, bought in Greymouth. My skin is honey brown and I have a radiant energy about me. I can feel it. I look and feel great! Mike collects me from the hostel in his car and we spend four most enjoyable hours together discussing business, the state of Maori culture and disaffected youth. Mike's older than myself and has a gentle, safe energy about him. He drives us along the coastline of Wellington, and then up to the Botanical Gardens Café, where he treats me to lunch. There's not enough time to cover all our interconnecting threads and themes around topics of interest, before Mike's due back at work. We part firm friends and promise to keep in touch!

Once back in the city centre I ask Mike to drop me off near The Beehive, a very royal government type parliamentary building. I've read that they hold tours at certain times of the day, and I'm interested in hearing more about the politics of New Zealand. Taking a gentle stroll up a long driveway, I arrive at the front of a majestic, dome-shaped building and book onto the next tour. It's starting in five minutes! I'm feeling very alive, after an interesting and stimulating morning.

CHAPTER 63

Our tour guide is young, enthusiastic and very keen. He starts the tour by asking everyone in the group where in the world they're from. We're quite a mixed bunch and a quick glance round reveals mostly couples and family groups, apart from one guy (in his 50s) who also seems alone. In my short 'eye candy,' I note he's smart and distinguished looking with groomed, short silver hair. When it's his turn, I hear him tell the guide he's from Canada.

Almost as soon as the tour starts to move on, Mr Canadian appears in my immediate proximity -after being seated quite far away in the room, where we started off.

I wonder vaguely if this is coincidental or not? The truth is that I'm in such a relaxed energy zone, after such a great morning and outdoor lunch in the sun, I'm not even thinking any 'man thoughts' today. I'm simply enjoying the experience of the tour. Our guide weaves his way through many fascinating and colourful rooms in the Beehive and adjoining buildings. As he leads us down into the basement, he proudly points out anti-earthquake shock-absorbers, on which the building rests. I'm enthralled as he explains how they will allow the structure to bend, sway and return to its original position, in the event of an earthquake. We tourists are well impressed with this bit!

All the time I'm vaguely aware that Mr Canadian is orbiting around my personal space and directing friendly conversation, concerning tour information and architecture of the building, in my direction. It's rather unexpected, but pleasant. I suddenly become aware that I'm enjoying a second day of conversation and company! Thank you, Universe. Once again you've given me what I asked for!

A woman with two small children tries to engage Mr Canadian in conversation, (probably as he's being so friendly to me) so I move away, to allow this to happen more easily. The tour moves on through large reception halls full of modern art and flags; they represent the multicultural nations of the world.

There's so much to see and experience. I love it! Entranced, I turn to examine a colourful display on my right when to my surprise, he's back again! It's then that I realise this is more than just coincidence or general friendliness. This guy is interested! Now, his conversation is more direct and asking questions like, "Where are you from?" "Are you travelling alone, or with a friend?"

He tells me he's here for 2 weeks, to spend a week on each island. Tomorrow, he leaves for South Island. I detect an accent that's not Canadian. He says he's Serbian but has lived in Canada for the last 20 years. His name is Stovan. I exchange light hearted and friendly conversation, and he asks further questions about me.

Our tour is drawing to a close when out of the blue, and unconnected to any thread of conversation Stovan asks, "So what you do now?"

Thinking he's meaning travel-wise, I say, "I'm in Wellington for a few days before…" But he stops me by saying, "No, No, I mean now, after this tour." I tell him that I have no immediate plans. I then make a split second decision to be less cautious than usual, as I'm painfully aware of missed opportunities, in the past!

I've already made up my mind that Stovan is attractive, intelligent and that I'm interested to get to know him more. So I ask, "Would you like to go for a drink or something?"

"Yes, yes, very much!" he replies straight away.

Well done Lynette, you're learning!

CHAPTER 64

Before long we're seated in the late afternoon sunshine, outside a very classy wine bar, watching rush hour in Wellington. This is a rather sophisticated part of the city and all around, men in suits and women in high heels dash backwards and forwards carrying briefcases and smart bags. It's pretty fun watching all this live entertainment! I ask for a coffee, but this bar doesn't serve hot drinks. Stovan suggest wine, and I agree. As he goes inside to order, I think to myself what an amazing day I'm having. And how deliciously divine it is! I lean back, take in the sunshine and relax, whilst thinking how blessed I am.

It feels so very much like the Universe is just waiting for me to decide what I want next, and that it's mine, for the asking. It's a pretty exciting feeling, I can tell you. Soon Stovan is back with two lovely glasses of chardonnay and a jug of water. As we sit there chatting in a relaxed sort of way, (for strangers) our mood is both friendly and jovial. He tells me he has two sons and shows snapshots on his phone. Both are grown men. I look at pictures of a garden in Canada with lots of snow in it. There's a beautiful lily pond and then Stovan shares photos of abstract art and Japanese flower arrangements. He informs me that these are all his own works of art. I'm fast realising that this is quite a creative guy. I like creative types!

Stovan begins to share his feelings, about the ending of his marriage, soon after a move to Canada. Of his grief and devastation, about how he missed seeing his sons, at the end of each day. These very open expressions of feelings from an estranged father, make me think of my ex-husband, and how it might have been for him following our separation. Suddenly my empathy seems to extend itself out to include all sufferings from all family break-ups across the world! It's a little overwhelming... As Stovan talks, it feels like he's a man of great feelings and I like that. It's a shame he's leaving Wellington and we can't spend more time together. I tell him about my daughters, the two lights of my life, and show him the note that Melanie gave, when I left. (I carry it with me

tucked safely in my rucksack, along with Gemma's guardian angel pin).
Stovan smiles and says, "She loves you very much…"

We've been sat there a good while when I check my watch and see it's
time to head back to shower, before meeting Jen for dinner. I think how
ironic it is, that I have a dinner date on the one day I get to meet an
interesting guy! I thank Stovan for the drink and tell him I have to go.
He must have been having similar thoughts, as he asks if he can have
dinner with me. But, I can't speak for Jen and it would be unfair to invite
him without asking. So I say that I'm sorry, but I've arranged to eat with
a girlfriend.

I comment that, "We could have made another arrangement, but of
course you're leaving tomorrow." As I make to leave, Stovan asks if he
can walk with me. I happily agree. As we walk he chats about his
arrangements for car hire and accommodation on the South Island. Here
in Wellington, he's staying in an Ibis Motel. "Come with me!" He says
suddenly, (again out of the blue). I stop and look at his face to see if he's
joking.

"Travel with me on South Island for a week. You have lots of time to
return to North Island afterwards." I'm stunned. I'd not expected this
unconventional offer, and it takes me back. I then find myself giving a
variety of 'conventional' reasons for why I can't. Stovan dismisses them
all and says, "You could, if you really want to."

He's right of course. But I also have another arrangement, (beyond my
dinner date) also with Jen. We've made plans to spend tomorrow
together and this commitment is also nudging at my conscious. So in the
end I thank Stovan for his kind offer and say I'll think about it. (I've
learnt not to say no straight away to anything anymore!).

And, this is *so* out of the blue that I really *do* need a bit of space, to find
the answer. I suggest that maybe we can meet up for a drink later on,
after my meal with Jen. He gives me the hotel address and his room
number. We say goodbye and Stovan says he hopes he'll hear from me.
I'm flattered by his attentiveness and crazy offer – it intrigues me! I walk
quickly, through the city, shower and change before heading straight back
out, to meet Jen.

CHAPTER 65

It's a lovely warm evening. I dress smartly in white linen trousers and a silk, lime green strappy top. Jen is already at the pre-arranged spot, so we head straight off to find somewhere to eat. Through the many streets of Wellington we tramp, laughing about the fact that when we've found a friend to enjoy eating with, now we're having difficulty finding somewhere nice to eat! As we walk, I tell Jen about my encounter with Stovan and she listens in awe. She offers to help me decide what to do, and we discuss options around my dilemma. Jen has a mature head and very open to viewing things from lots of positions. I like this about her. She suggests we arrange to meet up with Stovan later for a drink, so I can get to know a bit more about him.

How thoughtful of her to make this offer! But still, I tell Jen I'd feel bad that our 'girly' time would be cut short, if I make this choice. Jen dismisses this and encourages me to ring his hotel, to confirm the arrangement. So I do, and Stovan's delighted to hear from me. We arrange to meet in his hotel lounge at 9p.m. Jen is turning out to be such a good friend. (Thank you Universe) We enjoy an easy and effortless chat. She's very caring, makes helpful observations and seems to have a good understanding about men - even though she's not married. I comment that Stovan seemed to be a little forthright and matter of fact with words and that I'm not so sure about this.

Jen tells me that it's different in Serbia and men approach emotions differently there. She goes on to speak about cultural differences between her own country and mine, telling me she believes English men to be very romantic. I laugh at this, but Jen assures me that in relation to German men this is certainly true. I'm not convinced!

As the evening wears on, I find myself becoming more and more open to the idea of returning to South Island for another week, simply to have the experience of travelling with this unusual man. Jen and I discuss how things might be and we think of a few questions to ask him. Accommodation would need to be spoken of. I know I can't afford to pay the kind of hotel room rates that Stovan pays. Then there's the expense of ferry travel (both ways again) to consider although Stovan had already offered to pay my ferry fare – when I used this excuse earlier.

Jen and I finally decide to eat in the Irish Bar. I have Irish stew and a glass of Chardonnay. Lovely! We then leg it all the way back across the city, checking our map as we go, to find The Ibis. Stovan is waiting for us in the lounge area dressed in beige trousers, a white linen shirt, and smelling of classy aftershave. I introduce Jen to him, and then straight away she makes her apologies then leaves. I try to get her to stay longer, but she just smiles at me and is gone.

This suits Stovan more than me! He suggests we go look for a bar. Suddenly, I'm feeling a little shy - like being on a first date, as well as realising that this is to be (yet another) speedy information gathering/ intuitive exercise, to help me make a decision about the trip. We wander around, and find it's just as difficult locating somewhere nice to have a drink, as Jen and I did, finding a good place to eat. Stovan says he has a bottle of red wine in his room, so shall we have a drink there instead? It seems a harmless suggestion and quite practical really, as finding a bar in this goddamned city is proving impossible!

CHAPTER 66

So we go to his room and drink a glass of wine. I observe his suitcase and his belongings and gather more information about him. His aftershave is Fahrenheit. He has a small diary with Serbian writing in. I think it's strange he doesn't write in English, after all those years in Canada…

The conversation turns to my decision. I take a deep breath and ask my question about sleeping arrangements. Stovan asks, in a matter of fact way, "Why, you can share the rooms that I have booked." (Gulp)!

I say that I don't know him well enough for that, so he makes the (valid) point that I share mixed dorms with strange men all the time on my travels. (This is of course, very true). So then I suggest there might not be a place on a ferry crossing so maybe that will decide? As if I did decide to go, I would honour my arrangement with Jen, tomorrow. Stovan reassures me he'll pay for my ferry and pick me up from the terminal when I arrive, (but doesn't offer to check availability on the hotel Internet downstairs, or give me the money).

It's getting late now and I'm meeting Jen quite early. I tell Stovan it's late, I'm feeling sleepy, and need to set off walking back to my hostel, at the other end of the city. He invites me to stay. I quickly say no, I have to go back to the hostel to get my stuff ready for tomorrow. Again, he comes up with an alternative. This man is so matter of fact with his solutions; it jolts my habitual thinking patterns! Now Stovan states the simple fact that I could get my gear ready in the morning instead of tonight and he'll set the alarm for whatever time I wish.

This is all pretty unusual, but a part of me is very curious to step outside my conventional box and consider his 'alternative,' but very simple, solution focused options. Weakly, I state that I don't have any nightwear with me. Stovan says I can borrow spare pyjamas, if I want, and he's also got a (new) toothbrush. This man's got all the answers and its getting to feel like this is a pretty daft sort of a discussion to be having, as grown-ups. So my last stance is to ask where I would sleep, if I did decide to stay. He points to the far side of an enormous king sized bed and it all seems quite simple, really. I 'feel out' the energy in the room and it doesn't feel weird or anything, and so I think, why not? Stovan moves silently around handing over toothbrush and pyjamas, and off I trot to the bathroom. When I return he's wearing a tee-shirt with underpants and sat up in bed. Ah, this feels okay.

I'm as far away up the other side of the bed as you can get, before I call out "Goodnight." It's quiet for a bit before Stovan asks what I'm doing so far away and I reply, "Sleeping." He begins to speak of the afternoon (was it really only this afternoon?) of seeing me on the parliamentary tour and feeling very attracted to me. I ask why? He says I'm attractive, pretty, and smart. He goes on to tell me how he felt more strongly towards me after reading my little note from Melanie. "Here's a woman who is a good mother, a woman with a heart," he says with emotion.

I lie there and think this is a pretty deep thing for a guy to say on a first date, and I like it. Stovan asks if he can hold my hand, as we sleep and (naively) I offer the hand, thinking that he'll just hold it and go to sleep. Not so. He begins to caress and kiss it, intimately. "That's not holding it!" I say as I take my hand back and turn away from him. It's not feeling so straight forward anymore but still, I feel relaxed, and confident that I just need to keep communicating boundaries. Stovan carries on sharing his feelings of affection for me. He says he likes my hair and my face. Suddenly, he reaches over and says "Can I hold your face, please."

Well, I am not at all used to being 'wooed,' in such a way; and he is *so* persuasive! Stovan starts to caress my face intimately and then tries to kiss me. But I move away and push against him as I do so, to give the message that I don't want this. Stovan seems a little confused and asks why I push him away? I tell him that I want to sleep, and that this was what we agreed. All is still for a while. I relax, turn away and try to sleep.

CHAPTER 67

A thought crosses my mind that it might be best to leave now and head back across the city, but I ignore it, as it's late and the thought of walking dark streets isn't appealing, and I'm not sure I have enough money on me for a taxi, from here. After a while, Stovan turns towards me again, and puts his hand around my waist. I let it rest there; (naively) thinking that maybe he'll go to sleep like this.

Oh, how little I have learnt of men and their passion, over my adult years...

But, to be fair to the species, I have shared a bed with other men, in the past, without anything physical happening, so it was reasonable to think I could do so again. Stovan's hand isn't around my waist for long, before it's seeking the skin line of my pyjamas. Boy! You have to give this guy 10 out of 10 for persistence! I move his hand away, again and again, and he gently chides me. Then I push him away (more forcefully now) to try and get the message firmly across. He's upset, "Do not push me so hard!" I explain it's because he's *not* getting the message – with words.

Mr 'Golden Words' now explains that it's not easy for him, as he's so attracted to me and what is the problem with a little closeness between two people who like each other, anyway? It goes this way, backwards and forwards for a while and I'm fast loosing reason (and argument) as to why I am actually keeping up this resistance? I'm also starting to feel some attraction to the passion in him. I like a man with passion. And after all, there's been one too many 'lukewarm' kind of guys, in the past …

It's been a long time since I've shared intimacy with a man, and Stovan has a handsome stature. I start to think that if I'm seriously considering taking a week out to travel with him, maybe I should just go ahead and 'sample' a bit of what might be on offer - to help with the decision! I don't exactly know what shifts in me, but the next time Stovan seeks my lips, I return the kiss.

Throughout the night he rises easily in passion, again and again. But Stovan's passion seems all consuming; with such urgency for expression but with little tenderness or soft words to accompany it. I feel a stark absence of connection. My mind begins to go blank and there's a sense that my spirit is withdrawing from the experience. The darkness of our hotel room casts shadows across Stovan's face, making its appearance a little menacing. His facial features scrunch up in an almost pained like passion. They are strange and unfamiliar.

Throughout the night, this man remains a stranger to me. There is no connection on an emotional or spiritual level and therefore little connection on a physical one - almost nil. I speak not a word or show much response. It feels like I'm observing myself from above. The lack of warmth and affection has such an adverse effect on this beautiful act. Without these things, I realise it has no value or meaning to me, at all...

CHAPTER 68

The alarm goes off. Stovan gets up and I say, "A coffee would be nice." But it lands on deaf ears as he heads off to the shower; calling for me to join him. He can call as long as he likes – I'm not going! I get up to make a coffee and ask if he'd like one. Stovan says he wants tea, but there's no "Please or thank you." His manner seems void of warmth and affection, and I recall the cultural differences Jen spoke of. Maybe this way is normal to him?

Stovan comes out of the shower and asks why I didn't shower with him? He comments that I could have scrubbed his back! I laugh and say, "What do you think I am, a bloody servant?!" As Stovan dresses, I sit in bed drinking my coffee and can't help notice what a nice bum he has. So I tell him. He stops dressing, looks directly at me then says in his clipped Serbian accent, "You tell me now!" It then comes home to me how little I've shared of myself with him. I shower and dress.

He's packing his things now, throwing worn t-shirts into a wastepaper bin. I ask what he's doing and he replies that he doesn't carry dirty clothes around; he'll buy more. I'm a bit taken aback by this! But then I think that I admire his attitude of non-attachment to material things, and the ability to spend money easily on new stuff. Stovan doesn't have the money limiting issues; like other men on my travels. (At least this aspect is good!) Maybe my mirror of 'lack' is changing – I *have* been buying myself more things, lately!

There's wine left in last night's bottle. Stovan doesn't attempt to drink or decant it, to take with him (I would!). In Stovan's world it's simple. Don't need that. Do need that... He methodically packs his suitcase and prepares to leave with a relaxed ease. There's no mention of checking the Internet for ferry availability. No mention of money to support purchasing a ticket. So I don't mention it either, as my mind is not so open to the idea, after last night.

The decision seems to be making itself. Unexpectedly, (like he knows what I'm thinking) Stovan turns away from his case, holds my face in his hands and studies it intensely. I ask what he's doing. He tells me he's trying to memorise my features. I sense he knows that he won't see me again. I laugh and say, "I'm here! You don't need to remember me." He returns to packing and (again) I watch, trying to find any connection, or potential that could encourage me to change my mind. I try nuzzling into the back of his neck as he bends down, and kiss it gently. No response. I comment that I like the smell of his aftershave. Stovan stops packing, studies the bottle briefly and says, "You like?" before continuing to pack.

CHAPTER 69

I sit on the bed, watching him iron a shirt, still trying to find a glimmer of connection and understanding of this unusual man. "Why you look at me this way!" He demands, feeling my eyes on him and sensing my enquiry. "What way?" I ask. "This way," he mimics a lowering of eyes in scrutiny. I'm not able to explain what I'm searching for with my look. Instead, I find myself asking, "Do you think we could have a nice time together in the South, Stovan?" He makes a non-attached kind of statement like, "Maybe or maybe not, who knows?" Still, he offers little evidence that he wants this. But then I think that if he's actually achieved that non-attached state of mind, then of course it would be okay either way, wouldn't it? I conclude this might be the reason. Interestingly, I observe myself, as I try to extract some sort of affirmation that he wants or needs me – but of course in the world of non-attachment there is neither. It's all good.

Stovan's ready to go and so am I. He suggests we leave together and take the lift to the lobby. I already know deep down that I've decided to not go with him, but if I'm honest there's still a fascination in the magic of our meeting and initial attraction. We share an unexpectedly tender kiss and I look deep into his brown eyes, as a rare moment of tenderness passes between us. Stovan is gentle in this final kiss. We leave the hotel room together, like a regular couple. He says good morning to passengers in the lift as we enter, and I feel unattached from him. Stovan pays his bill and we head towards the entrance to leave. As he turns to go, I tell him I'll let him know my final decision, via email. He simply states. "You will be welcome if you come but also welcome if you don't." What a strange goodbye! Yet what a totally wonderful Law of Detachment response!

I head back through the early morning streets of Wellington, buying breakfast on the way. In a very short while, I'm meeting Jen. As I shower I notice a small friction burn on my left elbow (reminding me that what I had hoped was a bad dream, actually happened). I pop a band-aid over the area to protect it. Jen greets me with a smile and notices it, straight away! I'm still coming to terms myself, with the bizarre events of last night – and have been considering not telling Jen about it, as it feels so surreal. But she's my friend and besides, I don't like to lie. Jen listens, wide eyed and quietly, (as a good friend does) and doesn't judge me. She's a wise counsel to have as I digest my various thoughts, during our walk by the ocean. I'm trying to find some inner resolution and understanding to it all.

There's a part of me that wants the experience of non-attachment that this man seems to offer. It stops me dismissing the idea of going with him, completely. But as the day wears on, my 'inner council' make their final decision. I recall the lack of respect for my personal space, at the beginning of the night and Stovan's constant persistence, during earlier attempts to ward off his attentions - before I changed my mind.

On reflection now, I believe that I would not have moved our relationship on to an intimate level so soon, if Stovan hadn't been so insistent and persuasive. Of course, I realise it was my responsibility to have left, when I felt his advances became unacceptable. *So why didn't you?*, I ask myself. At this side of the encounter, I can see clearly how communicating my needs and being assertive over boundaries, in relationships with men, is something I've always found hard to do – and clearly still work-in-progress!

CHAPTER 70

I decide to take this experience as an opportunity to take any learning into my next relationship. After what seems like a lifetime of carrying the belief that men's-needs-are-more-important-than-mine, I see that this *must* change, for me to experience a healthy relationship. I catch my mind slipping back into old memories then pull it back. I make the intention to let go of any blame or criticism and take full responsibility for this experience, with its gifts of new and heightened awareness.

There's no blame. There's no right or wrong, just what *is* and a chance to make a different choice next time.

I reflect on the clues that were given to me (early on), about Stovan's lack of emotional warmth and connection. I see another piece of learning here for me in that, (despite my desire for connection, love and warmth) – to move into an intimate relationship, without it, is not helpful. Until a deeper connection is made outside the bedroom, to move into a union, that's both an emotional union as well as physical one, is a recipe for disaster. Feeling safe and feeling respected, I now realise, are two essential needs of mine. And I can't feel this with a man that I have only known a short while, however attractive he is, or nice it feels to have his attention. My wounded spirit is afraid to be hurt again, and still finding it hard to trust. I recall my meeting with Ian and how my 'policing' and setting of boundaries in the early stage of our relationship, was meeting this 'need' - but at the other end of this extreme! I laugh to myself at these insights, *hey, well at least you're trying out new approaches and learning, (hopefully).*

I know that as I get more enlightened, then this stuff will become easier. Then, I'll be able to balance my needs, give of myself (or not), without having to 'police' boundaries and manage time scales around when to move closer in intimacy – I'll just 'know'.

But up until then, my heart is still learning how to stay safe as it opens itself up to love again. The main thing is that I don't take this personally or beat myself up for making a mistake. And that I see the bigger picture of me (so to speak) and how to value myself more.

After a period of walking silently, side by side, with me deep in thought, I announce to Jen that my decision is made. I'm not going. She's delighted! Back at the hostel I send a polite email to Stovan saying that I hope he's had a good crossing. I add that it didn't work out for me to join him, but I wish him well.

That evening, Jen and I meet up for our farewell meal together and find a nice restaurant to eat. The mood between us is buoyant and jovial, even though we're both feeling somewhat tired from our day out walking, with strong Wellington winds pushing us in opposite directions to our step! (A bit like life does, sometimes). I buy aperitifs and we toast each other's *new beginnings* in relationships and life. We plan to keep in touch. That's nice.

CHAPTER 71

14TH January Today I'm moving from Wellington to a little seaside town called Paraparaumu. Before I leave I check emails and there's one from Stovan with friendly greetings, saying he was waiting for me at the ferry port. He wishes me happy travels on North Island and says keep in touch. It's friendly and okay. I send out appreciation for the nicer aspects of our time together.

Before leaving windy Wellington, I buy an elaborate piece of jewellery that I've had my eye on for a few days (a treat to myself) and mail off my next 'newsletter' to dad, complete with an 80th birthday card for mum's birthday. I'm looking in shops, (killing time really) before my bus leaves, when a text comes in from Ian. It must be the next time he's in range of a mobile signal since I sent my last text, when I left South Island, as it says: *Awesome! Hope the North is as much for you as the South. Take care. Luv Ian.*

I reply with a chatty text about meeting Jen, and then ask about Zach. Ian's playful reply comes in by return: *Watch out, you might change camps! Zach the same but very tired 2 day. We went to top camp and back yesterday. 6hr walk. I had to carry goat home for him! All good!*

Interesting... As soon as Ian says something that may be a little less than okay or negative, he cancels it out with the positive affirmation *it's all good'*.

So this is how he stays so positive all the time! He converts negative thoughts and energy to positive, straight away. I'm enjoying my unexpected contact with Ian, and text again telling him that I don't think there's any danger of me 'changing camps'. Then I make a joke about him *still carrying that bloody dog's' food for him!* His last reply says simply, *Yep.*

The bus takes me one stop up the coast, and then I catch a connecting bus to Paraparaumu. Barnacles Inn is a sweet little light blue and cream painted, cottage hostel. It is run by a gentle natured and friendly woman called Sue. Instantly I feel it's good energy and things get even better when Sue shows me to a four bedded room, complete with sea view and informs me there's only me in it, tonight! This quirky little seaside hostel is so cosy and relaxed, I feel at home straight away. It's clean and well decorated and there's a nice mix of ages, which I like. In the kitchen I find a couple (they appear like newly-in-loves) full of passion and energy for each other. It's amusing to watch. She's clearly trying to impress her lover, as she works with great care and intensity preparing a perfect meal. Her guy skirts around (doing nothing much really) as he 'bills and coos,' making *ooooohh* and *ahhh* sounds of approval – and the occasional token gesture of help. After eating and lots of eye gazing, the lovebirds wash their dishes and disappear – sharing knowing glances and giggles.

Lucky buggers!

CHAPTER 72

I go out to explore my new location. I take a walk on a beautiful beach. I cook a nice meal for myself and eat, alone. I watch a bit of TV and then make a nightcap drink which I take to my room. Sue keeps popping in and out of the kitchen and lounge, all night. Maybe we backpackers are her only family? She's a sweet woman with a caring energy that seems genuine. As I sip my bedtime drink tucked up in my (unexpected) single room, I think about the many new people I've already met in such a short time. There's a man here called Toby, who seems interesting. His room is opposite mine.

The next day I awake from a wonderful night's sleep and discover an overcast day, so I have a peaceful (and private) slow start – in a room all to myself! Such bliss! I reflect on how I appreciate little things now - that I used to take for granted back home. After sharing bedrooms and dorms for weeks, a bit of personal space feels such a luxury. I meditate and decide that I'll use today for relaxation and reflection, while I soak in the surroundings of my new home. I want time to think about the next stage of my journey and also reflect on the learning of the past few days.

The afternoon is spent on a small terrace in the garden. I find a nice comfy sun lounger and lay back in the sunshine. I relax; I drink beer and eat cheese and seaweed rice crackers (another of my NZ finds). Whilst topping up my drink in the kitchen, the guy in the room opposite me begins to make conversation. I discover that he's not called Toby, he's Alan. That he's English and been in NZ for a couple of years. I return back to my chair in the garden and in a short while Alan comes across, and we talk for a long while. I sense a 'tired' energy around him, although he's much younger than me, (I would say) and otherwise fit and well. As he talks, he tells his 'story' and I discover where his depleted energy field is coming from.

Alan 'left it all behind' to make a life with a girl from New Zealand. He visited her for some months before making the decision to move here. After much thought, he left Wales and bought a place in Wellington with his new love. Almost immediately, their relationship became abusive. He speaks of things that she'd hidden from him on their 'dates,' but also acknowledges there were enough 'warning signs' – which he ignored, (as we do). Changing the subject, Alan tells me he's a sculptor, and that he's brought tons of alabaster with him from Wales to work on, but not been able to do any for a while. He goes on to tell me that he has come to work-trade at Barnacles for the summer; to "Get his head straight."

Alan has done counselling studies, so now the conversation moves on to therapies and behavioural change. I talk about the importance of taking responsibility for our own healing, and I talk a little of my own journey with this issue. As he talks, Alan is softly reflective and I 'feel' his gaping wound...

Later, I gain greater understanding of the depth of it, when Alan reveals to me that he has three young children, back in the UK, that he hasn't seen since he left, due to difficulties. I take a moment to think of these three young children, a boy and two girls. Their daddy far away, not knowing when they will see him again and this sadness almost consumes me. I try to stand back from it. Try to listen and not judge or give advice. Eventually it grows late and Alan goes in, to make food.

I go back to my room and discover that I have a new roommate called Dot. She's from Auckland and, "Just passing through." Dot is a thoroughly middle class, middle aged woman with a sort of Colonial Brit energy about her! A teacher in a private school, Dot is very 'jolly- hockey sticks!' We chat first, sat on our beds and then later, tucked up under duvets, before saying goodnight. Our talk is about moving comfort zones and travel; alone or otherwise. Dot has been to the UK a lot, and is fond of it. She shares gusty chat until finally, we fall silent. But *Mischievous Mind* plays around with images of my 'St. Trinian's type roommate and school dorm scenes, with gentle humour, until I'm fast asleep.

CHAPTER 73

<u>Wednesday</u> The morning sunshine is bursting through the little bedroom window! I peep out with delight onto a pretty seaside view. It's surely a day to pack a picnic and take an expedition up the shoreline, to see where it goes.

Heading north up the beach, my journey takes longer than I anticipate as I'd hoped to easily cross the sea estuary, a couple of miles further on. But instead, I find I need to head way in land and then out again (using only intuition and common sense to guide me) as I don't have a map. I walk for miles inland and then out onto the beach again; before attempting to make my way back – hoping the tide is out far enough for the water to be shallow enough to cross. But the depth of this estuary is deceiving, and I spend a lot of time testing areas that look shallow, but then become too deep for me to continue. First it looks like I can, and then suddenly the sea bed drops a lot lower!

Determined to not retrace my original route, I try taking my shorts off, (have a bikini underneath) and holding my rucksack high above my head, I wade in deeper. It's frustrating to get so near (I can see the other side very close to me now) only to discover I just can't make it. It's getting far too deep to risk it. I have my camera in my bag and it's just not worth it. I glance around to see if there are any kayaks about to ferry my bag across. No. Eventually, there's nothing to do but re-track round the coast line. Phew! The heat of the day is so blisteringly hot and then I discover I've used up all my water.

Not a bloody café or ice-cream parlour in site!

Once back on the other side of the water, I find some amazing shells and driftwood on the beach. As soon as I hit 'civilisation' again, it's a cold can of Coke and enormous chocolate bar – to reward the explorer's efforts. Ah, heavenly! Alan is outside the hostel when I arrive back, munching chocolate and we greet each other. He follows me in, exchanging small talk. I feel for this guy! His gentleness and creativity, always clothed in such a weary, sad energy, is starting to become the predominant sense I have of him. I realise more and more, how sensitive and receptive to energy fields I've become since travelling, as well as an increase in my intuitive senses.

I make a mug of fresh coffee and enjoy the last rays of sunshine on my lounger in the garden. Sue calls over a friendly greeting to me, as she weeds the garden. Looking around, I notice that Alan has uncovered one of his half-finished sculptures, (that are all under covers) at the far end of the garden. I think he wants me to look, so when I see him later I tell him that I noticed it was uncovered. Alan says it's not finished, but that he has two smaller ones which are, if I want to see them. I do. He takes me to his room, to look. The statues are very smooth, highly polished and really quite good. I comment that one looks very peaceful. Alan screws up his eyes as he tells me he's not sure yet; if he's done with it. His soft voice, still tinged with weariness, seems happy to be sharing his artwork with someone. I take a quick look around the room and see photographs of his children, dotted around. Such a sad and heavy energy about this room – I'm glad to be out.

I muse on how magnificent a day it's been! I recall the extraordinary shells I found, washed onto the beach and decide to take an evening walk. I have my camera with me and capture the brilliant fireball, as it sets fiercely across the ocean. Oh, nature, how you create such magical and beautiful sights!

CHAPTER 74

<u>Thursday</u> After another great night's sleep, with no snoring and no night noise, (such blessings!) I awake to more sunshine. *Another day in paradise!* I think to myself. *Hmmm, what shall I do today?* A big blister has appeared on my left toe from yesterday's walk and I'm sporting a couple of bites of some sort too. I feel like just lazing around this lovely place again, to catch up on writing, washing and reflections. So I do.

I'm washing shells in my bedroom sink with the door ajar, when Alan comes out of his room opposite and asks what I'm doing. I walk across to show him my shells. He invites me in again, and we look at the shells, together. Alan examines each one slowly, with his artistic eye and seems surprised at their uniqueness. Again, for a minute, he's lifted out of his low state and asks what I'm doing today. I tell him about my blister and that I've decided to have an easy day. He makes a little smile and suggests that taking a walk barefoot on the beach, may help. As I leave, I call back to him to say, "A blister is a small price to pay for such wonderful shells!" He laughs.

Later, 'The Lovers' come in with lots of cooing and enthusing until their sexual energy is bouncing all over the kitchen walls. I ask myself why I find them so annoying and making judgements about them. Perhaps it's my ego trying to feel superior and naming the guy as a 'jerk' helps me not ask myself, *how come this woman is with a guy and you're not?* I decide to make more of an effort not to judge. After all it would be nicer to acknowledge they're giving each other such happiness. And so I send them a silent blessing. And one for Sue and Alan too...

Today I will continue to reflect on my journey so far. Which areas I've had the opportunity to grow in, and whether I feel I am any further along the journey to knowing myself, than when I first came? The worst thought I find myself having is that I might enjoy all these experiences, then not take the learning back, when my trip ends. Will I make the effort to use the gifts to sustain these wonderful changes, in my life back home?

As new insights about me, my reactions and responses become more and more apparent, I feel blessed to have this heightened awareness, as well as some discomfort, with what I'm finding out about myself! I realise that there are still things I don't understand about some of my reactions and behaviours, and I want to learn more.

At lunchtime I ask Alan if he'd like a walk on the beach later, to look for shells. He agrees but when the time comes, he's changed his mind and says he is busy. That's fine. I take the walk anyway. Gone are the days when I don't do something because the other person changes their mind. I walk the opposite way to yesterday and find beautiful coin shaped blue shells. There was a storm here, last week, and the beach is strewn with enormous pieces of driftwood, but also lots of smaller very smooth, washed pieces of wood, too. They remind me of the karmic process of washing and washing until something is gone...

It's such a hot day that when I return, I put my swimming gear on and go back to the beach and wade out into the Tasmanian sea. It's extremely shallow for a long way, but eventually it gets deep enough to swim and the water is lovely! Waves lap over me as I swim further out and I begin to feel really small in this vast ocean (which of course I am!). Kapiti Island is in front of me. The hills are to one side and the shoreline to the other. This is a beautiful place.

After getting out, I dry off in the sun and end up sitting for a long time on a fallen tree, just simply 'being' and marvelling at the beauty of this place. Gulls dip and swirl, almost like they're doing a show, just for me! There's a feeling of great peace and calm within as I sit. Out of the corner of my eye I become aware that one of 'The Lovers' is here, alone. She sits amongst the sand dunes, only a little way from me, reading. My mind idly wonders what she wonders... Of her lover? Of me? I think of how we never know what others think – and yet our mind likes to guess (and how this is sometimes our downfall, when we get it wrong).

On my return to The Barnacles, I make a meal and as the room is, once again, my own I take my food and eat it in bed, whilst reading (a real treat). I write out a new list of the things I desire to manifest and read them out loud. I wash up and hit the sack.

CHAPTER 75

<u>18 January</u> Another walk on the beach, more shells and driftwood! Oh, what fun! I'm like a child, once I get on a beach. Must stop this collecting though, as I am not allowed to bring this stuff out of the country! Yet (like a child) I can't resist... I make a conscious decision to be more careful about being in the sun today (during its hottest times), as I mustn't underestimate its power.

As I continue trying to draw out learning from all my experiences and meetings, I realise that the space I have here (for reflection) is conducive for this to happen. Walking back to the hostel, (I don't know why) but I find myself feeling a little low. I'm not sure if it's Alan's negative energy or what? When I get back, he's working at his laptop on the dining room table and looking smart. He tells me he senses I'm a little grumpy or pre-occupied today. I laugh and say no, not grumpy but yes, I'm a little distracted, with many thoughts. I gift him some driftwood I've found that's a dome shape with a hole through the middle and say, "A piece by the sea sculptor."

Alan asks me what I see in the shape. I say that I realised it was for him when I saw the hole. That it's symbolic of the hole in his heart, which I hoped, would heal soon. "Ah, that's a different story." He replies, as his eyes wander off somewhere into his mind. My low mood doesn't lift, and after supper, I go to my room to pack and get ready for bed. Out of the blue, I find a tear in my eye and it surprises me. I've been here over two months and this is the first time I've felt down – like this! I email my girls and tell them I love them; suddenly feeling the need for connection...

During the night I dream that I'm lonely. I am searching and I find a house. An ex-boyfriend of mine is asleep inside and I stand by his bed, talking to him. I wake up and wonder what on earth the dream is about? Finally, morning comes and I'm up and away before anyone's awake. No goodbyes. Glad to be moving on, away from this strange, low energy field.

On the bus to my next destination Napier, the inner journey continues, full of reflection. Now, I find old understandings of events are being replaced with new awareness and insight. Past issues around my children and marriage difficulties are given new viewing positions. This allows greater understanding about some of my ex-husband's negative behaviours towards me over the past years. My empathy is so strong, it's like I experience myself as him. As our bus bumps along the hot and winding road to Napier, I find tears in my eyes and a powerful release of something occurs; from deep within.

Arriving in Napier I make my way to The Stables Lodge Backpackers, my next home. It has a nice friendly feeling about it, and I'm glad to be having a fresh start. There's a new feeling about *my* energy field too. A sign outside the hostel says: 'Best Plan is no Plan.' Sounds like my kind of a place...

This time I'm sharing a mixed dorm with two Japanese guys, a girl and an English bloke (about my age) called Ian. As I unpack, he sits on his bunk across from mine and starts chatting right away. I discover Ian is also taken a career break and making his way around NZ, then over to Canada. Pretty soon I have the basics of his 'story' (speed friendship or what!).

Divorced last year after 25 years of marriage; with two grown up children Ian is now looking to make a new life. As he talks, my initial feeling is that he seems to have a bit of an uneasy, but young spirited energy. Yet something feels a bit odd about Ian. He looked me up and down intently, when we first spoke - which I found most disconcerting! Still my intuition is telling me Ian is harmless, he's keen to tell me that he's just come from Taupo (which is where I'm going next!). He goes on to say that he's also crossed the Tongariro Crossing (which is a trek I'd like to do) so we get into conversation about the route and Ian offers to show me his pictures of it. I then go off to do my usual new-in-town shopping trip.

CHAPTER 76

There's a real big supermarket, just a short walk away, full of wonderful tasty things. I make a split decision to work on changing 'fear of lack' and financial limitation issues, by just buying what I fancy and really enjoying the food I choose – not just buy economical stuff. There's a colourful array of produce and I delight in picking out enormous giant prawns, assorted sushi, a bottle of Chardonnay and wonderful fresh crusty French bread, for my evening meal. Passing yummy smelling cooked chicken, I pop one in my trolley, before picking out fresh fruit and veggies, for the rest of my stay. I'm pleased with my purchases and triumphant over meeting the challenge of pushing my financial comfort zone out a bit further. My energy is joyful and flowing. At the till a Kiwi guy in front, smiles and starts to chat. We share easy flowing and playful banter as he packs away his groceries. Outside the store, a few minutes later, he drives by in his car and smiles as he calls out, "You made it!" I wave and smile back. That negative energy field has definitely moved on. I feel great!

Back at the hostel I label up the bottle of wine, with name, date of stay and room number, before placing it in the communal fridge to chill.

Ian's in the lounge area when I return and shows me his photos of the Tongariro Crossing, and then asks what I'm doing for food, tonight. I tell him I already have my meal sorted, but that he's welcome to share what I have. He accepts my invitation and we lay out the mini banquet of fine food on a picnic table outside. It's a warm and balmy evening and across the courtyard a couple of young hippy kids are strumming at guitars and singing gently. What a wonderful setting for our meal. Soon the bottle of chilled wine is open. It tastes so good in this sweet air, with such succulent and tasty food. I'm enjoying the creative ambiance of this place and the wine mellows my mood even further as I sit back, take it all in and relax.

In the bus station, on arrival, I'd picked up a leaflet about wine tasting tours, as this region is Hawke's Bay; famous for fine wine and vineyards. I think it might be fun to take a tour and see some of the area, so I ask Ian if he's interested in going too. We book a tour for the next day – and so it seems that my next travel buddy has arrived, via the Universal Express! But as always, there's a mirror experience to be had (as I'm fast finding out) when someone new arrives into my life. It's not long before I realise that Ian has limitations around spending money, when I watch him tuck heartily into my free food, with no offer of food contribution or splitting the cost.

Then, at the end of the day I find him entering figures in a small black book! When I ask what he's doing, Ian tells me it's his daily record of expenditure! Oh my! I don't find this at all attractive but make no comment and smile to myself, as I realise we're all at different stages of our journey out from the 'Valley of Limitation'. I have my challenges and Ian has his...

Back in the dorm Ian stretches out on his bunk, wearing only his underpants! This is a bit in my face [pardon the pun] and not at all what I want, or have experienced in other mixed dorms. I decide to ignore it. He's just out of a long term marriage, clearly still in transition, and a bit needy. But still, a lot braver than most to step out of his comfort zone and take this trip. I admire him for that

20th January It's a rainy day, but the tour's booked so off we go, on *Vin's Vineyard Tour*. It turns out to be an enjoyable day, with Robert our Canadian host, a jovial bus driver Bill and two other couples (English), who are both quite friendly. Our little minibus takes us to four vineyards, to sample six different wines at each. By the end of the tour, we are rather 'tanked up' – to say the least! Despite drinking lots of water, in between glasses, I'm already carrying a left over headache from last night's wine. Still, it's a great tour, but even the small feast of local cheeses, pâtés, olives, and fresh crusty bread for lunch, doesn't manage to soak up the wine and prevent my head developing into one huge throbbing mass.

On arrival at the hostel, I go to bed, with a couple of headache tablets and a coffee for a few hours to try and shake it off. Ian follows, with a mug of coffee, telling me he wants to do the same. Hmmm…I close my eyes and try to rest. Ian's sits on the edge of his bed, but keeps engaging me in conversations about this and that. He comments on how at ease I seem with myself and I sense he finds this attractive. I can't say I find Ian attractive but he's a nice friend and easy company.

Now he's telling me (again) that he's just come from my next destination Taupo and stayed at the same hostel (that I'm visiting next). And that he liked it so much he's going straight back there — so he can show me around when I arrive. (?) I thank him for his unexpected invitation and think it would be nice to have a walking companion, but I don't really want Ian getting attached to me in any other way.

Suddenly, I realise that here is an opportunity to let go of the need to 'police' boundaries like I usually do and just let him take responsibility for his own feelings and actions. Ian thanks me for my company, and says how much he's enjoyed it today. I make a polite reply of, "Yes it's been a nice day – the group and the wine tasting was fun!"

Later that evening he's strutting around the room again, in underpants and t-shirt. I keep the covers pulled up tight around me so he doesn't get any ideas. His energy is harmless though, and not in the least bit intimidating. More amusing really, and I smile to myself as I think perhaps it's just his way of 'saying' he likes me.

Men are so funny!

CHAPTER 77

21st January Another lazy start to the day. How I love them! I brew fresh coffee for breakfast and toast my left over French bread. Ian surfaces later and we take a walk along the seafront together, past all the quaint coloured wooden houses that line the streets of Napier. It's a chilled out energy town, and despite the fact it once experienced an earthquake, there's lots of beautiful art nouveau features that have survived enough for us tourist to enjoy.

Ian offers to buy our morning coffee, at a little side street café (he did this yesterday morning too after saying, "As a 'thank you' for sharing your food, again." I'd shared my food with him for a second night in a row; and there was my mind, judging him for not contributing in the way it wanted!. We sit in bright, sunshine, at an ornate street table and watch the jolly world of Napier go by. Ian tells me that he couldn't sleep last night and that he feels restlessness within. I encourage him to, "Just be easy with it and let it speak to you – don't push it down."

Suddenly, he's crying. Hearing gentle and supportive words seems to have touched him. As tears flow, Ian blurts out difficulties with his son and how he misses his ex-wife. Out it all tumbles, fast and disjointed. He's clearly in pain and without thinking, I reach out to hold his hand and tell him it's okay to cry. I say that he's clearly emotionally fragile and processing his pain and confusion. I tell him how brave I think he is to be here and open to search for something new.

Ian leaves for Taupo this afternoon but my transfer arrangements are not for another day. As he packs, a new guy checks into our dorm and I sense Ian's hostile non-verbal language towards him; almost like 'marking out territory' around me. Yuk! But how amusing! Before he leaves Ian offers to collect me from the bus station on my arrival in Taupo. I decline his offer.

I'm feeling a little uneasy at the growing signs of his attachment and although it's nice to have companionship, I don't want to be with Ian all the time – as I like to do my own thing too. Once again, I make an effort to try and be at ease with this and realise it's simply the Universe giving me another opportunity to learn about communicating my needs to others. I resist using defence mechanisms of turning hostile and unfriendly as a way of putting down personal boundaries. Instead, I tell myself that here's an opportunity to communicate at each stage of things unfolding (not ahead of knowing) and that it's about checking-in with myself on how I'm feeling and what my needs are, in a relaxed way. After all, Ian has only made a simple friendly offer; the rest is purely my own fear and imagined reality.

When he leaves, Ian gives me a hug and I say cheerfully, "Goodbye. See you tomorrow." After he's gone it feels nice to get some space. I do hope we can be friends without it all getting too needy or heavy...

CHAPTER 78

Well, it's another great day! After Ian's departure I pack a picnic lunch and set off walking along the pebbly seafront and up to Bluff Hill. The road climbs steeply up and at the top I'm rewarded with views of the busy working harbour, below. An enormous white cruise liner sits majestically in residence. It's so lovely feeling the sun and wind on my face, experiencing freedom of sky and sea, from up here. Far below, the waves rise and break. I eat my picnic and stay a while, just soaking in the peace and beauty around me.

When I return to Stables Lodge a new Israeli guy is in my room; and it's all change, again. As is the way of backpackers we begin our communication as strangers, curious to learn (initially) about each other's outer journeys, as fellow travellers and like-minded spirits. He asks where I'm going to eat tonight and I tell him I have food that needs using before I leave tomorrow. This young guy gives off a lonely vibe as he confides in me, "It's hard to find friends that are the right company sometime, when travelling." I agree with him in parts, but say that it's about just being easy with it all and letting the Universe works some of it out. He smiles.

22nd January I travel on to Taupo. It's a fairly uneventful journey. As I arrive and check in at Rainbow Lodge Ian suddenly pops up and says, "You got here, then!"

Fairly obvious, I would have thought…

He now has a nervous, over confident manner that feels like it's a bit of a front and that underneath he is not at all sure. Ian makes coffee and then offers to take me on a tour of the area. He's telling me he's arranged to stay on until Friday but I can't say that it's a *wow, great* feeling. More like: *I hope I can find the balance of 'me' time* as it's starting to feel a fairly heavy energy field of me 'giving' (emotionally) and Ian 'receiving.'

But, I tell myself this maybe unfair of me. Maybe it's my fear that I won't be able to communicate, in good ways to him? Ian seems enthusiastic as I sip my 'welcome' coffee. And then he throws into the conversation that he had the brilliant idea of enquiring about availability of a twin room, for us. I nearly choke on my drink, before informing him in a very firm tone that we do *not* have that kind of relationship! Suddenly Ian is stuttering that he didn't mean to be forward, that he just thought it would be a way to have more privacy – sharing a twin with someone you know. I say that I'm perfectly fine in my three bedded shared room (separate dorm to his). I get the feeling that Ian wants to 'claim' me (again) so I focus on trying to make my communications that of the 'energy of friends' (but no more!).

CHAPTER 79

With the 'failed' room idea behind him, Ian moves on to tell me how he's bought all the ingredients to cook us a nice meal this evening. I thank him and say, "That will be nice." But inwardly I groan, as I'm realising how hard it is to have men as friends sometimes, and how necessary to find ways to keep communicating the type of relationship I'm offering; without them taking my friendly gestures as a sign of something more. Later, whilst taking our 'tour' around town, heavy rain showers drive us into a little Irish bar tucked back into the shore line. We decide to have a beer as we wait for the rain to pass. And I make the suggestion that as we'll be spending a few days together, shall we agree now to pick up our own tab when out, together? Ian doesn't like this idea and makes a comment like, "Remember I'm doing the meal tonight..." - as if there's payback attached to it!

I say nothing except, "Yes, that was kind of you to offer", then buy my own beer.

He soon gets over it and starts chatting merrily again; telling me how he emailed his son after our conversation yesterday and got a reply straight back. I'm delighted for him and we talk again about father-son relationships and other related stuff. Then suddenly, he says, "Don't you ever get drained spending time with these pathetic men you end up with?"

I'm guessing he's talking about himself, in the third party, and so I reply, "When I need space to recharge I communicate this. And no, I don't see them as pathetic. Brave; not pathetic."

I call at a supermarket for fresh supplies and a six pack of beers to go with the meal. Ian's pasta dishes all tastes very good. He keeps on talking and talking about his marriage, but there doesn't sound like much togetherness in it all. From what he's saying he sounds to have been lost in his own world, inattentive to the needs of their relationship. I hear how he went kayaking on their 20th wedding anniversary, but then couldn't see why his wife was so annoyed! Ian seems to be mirroring the other side of the balancing-your- own- needs-with-others' challenge to me. Ian confides that it might be hard for him to find a woman flexible enough for him...

I'm kind of inclined to agree – unless of course she's kayaking mad!

CHAPTER 80

January 23ʳᵈ It's good weather today. The showers of yesterday have moved away. Ian suggests we walk to a famous hot springs that bubble out of a fresh water river. I'm curious, so off we go. They turn out to be a pretty long walk away, but Ian volunteers as chief map reader, then beats himself up (verbally) whenever he takes the wrong route! Oh dear. Still, I've noticed he seems to be relaxing down a bit more. It's evidently hard for him to let go and relax. Ian is very self-conscious (not as much now, with me) and often stutters in conversations

This walk is turning out to be a good decision. We pass a bungee jumping platform, and decide to stop off for a while to watch a few crazy leapers plunging into the river far below. Then we walk on to the hot springs and it's so unusual to see steam rising off of bubbling water, as it spills into a cold river and cools itself down! People are bathing underneath a bridge and Ian's quick to jump in amongst groups of bikini clad women. I relax on the water's edge in the sun, while he takes a soak and then we decide to walk further on, to Huka Falls.

Wow! What a sight to behold, it is! As the gentle, winding river current begins to build, it suddenly turns into a vast volume of energy and water that forces through a narrow part of the riverbank. What power! So full of urgency, the powerful force of nature driving this enormous energy field. The noise gives off as much a sense of urgency as the speed that this white mass of water is flowing with. For a while, other conversation is put on hold, as we exclaim excitedly about the wonder we experience before our eyes.

On the return journey Ian starts to ask insightful questions and I realise he's growing more emotionally aware. This guy's a bit of a contradiction really, in one way he's brave to be on this trip (never been out of Europe), not at all the independent traveller 'type'. Yet in another way he seems scared, unconfident and very unsure of himself. I almost splutter in amazement when he says he has a £12,000 budget for his six months trip (almost as much as I have in my entire saving accounts back home to last me a life time! Yet still, he keeps on totting up and recording the daily spending in his little book, so I conclude that it must be a way of feeling in control, to explain why he does his penny-pinching act. As I well know though, such feelings of control are not real but illusory and it sounds like the Universe is playing its little 'awakening' game with Ian, too around the 'fear of lack' theme. I smile to myself when he discovers that he's left his walking boots back in Napier and now has only trek sandals for footwear. Reluctantly, he says he'll need to buy boots before going any further. To give him credit, he takes the news really well and tries to be easy about this big 'blow' to his finances. Ah well, the Universe gives and the Universe takes away, eh?

Later, after eating I take a shower and begin to arrange Internet travel for my next stopovers. Ian suggests an evening walk, so we set out (once more) into the beautiful evening in the direction of Taupo lake. A deep evening glow from the sunset casts gentle but stunning hues over the distant mountain range. With my full attention transfixed on this scene and not watching where I'm going, I stub my toe on a metal ring that's protruding out of the ground. Ouch! I start hopping about and a few blue words fill the air, as I try to distract myself from the pounding sensation that's growing in my foot. Ian seems concerned and bends down to look. He examines the toe more closely for damage then rubs it to try and get circulation going again. We both come to the decision that it's probably just bruised, but boy is it throbbing!

CHAPTER 81

As I wait for the pain to stabilise, we sit on a bench next to the inky, moonlit water for some time; silently surrounded by (outer) tranquillity. Ian starts to get melancholy. With tears in his eyes, he turns to reminiscing over his failed marriage again; spurred on by the mood of water and deep reflection. I let him talk (remembering that feeling of a need for closure, after my own relationship endings). To lighten his mood, I suggest we go to the Irish Bar. Once there, Ian's suddenly generous and wanting to buy drinks.

At first I decline but he insists it's, "His treat"! So I order a half of beer and he returns to sit across from me; screwing his baseball cap round and round in his hands, like a nervous teenager on a first date! Tearful again and full of emotion, Ian tells me it's going to be hard to leave (after these days with me) and says how much I've given him.

This touches me and I try to reassure him that this is just the start for him; that he'll go on to have many more such experiences, adventures and friendships. All at once, I realise that I have repeated almost word for word what 'Mountain Ian' said to me when I got sad, at our parting!! How spooky. It's a mirror. I see it clearly. I have no emotional feeling for this guy other than friendship, I wonder if that bit's the same for the other Ian? I see how (like this Ian), I too would have gladly carried on being with him for longer, and I see that this Ian also (like me), is unconvinced that he'll have any other relationships or experiences as wonderful as the one with me. Ian goes on to speak of how refreshing it's been spending time with someone who's clearly happy with themselves and in the driving seat of their own life.

I thank him, but don't want him thinking I've 'made it', so to speak, and assure him that I am also on my 'journey', with much work still to be done, to learn about myself. But yes, it's true I'm much easier with myself now, than in the past. So much more full of hope for the future. There seems to be a gentle loosening of attachment to outcomes and I feel happy to share my learning with others. With much relief on my part, Ian ends the conversation positively and brightens up. Thank goodness for that. I really want to sign off as life coach for today!

Thursday Our backpacker's hostel offers a facility for booking local trips and I would like to do something that involves going out on the lake. One of the trips advertised is on an old restored sailing yacht. Ian and I both book a ticket and today we experience Lake Taupo in a fun way. Once again the morning is sunny and bright as the yacht casts off onto the azure lake, with white clouds billowing across a turquoise sky. I feel a real sense of freedom and adventure as I lean over the side of the boat and the wind presses down on my face. Our captain announces an opportunity to jump over the side and take a swim, so I take it!

Ian follows close on my heels, after some initial reluctance – but not wanting to be out done by a female! The water feels quite cold but as I swim around I find little thermal pockets of warmth where volcanic activity beneath the lake is still active. One minute the water is hot and the next cold! The yacht sails past ancient Maori carvings cut out of the rock face and I swim over to take a closer look. Back on board after being hoisted up, I realise I'm the only older woman who took a swim. Ladies… you don't know what you're missing!

The crew serve up hot drinks and beers, and a party atmosphere takes over. I relax and try to detach from Ian's nervous energy field, which seems high today and definitely not relaxing to be around. I find myself thinking that I'm glad he's moving on tomorrow, so I can disconnect from it for good.

It's Ian's last night and he's keen for us to go out for a meal to say goodbye. So I shower, change and make an effort to smarten up a bit. When we meet however, Ian's still in the same clothes he wore earlier! We have a Thai meal at a lovely traditional Thai restaurant (not too far from our hostel). Again, Ian begins to share his feelings. Oh well, at least this time I have the comfort of a Tiger beer for support! Feeling immense compassion for this guy,, I say that I hope that his brave spirit wins through. Ian thanks me again for my help, we exchange emails, and say goodnight.

119

CHAPTER 82

Friday Ian has gone. The weather continues to be hot and sunny so I decide to hang out at the hostel, relaxing, reading and resting up, along with preparing my food for tomorrow's adventure. I've booked on the Tongariro Crossing day excursion and will need to be up at 5a.m to catch the coach. In an effort to get enough sleep, I take a couple of herbal sleeping tablets before going to bed. Ineffective is not the word as I toss and turn for hours! To add to this, it's Friday night and there's a party atmosphere around the hostel. My ground floor room has residents sitting, drinking, and talking, on its outdoor veranda, until the early hours!

After what feels like no sleep at all, the alarm goes off and I stumble about in semi-darkness pulling on clothes. Once in the kitchen I make toast in zombie fashion, gather up a picnic pack from the fridge and push it deep into my bulging rucksack. I move about in automatic pilot, but refuse to let my mind stress or focus on how little sleep I've had – as that wouldn't be any help at all. One and a half hours and a coach ride later, groups of walkers are assembling at the start of the Tongariro Crossing

It's still only 7 a.m. but already hundreds of walkers have spilled out of dozens of coaches and headed off enthusiastically, up a windy track. Mount Doom (as seen in Lord of The Rings film) towers menacingly above us. I start to walk. It's fairly cold and still quite dark; as the sun is over the other side of the mountains. There's an 8 hour walk ahead of me, over a variety of challenging terrains. I find myself anticipating ahead of time, the satisfaction of achievement I'll feel, on completion, with an inner tingle of delight. The rewards of pushing my comfort zones are always worth the effort. Less and less do I fear new challenges, but see them with more confident eyes. I feel that this lessening is matched with an increasing trust in the Universe.

I'm walking across the mouth of an active volcano, and before long, steam rises up from out of rocks and under the very ground I'm walking on! The smell of sulphur and enormous clumps of gnarled lava, beneath my feet are constant reminders of the ravaging effects on land by volcanoes. The first few hours of this trek involves a lot of uphill, strenuous effort (thankfully the sun is still not up) and I'm able to walk for a few hours, without its searing rays to add to my challenge.

After hours of walking across barren terrain, I'm rewarded with the sight of a glistening lake of stunning turquoise milky water. It feels like I've stepped into a storybook of ancient magic and mystery. These pools of brilliant blue, bubbling sulphur in the middle of nowhere, paint a striking contrast to the dark russets and blacks of their surrounding landscape. To add to this awesome image, is a sprinkling of snow on top of a distant peak. Slowly, slowly the sun begins to warm the cold morning air, and I'm able to peel off some of my many layers. These are quickly replaced with sun cream, sunhat and shades!

I enjoy walking alone with just my own thoughts for the first part of the day. Silently reflecting, and soaking in the stunning and dramatic beauty that surrounds me. After a group stopover near an emerald pool, for a rest and energy snack, I fall into conversation with two guys, Luke and his Asian partner. They are American and I learn how they're in New Zealand, working. One is a teacher and the other a lecturer. Somehow, the conversation moves on to the theme of Family Group Conferencing and Luke tells me he has a friend who attended one. Both of them are interested to hear of my experiences in this area of work. It's curious how many people I'm finding that know of this process and I begin to wonder if it has any greater significance for my future work, back in the UK...

I walk alongside them, until the last stage of our decent, when the old knee injury begins to play up and my walking pace slows right down; with the pain. I urge the two of them to push on and not let my slowness affect their chance of catching one of the earlier buses out of here. Listening to the needs of my very tired knee (and no longer having to match the pace of fellow walkers) I slow right down to a pace that's more comfortable. The challenge of the next half hour is pretty tough! Hundreds of steep steps down, for the final accent, pound and agitate my weary knee ligament injury. In the end, I manually lift my leg up and down each step (to assist the knee) which, by now, is refusing to bend much at all. Finally, I make it back to the bus. And what a blissful feeling this is

Missing the last bus out of here would not be fun! A blister on my big toe begins to complain loudly and rub, as a deep feeling of weariness spreads out through my entire body. I now allow myself to remember that I had virtually no sleep last night, and so I let my mind have a bit of a moan. But no worries! A sense of real achievement is mine. It's been 17 km of almost solid walking across difficult terrains, and once again I am pretty pleased with my amazing self!

CHAPTER 83

Sunday My last full day in Taupo and the sun just shines on and on. There's a young French guy in my dorm. He tells me that he's hitchhiking which is pretty amazing really, as he's on crutches and has some sort of palsy of the limbs. I enjoy his bright, chatty and positive attitude. He's clearly living life to the full and refusing to allow his physical disability to become a limitation. I admire and like his gutsy spirit. Later in the afternoon I take a final walk down to the lake and sit munching and slurping on small chocolate treats and ginger beer, as I finish my latest book. I'm moved to tears at the end, as an English woman and NZ guy, who meet on assignment in Antarctica fall deeply in love. Despite living half way across the world, they find each other again, a year later. Originally the guy had thought that he couldn't fit into her middle-class world, but after realising how much he loves her, he goes in search of his woman.

I'm moved (and surprised) to find the NZ and English theme back again. Tired now, (too much thinking and emotion) I walk slowly back to the hostel. People finding love is very moving for me; whether in books or real life. It is *so* my heart's desire to experience this (one day) for myself.

<u>The next day</u>, I move on to the town of Rotorua. Ben kindly drives me to the bus stop. He's a young English guy who works at the backpackers and has been such a helpful, pleasant guy. We exchange a few words and I thank him for his kindness.

The hostel in Rotorua is ultra new with leather settees, soft carpets and nice dorms. It's managed by a stocky Maori woman. This is my first experience of 'modern backpacking'. Most hostels have been in older more traditional buildings. In the hostel kitchen is a sign that hits me as soon as I walk in. It says: *Hope is a bird that knows dawn is breaking and sings in the darkness, until it comes*

Wow! Thank you, Universe. What a message!

CHAPTER 84

Boy is it hot in Rotorua! I take a walk down to the lake and look around. I buy fresh food but feel pretty much under the weather. My period has come and I have bad stomach pains. I decide I need wine for comfort tonight and choose a nice bottle of New Zealand chardonnay. Its mum's 80th birthday and although my family are sleeping (back home) right now, my thoughts turn to the gathering, I'm sure they'll be having later today. I think of how nice it would be to be there... I decide to try and give mum a call, if I can stay up late enough for her to have got up!

Later, it cools down a bit. I can't get through on the phone to mum so I go out to the lake front and watch the sun go down. There is beautiful clouds and immense stillness, out here. Couples are strolling hand in hand. I make the intention to set my alarm on my mobile phone and get up early to ring mum tomorrow morning (in the hope of catching her after the family party is over).

<u>29th January</u> Well it's still evening on the 28th back in UK. I have a mix up with phone numbers, so ring my sister, to get mum's phone number and we end up chatting for quite a while. Everything sounds fine, back home. Janet tells me how well the birthday meal went. I hear that both my daughters were there and looking well. I feel pleased. I ring mum, and dad answers. We chat away for a while. Dad sounds pleased to be getting my 'travel letters' and I'm glad I made the effort to connect with him in this way. Dad asks if I have plans to settle in NZ. I say not at the moment. He comments that he would! Then mum comes on, but she has little to say, except she wishes I'd been at her party. I tell her I was thinking of them all.

Later, I go out to find a camera shop as my digital camera has stopped working. The shop informs me they're not able to repair it and suggest a replacement. Gulp! *That sounds expensive* (is my first thought). But after only minutes of deliberation; (not hours or days, as before; while the fear of lack played out) I decide to 'cough up' the $210 for a camera without even converting its cost into British pounds! I need a camera, I tell myself. It's quite simple. I like taking photos of the beauty I see. The shop seems reputable and they even knock me $39 off the price. So out comes my flexible friend and the deal is done.

CHAPTER 85

Rotorua is well known for its Maori heritage and geothermal activity. I intend to invest a little money and time here, to make sure I experience both. There's a local shuttle bus that goes to a re-constructed Maori village where a cultural performance is held nightly. It's located on land where the first Maoris settled and is a site of considerable geothermal activity. So I hop on a bus and off I go, to spend five hours hearing about Maori history, dance and culture. It's fascinating! There's an active geyser on this site, called *Prince of Wales Feathers*. Every half hour it spurts huge plumes of hissing steam, high up into the air; as crowds of astounded tourists watch on in varying degrees of amazement. Walking a little further, I find a range of glugging, plopping, mud pools alongside bubbling hot spas. What an area this is! So alive with natural energy! But oh, so hot.

I had originally planned to stay much later, but the intense heat of the day gets to me, in the end. As I sit in the shade trying to cool off, I get into conversation with a fellow Brit; also female, traveller. She says she's not got long to 'do' both Islands and when I tell her about the Tongariro Crossing experience she gets up immediately to go and find out if she can 'fit' this in to her packed trip, tomorrow. I resist the offer of her free lift back into Rotorua (after checking inside first), by asking myself, *what do I feel like? Do I want to stay another hour or so here, or go now?*

I then make the choice that 'feels' right rather than make it from other motives e.g. saving money. I'll take the shuttle bus back later. I see how this freeing up from financial 'inertia' and limitations requires regular attention; to stop the mind from falling back into old patterns of fear and lack. Later, I notice a woman very stylishly dressed and I renew my resolve to rejuvenate my own shabby wardrobe, once home! The spending-money-on-me limitation keeps holding me back, but then I remind myself that I *have* bought a new camera today (without planning to). So I give myself a virtual 'pat on the back' for working on that limitation and stretching this comfort zone further.

Looking around the Maori village, I really feel the spirit of the ancient Maoris and am moved to tears by strong and powerful emotions. I learn that the most important thing to them *'is people, is people'*. That Maoris had a deep respect for nature and living in harmony with it. That their distinct greeting gesture of looking each other in the eyes and rubbing the bridge of their noses together twice, signified the combining of both energy and breath, in unity. Their carvings, their ways of life, their dress, dance and song speak to me of a deeply spiritual tribe who seems to have somehow become lost in the modern New Zealand.

I am amazed to learn that the Maoris have 25 generations of history in NZ and white men, but a few. Yet Maori ways are dying and Western ways are taking their place. The displacement of all these ancestral moral codes and values are being diluted. As I leave there is much food for thought swimming around my head.

Back at the hostel, I take a shower. Oh, boy it is *so* hot in this area! Any kind of activity at all seems to make me sweat! I pour a glass of chilled white wine and just lie on my bed and read. Later, I go to the shiny, communal kitchen and make a meal of Thai sweet chilli king prawns with pasta. It tastes so good!

CHAPTER 86

A Swedish girl called Daniela is also cooking. We sit together to eat our food out on the little wooden veranda. Daniela tells me that she's also travelling alone, and that she has a car. We get on and I ask if she wants to come with me on my evening walk. Daniela comments that she was planning to take a shower but does a double-take and changes her mind. I like her ability to be spontaneous! We stroll along in warm evening air, and get a bit lost but neither of us minds as we are having a good laugh together, about it.

Back at the hostel both of us drink deeply from glasses of cold water, and then head off for bed. We are in separate dorms and on entering mine I disturb an enormous bug! Daniela fearlessly comes to the rescue, catches the ugly creature and escorts it out of my room. We laugh a lot together about the whole incident, and then Daniela discovers that she's rushed out of her dorm without the key and is now locked out! It's very late, and try as she might, she's unable to rouse the caretaker to let her back in. We make our own emergency plan. I loan her spare sleeping gear and shower stuff and Daniela spends the night on one of the spare beds in my dorm. We laugh and laugh about the whole event, before finally drifting off to sleep.

30th January Today I'm leaving Rotorua and whilst this hostel is lovely, modern, clean and new it has no real life or heart in it. Daniela comes back as I'm packing and I say goodbye and happy travels. She says, "Maybe we'll see each other again in the Coromandel?" (an area we're both planning to visit). As the conversation continues, I sense Daniela would like to meet up again. So I tell her the location of my next stop, but that I have no definite plans or hostel bookings after that. Daniela says she can meet me at my next location, so we end up planning to travel for 3 or 4 days around the Coromandel together. Then she gets straight on the phone and finds some accommodation for us! So again (thanks Universe) I have a new travel companion for a few days. Today I move to Tauranga and Daniela will follow on tomorrow, to pick me up; after one more night here in Rotorua.

CHAPTER 87

I decide to telephone Mana Retreat, the place (back in the UK) that I arranged to spend my final month at. I would like to firm up on details around my arrival, pick up time etc. I speak to Vera the organiser and it feels good to be nearer to the time I'll be living and working at a spiritual retreat. I'm looking forward to it with excitement and great anticipation. The phone call prompts me to start musing about the experiences I'll have there.

I arrive in Tauranga around tea time and the place seems like a busy industrial kind of harbour town. The hostel is big and my four-bedded dorm is on the top floor, so I have to heave my beast of a bag up loads of stairs! There's a low energy feeling about the place too. It seems like a lot of the residents are not transient travellers, but fruit-picking workers. Thank goodness I have only one night here! Still, the hostel does have a nice view of the harbour from its kitchen decking area, so I try to look at positive aspects. But the deck turns out to be a noisy, smoky place to sit. Oh, well, this hostel *does* have a book exchange – that's always a bonus…

I take an evening stroll around the locality, and find a little harbour fish and chip shop that's buzzing with customers. I eat fresh and yummy sea fish, seated in an outside eating area that's alive with people. Back at the hostel I pay for thirty minutes of Internet time and check emails. There's one from Wellington Jen and friend Heather, back home. Daughter Gemma has been silent for almost a month. I really don't know what to think about her lack of contact – so decide not to (think that is). Just let it be. Surely if I trust in the synchronicity of Universal timing then all will be perfect just as it is? I shouldn't need to hear from people at certain allotted times to feel okay. In the world of non-attachment I can love and be at peace with 'what is'. That's all well and good in spiritual theory, but I still find myself wanting to text anyway…

What if she's not okay says the inner voice of Mr Fear. I remind myself that I heard from Janet, that both daughters seemed well. And I know that she and her sister have now made friends again; so that's reassuring. The old feeling that I'm responsible for my children's happiness surfaces again. I resist it. If I'm to learn from this time away to really let go of dependency issues, attachment fears and needs, with my daughters – then I must use this 'gap' wisely. Gemma (and everyone else) will be in touch when they are. And that timing will be perfect for the greater good of all. I am not the orchestral conductor of the Universe I realise, now. (Never was – but thought it!!).

CHAPTER 88

31st January So here we are in the last day of January. Where *did* that month go? I was working in Franz Joseph four weeks ago… Today it rains hard. For the first time in a long while, but by lunchtime it begins to brighten. I spend the day wandering around shops, buy my sister a birthday present and mail it. I look at pretty clothes and buy a silk blouse that's unusual in colour. (And yes… it's in a sale!!)

I try a classy waistcoat on but an inner voice informs me it's far too expensive! Even though it's in a sale, a big tussle begins inside my head trying to decide if I should buy it. Surely there are other questions I need to learn to ask myself first, like: Do I *want* to buy it? Does it *fit* nice? (Not just can I *afford* it?)

I remind myself that I seem to be spending quite a lot of money at the moment and of the fact that I have no salary coming in at all, from my job back home. Still, I do have the small income from renting out my house. I'm still fighting with the same old 'fear of lack' and I *know* that until I 'act' as if I *am* abundant... I never will be. But it is *so* HARD to let go of this!!!

I return back to the waistcoat shop to re-try it and ask myself those new 'decision making questions'. The shop assistant remembers me and after a brief conversation with her, I try on the waistcoat again. This time, I realise that it's actually not a very good fit, a bit on the small side. After this realisation I quickly exit the shop, relieved that the new decision making process is over and that my decision 'feels right'.

At 5p.m. I sit on the wall outside the bus stand swinging my legs out over my holdall, in the late afternoon sunshine as I wait for Daniela to pick me up at our pre-arranged time and place. I sit, and I sit. The time grows late...Then I realise that I've not heard from Daniela at all today and begin to wonder why. But before I have much time to worry, here she is walking towards me, smiling her big smile. She tells me she's been waiting for a while, and had sent a text, with no reply. Have I not received it? For a moment I'm confused, then suddenly realise what's happened. Earlier in the day, I changed my NZ Sim card back to my UK one (to check UK messages), and forgot to put the NZ Sim back in. Dippy me! We laugh together about this and I thank Daniela for waiting. Heaving my bags into the already full boot of her hire car, we're soon on our way.

It's a real treat to be travelling by car and I soon realise we have much more freedom in our choice of places to visit and accommodation. Our first stop is an overnight at a little home-stay place in the hills. It has horses, a view of the sea and its own little swimming pool. It turns out that we have the place to ourselves and is a perfect place to relax and spend our first night. Daniela and I are getting on really well and soon she tells me all about her life and career as a landscape architect. Later, she confides how she was madly in love with a woman that she's no longer in touch with, but still has feelings for. We talk for a while around the theme of 'being true to yourself' and brave enough to let people know how you feel, even if it means risking rejection. I reflect on how I had a hunch (before Daniela spoke of her love for a woman) that she was gay. My intuition is yet again working well.

CHAPTER 89

<u>1st February</u> Wow! A brand new month. Amazing! I take an early morning dip in the outdoor pool and listen to distant melodies of goats and sheep calls on the surrounding hills. I recall those similar sweet, early morning sounds in the mountains with Ian. He is also now silent, in his texts... Again, I remind myself that it's about letting go and not attaching to outcomes or expectations.

Daniela and I are making our way up the Coromandel, driving slowly to take in all the pretty scenery. It's carefree and it's fun. Daniela drives and I map read. We make a good team.

Pulling in to have coffee at a quaint little hamlet, we take a quick look around the local stores. Danielle is slim with a good figure, but seems not to care much for clothes. However, she's soon looking at Indian type clothing (with my encouragement) and even trying on a few things, with some coaxing! She looks great in a pair of baggy cotton navy pants and white blouse but seems not sure. I can tell she likes them, even though they're different (more feminine) than what she normally wears. Then, she takes a big leap out of her comfort zone and decides to buy them. I give loads of praise! Daniela beams and appears so happy, that her happiness gives me great pleasure too. I see a mother of pearl and silver necklace. It's so beautiful I decide to buy it Gemma for her forthcoming birthday.

We carry on driving up the coast and our next stop is Cathedral Cove. It's a forty minute walk down to the beach from the car parking lot, but the stunning beauty that awaits us, is well worth it. We both agree it's a shame we haven't brought our swimming gear; the water looks so inviting and the sand is so soft, white and beautiful. We pass through an archway of magnificent rock and look out at tiny tree adorned volcanic islands; jutting out of the sea. People are snorkelling, kayaking and swimming down here. Daniela has a travel guide book that says: *'this is one of the most beautiful places on the whole North Island...'*

We stay a long while in our paradise cove, trying to delay the delicious experience, before making our way back up the cliff side and along the coast to our next hostel that Danielle has pre-booked for us. It's called *On the Beach* and oh, it's lovely!

We're in a dorm that has a sweet ocean-view window seat and the lounge has a view of the sea, too; and so do all the terraces! It's a great place to relax at for a few days. I start preparing our evening meal whilst Daniela takes a shower. As I chop and cut the vegetables, I reflect on a number of aspects of myself that I do *not* find attractive. They just keep popping up!

Annoyingly all of them can be traced back to the 'fear of lack' (mainly of money)! I really don't like this side of me. It's not nice and I find myself trying to resist it when it surfaces. Then I think that pushing a way a part of me, is probably not going to help it change. Maybe I could try to talk to 'it' and reassure it? Thank it for taking care of me, before I tell it that it's not necessary for it to think or act this way, anymore as the Universe will take good care of me, now. I really would like to try and get this new thought pattern to become more of a first thought; when old limitations and fear comes up.

Daniela and I eat our meal on the terrace, looking out onto the sea. It's a funny kind of energy between us sometimes with her appearing a bit aloof, and somewhat surly. I wonder if maybe Daniela misinterprets my actions or words sometimes... Now, I find myself struggling with the feeling that I analyse too much; rather than simply sitting back and relaxing. I'm fast realising that the experience of travelling with someone else has very intense 'mirror' effects and presents its own challenge for considering another set of needs alongside one's own) – which is something new to me on this trip! Still, I want to try and learn from it and grow.

CHAPTER 90

2ⁿᵈ February I had a great night's sleep last night, if not somewhat odd! I slept with the packet for my ear plugs in my hand all night, rather than putting the plugs in my ears and dreamt I was wearing a wedding dress and waiting for a photographer to arrive before finalising makeup. Wandering around in a wedding dress, that's all I recall! We go to the beach after breakfast and it's a perfect day for it. I wander along the beach for a while and then read, whilst Daniela stays for only a short time, then heads back to the hostel. Later I take one of the hostel kayaks out onto the sea. This venture entails loading the vessel onto a little trailer and then pulling both trailer and kayak across a main road and onto the beach. Once on the beach, I struggle to get the kayak launched off the trailer and into the waves. A friendly local kindly comes to my assistance.

The view back to the shoreline in the kayak is beautiful and so clear. I can see hills as a contrast and backdrop to little rows of beach houses, shops and hostels. Once I'm further out into deeper water, I lie flat along the body of the boat and relax. Basking in the sunshine, I gaze up at the sky. Stillness is all around. No wind, no sound and hardly any movement anywhere. The clouds are amazing shapes! Large and billowing, some elongated and others flat. New Zealand clouds are really quite special.

After a short while of experiencing a vast empty space, (both inside and out) the mind kicks in again, and starts to 'chew over' new awareness's, that the 'mirroring' experience is bringing. It's proving strange and somewhat alien, being with another human being for 24/7. I realise that I am tired with all this talking, and the energy it takes. And I'm alarmed about how the money 'thing' has reared its head again, in relation to an 'other'. The heightened awareness around not wanting to share my possessions has been such a shock to me. Maybe I'm not such as nice a person as I'd thought, after all? I consider the advantages and ease of lone travelling without all these personal dilemmas, or stuff coming up to unsettle me. My conclusion is yes, it's true that things are simpler alone, but how does that help me grow as a person and learn how to live in rewarding and healthy relationships with others?

I buy all the food and wine that evening and we sit together in the soft evening air, with its occasional whiff of seaweed carried to us on faint ocean breezes. We are talking about relationships. Daniela talks (again) of the woman she is still in love with. I talk of my experiences of men I have met in New Zealand. I reflect on the 'Stovan Experience' and still don't seem to be able to make full sense of it. Perhaps that's a sign that I'm not ready for another relationship, yet?

CHAPTER 91

The next day it's raining as Daniela and I move on to the final destination of our joint travels, the town of Thames at the mouth of the Coromandel. The road we take passes the main entrance to the Mana Retreat. Today I'm really not feeling so great – maybe the effects of last night's wine? But also, there's a weariness of travelling, that's growing inside me. I'm really looking forward to being in one place, for a longer period of time, soon. But after passing the entrance to Mana (in the middle of nowhere) I find myself wondering what on earth it's going to be like living in such an isolated place. The gateway bears only a plain sign with its name on it and no other clue as to what lies beyond its long narrow driveway winding up the steep hillside. What will it be like living and working in a community? And what kind of people will I meet there?

Daniela and I go out for a farewell meal. Tomorrow she and I go our separate ways. We choose a small downtown Indian restaurant. She wears the new clothes (I encouraged her to buy) and looks great! I loan out my little lacy snug to complete the outfit and comment how lovely she looks! We take pictures of each other, together and apart. When it's my turn to pose for the camera alone, I suddenly become aware that I'm extremely conscious about having my photo taken. It's like all the things that my ego has tricked me into believing (that I am), are cracking open, to expose a thin veneer. It threatens to reveal that I'm not anything like as far on the self-development road, as I appear to be. Back at the hostel, in our twin room, we chat and laugh late into the night. Daniela leaves in the morning for Auckland and I'll miss her.

After saying goodbye, I start to feel a bit lost almost straight away. My thoughts turn to home again and my family and friends back there. I suddenly realise that there's still been no email from Gemma, for longer now than I care to remember. My thoughts fast turn to worry ones. I try not to. But I do. Maybe I should call? What *is* happening with her? Finally, I decide to send a text, but her one word reply only makes me even more uncertain. Acting on impulse, I telephone. Gemma answers in flat mono tones and one word responses, as I keep chatting away and she keeps telling me she's okay. It doesn't sound at all like she's okay to me! I ring off and soon, I'm troubled again. I feel like crying! What on earth to do now? I panic, and decide to ring back. This proves no better at all really, as Gemma gives no further clues or anything to help me know what the problem might be. I ask if she's doing okay in her studies at University. The reply is *yes*. I try and try to encourage my daughter to talk – but with no success. I ring off. The disquiet inside grows even more. I feel such a long way from home (which I am) and oh, such a long, long way from my precious daughter who despite being 23 now feels like my baby again. *Keep calm. Try another approach Lynette.*

I text my other daughter but Melanie only dismisses my concerns, says Gemma is fine and not to worry. What a dilemma! I had said to Gemma (on my second call) that I'd fly home early if necessary but she'd dismissed the idea. So many feelings are coming up and threatening to destroy my new found peace of mind. *Should I go back sooner? What to do? How to decide?* After a turbulent half hour I make a serious decision to try and detach from it somehow, to try and leave it to sort its self out.

Why do I feel like this? What has happened to my trust in the Universe; that it will take care of me and my family? I want to cry. I feel so sad, so alone. It's like all the positive feelings of the last few months are slipping away. I resolve to not let this happen. I begin to focus on regaining balance in my mind and reconnecting to Universal care and love. For a long, long time I lie motionless in a swing hammock that's strung to a tree in the hostel garden. I think about taking a bike ride to channel some of the restless energy in me but 'thinking' is as far as it gets. As I lay there, the guy who owns the hostel passes by and says, "Hi I thought you were taking a bike out this afternoon?"

It's true, I did ask him earlier about the procedure and cost of loaning a bike. Now, Chris encourages me to still go and starts to gets a bike ready for me. As he adjusts the seat height he comments, "You have long legs, eh?" I make no comment, except to thank him for his kind help before pedalling off down the road in the direction of town.

I cycle into Thames and take Gemma's birthday parcel to post. I send my latest newsletter off to Dad and then just cycle around the area. Despite it being well past midday, the sun is still very hot. I perspire a lot and soon feel quite fatigued, so it's not long before I head back. Chris is on reception as I check the bike back in. He gives me more compliments, this time about my blue eyes and out-going personality. Now, my mind starts to collate other information around Chris's attentiveness towards me since my arrival that I've failed to recognise as such at the time, or simply passed it off as him being a friendly proprietor. Now, I'm not so sure where this guy's coming from, but with all my other distractions today I'm too tired to even care.

CHAPTER 92

The next day, I'm feeling a bit more centred again. I take the bike out once more, this time for a good few hours along the coastal roads and river tracks. Again, Chris's very chatty, asking me about myself and what I'm doing here. He makes general conversation about this and that, then out of the blue asks if I'd like to share a beer with him, "Maybe tomorrow night?" So I agree, as this sweet guy seems keen to spend some time with me! When I return the bike, later in the day, Chris offers to give me a lift to a local swimming spot that's on his route, to pick up walkers returning from a nearby trail. This is all a bit sudden; but the idea of a river swim sounds nice (and fun) so I check out the vibe and intuition about how 'safe' Chris feels. The message comes back that he's okay, so I accept his kind offer and go get my swim gear. We drive in Chris's minibus on bumpy roads that lead out of town and up, up towards the Pinnacle trail. Kiwi-Chris keeps glancing over at me and smiling as he asks lots of questions about me and my life. He wants to know my age and is surprised when I tell him. He tells me he's 36 and that I only look in my early 40's. I laugh. Chris then goes on to tell me that ever since I checked in at the hostel he senses that I'm different. That he finds me an outgoing, friendly and interesting person. I thank him for his compliments.

As he drops me at my water hole Chris tells me the time that he'll be back to pick me up. So I wave him off and make my way down a path to the river bank and jump into the cool, inviting, clear water. I have a great time, watching groups of teenagers jumping and diving in quite fearlessly from high rocks. This unplanned excursion is so much fun that I find my mind gets totally distracted from yesterday's worries and fear thoughts. True to his word Chris picks me up at the appointed time. The minibus is now full of hikers, so his conversation is more general than personal. I sit up front and listen to a group of German walkers chatting in the back. Later that evening I'm curled up reading in a chair in the hostel lounge, when Chris comes in and says he'd like to show me photos of dolphin shoals taken from a boat he goes fishing on. As I comment with glee at his beautiful pictures, Chris tells me that he'll take me fishing with him, if I'm still here at the weekend. But I am not. I'm leaving soon for my month at Mana.

A woman from Buxton arrives in my dorm today. Soon we're chatting away and discover we both want to hike a seven hour local trail called The Pinnacles. We start to make our arrangements to go tomorrow. Jill has a car. She's a year older than me. We get on quite well. She gives me a work experience contact for Gemma back in the UK and this makes me happy as I email it over to her. Perhaps this will cheer her up? The next day Gill and I set off on our hike together. It's a long walk through heavy bush and across swollen rivers but the views are beautiful and well worth it. Right at the peak of the Pinnacles we come across a large, wooden hostel hut. People clearly stay here (it's furnished) but today it seems deserted, no one is home. We eat our sandwiches on benches outside the hut and I make a comment something like: "I would *love* a cup of coffee right now!" When out of (what seemed like) nowhere, a Ranger appears from around a corner and invites us to join him at his cabin, for coffee! Wow! There I go again manifesting what I think about! Even works for a cup of coffee!

We sit drinking wonderfully percolated coffee in the middle of this wilderness and chatting with a most charming and most interesting Ranger called Charles. He's half Maori and half English. Charles grins as he tells stories of how Billy Connelly's helicopter landed here one day (quite unexpectedly) and how he invited him in for tea. Gill and I look at each other in total surprise and laugh as Charles announces, "Billy Connolly sat right there where you're sitting, drinking his tea!" It's hard for us to tear ourselves away from the stimulating conversation and comfort of the little hut, but eventually we continue our trek; waving goodbye to this sweet little guy and his tall stories.

The walk back is a much gentle one. I am tired and ready for a warm, refreshing shower. Back at the hostel, it's late before I see Chris. He asks again, about our beer date. I remind him that as I leave tomorrow, it would need to be tonight. Chris readily agrees and soon we're chatting in a small bar.   Chris's makes it pretty obvious that he likes me.   My beer has a pattern on the top of it and I comment how nice it is.   He responds "A pretty pattern for a pretty lady." Then later, "You really are nice aren't you."

Chris talks of the many places he's travelled to in the past and of conflicting feeling of obligation to care for his mum after the death of his dad.   Chris is clearly in a low energy space and seems quite unhappy to me.   He starts to talk about an unfulfilled dream of gaining a pilot's licence and I encourage him to, "Go for it!"   Chris talks quietly of past relationships that went wrong, but doesn't know why, then he starts asking about my ex-husband and makes the comment, "He let go of the most special thing in his life, when he lost you."   I laugh and say I don't think my ex saw it quite like that himself…

After a couple of beers we go back to Chris's house adjoining the hostel and drink coffee.   I check inside myself on what I'm feeling and find it's the energy of friendship.   Chris has nice eyes and face.   He has a muscular body, but his tired energy field is not attractive to me.   I give him a friendly hug goodnight and he hugs me back, his strong body holding on to me for a few seconds, before I return back to my dorm for one last night in Thames.

CHAPTER 93

7th February To Mana! Goodbye Gill. Goodbye Chris. His mother sits in reception, as I check out (she knows her son has an interest in me, even though she says nothing to give this 'knowing' away). I sense Chris can't really say what he wants to me because of her. Instead of speaking, he silently hands me an email card with an address on as he returns my deposit. Smiling, and in return, I give him a pretty rock that I found on my river swim, along with a scrap of paper with my email address scribbled across it.

Later, when I take my bags outside, to wait for the bus Chris is already outside waiting to say goodbye. I sense his shyness. Gill has also come out to wave me off. I feel for them both as they stand, one on each side of me with Chris trying not to make it obvious that he's just here for me. Presently, my bus arrives and I hug Gill quickly and say goodbye to Chris quite formally. He offers me work back at his hostel, if it doesn't work out at Mana, and says, "See ya…"

The bus ride is a mere half hour gentle drive back up the coastal road. It drops me right at the gates of Mana. I can't put my finger on why, but I feel really happy. The ocean is on my left and a long windy road is on my right, as I wait patiently and expectantly for someone to pick me up as arranged by email. I'm thoroughly enjoying the anticipation I feel about living in this mysterious looking place, when a minibus arrives and a smiley middle aged woman gets out to greet me. "Were you worried no-one would pick you up? Have you been waiting long?" she asks. "No, not at all," is my reply (to both).

At the end of a long, loopy road rests Mana. The beautiful spiritual retreat centre I first fell in love with over the Internet many months ago and somehow knew right away, it was the place for me. My online application to become one of their wwoofers (willing workers on organic farms) had been accepted and I hope to stay for up to a month here to experience living and working in this little community of multi-cultural work-trade volunteers, resident staff and paying guests.

I'm shown round the main lodge, with its stunning views of the ocean, by Ed, a friendly retired Canadian wwoofer. He takes me to my accommodation; a wooden cabin which I'll be sharing with other wwoofers and I drop off my bags. The place seems fairly quiet. One residential course has just finished and another is soon to start. I'm informed there's a free talk tonight that I can attend at 7p.m. A smiley, long haired girl who introduces herself as Bev, tells me it's her birthday today and I'm invited to a little party, after the talk. It feels really good to be here. Even at such a quick glance, I can see what a beautiful place this is. I know it's good here. I can feel the energy of the place, so strong. Lunch is an amazingly tasty meal of lots of strange looking colourful and wonderful things, many of them taken from the organic gardens. It's completely vegetarian here. I'm looking forward to this experience too along with their no alcohol, smoking and all other drugs rule. After lunch, I enjoy freshly made coffee and newly baked carrot cake. We all sing *Happy Birthday dear Bev.*

Afterwards, I help clear up in the large, open plan kitchen and am asked if I'll go pick flowers from the garden, to replace wilting ones that are dotted around the dining room in little tiny vases. The sun is really quite fierce today, and what a wonderfully long hot summer this year has been! Vera, the co-ordinator, is away today and so it seems that I'm to be pretty much left to settle in, and not put on the rota for work until tomorrow. (Thanks for that little extra holiday Universe!) I wander around a well-stocked library, acquainting myself with its 'booty' and pull out an interesting looking book to read. I've been encouraged by Ed to view the facilities and resources of Mana as mine to enjoy; especially when there aren't any groups using the Centre, like today. A huge dome shaped meditation room looks out onto a large expanse of sea and sky. I hear that this room is a place people sometimes spend the night. It is truly an inspirational setting and the whole place vibrates with such a beautiful energy. Very special!

CHAPTER 94

There are about eight wwoofers at Mana right now, whose nationalities are German, English and Canadian. I learn that I will share a cabin with two German girls, called Tanya and Suzanna; both in their early 30s. It's a peaceful little lodge with cute wooden verandas set in a semi-circle of other cabins. I am shown to my sleeping area, which is a mattress on the floor by a window. I almost fall asleep, resting after lunch as it's so very cosy and peaceful. I hear the gentle noises of a forest and see trees rustling in the breeze, as I lie gazing out of the window. The soft sounds lull my mind into a restful place.

When I return to the large communal dining hall, Al and others are chatting excitedly about a show they're going to see by The Drifters. They're performing in Coromandel town next Sunday. What a treat! I ask if it's possible for me to get a ticket too. Al says he's going into Coromandel today and will see if he can get one. Such a friendly crowd! It feels almost like family and so lovely to be surrounded by such a stable warm and friendly vibe, after my transient time 'on the road'.

I feel so very at home here, already. This evening, after a very interesting evening talk about healthy eating by an old guy called Earl; I leave the main hall and head for bed. I decide to decline the party invite, as I suddenly feel quite tired. I say my goodnights to the group, as they head off to Bev's birthday dancing party. I lay in bed that first night, feeling very relaxed, as I listen to distant rhythmic beats of drumming. My mind begins to wonder at all the learning, wisdom and growth that I'm about to experience in this community of interesting and spiritually minded folk.

The next day Sleep came quickly, last night and this morning I'm up early, in time for the daily 8a.m. circle gathering of Mana staff. We meet in the library and sit cross legged on the floor, holding hands in silence as we strain to hear the faint peel of bells from up the hill. Each of us takes turns to choose an angel card and share any thoughts (if you want).

My card is gratitude, so I share that I have immense gratitude for being here at Mana. We are invited to share thoughts on the talk last night and a few of us do so. Then it's time for healthy muesli, fruit and weird tasting bread for breakfast, with hot Chai tea. After, a chubby and cheerful girl called Katrina gives me an hour of induction on how to make up cabins for guests on residential courses then Vera comes in and introduces herself. After this, I get to take time off until 4p.m. when I will shadow Tanya in the kitchen.

I enjoy free time to read, soak in the atmosphere of this place and lots of glorious sunshine from the deck of our cabin. My stomach seems a little gluggy (and also a little windy) but I decide it's probably in shock from all the fruit and vegetables in my new vegetarian diet!

After lunch I take a short walk down a path called The Goddess Trail and meet one of the paying residents called Haleakala (aka Hale). He is a rather strange, but interesting American guy who now lives on the Hawaiian island of Maui and has adopted the Hawaiian name; Haleakala which he tells me means *house of the sun*

We start to exchange small talk and very quickly discover similar life themes. Hale has intense eyes and wild shoulder length grey hair. He wears scrunched up, strangely put together eco outfits. Hale tells me he's a strict vegan and also a Sufi. (?) During our lengthy chat we exchange details of books that we recommend to each other. I'm intrigued by Hale's book as it's by an author I haven't heard of before called Krishnamurti. When Hale tells me that he's here for up to a month, I think to myself that it could be interesting to study his book in my non-working time. After this most unusual conversation, we both go our separate ways in opposite directions.

Once back at the wwoofer cabin, I shower and go to work on my kitchen shift. After dinner and clear up there's time to relax and sit about chatting with Suzanne, Tanya, Hale and a few others. Later, my two housemates invite me to go for an evening sauna with them but as I am still finding my stomach a bit achy I decide its best to go to bed

CHAPTER 95

<u>9th February 8a.m.</u> I attend morning meditation and pick out an angel card. It's *Communion and Inspiration*. After breakfast Hale (the American-Hawaiian-Sufi) invites me to take a walk with him. I have no work or any other idea what to do, so I accept. He knows the trails around here well, and after an enjoyable walk we spend the rest of the morning reading Krishnamurti (his favourite author) and discussing the text.

For some reason, Hale's energy field seems to resonate deeply with me, even though I still find him a pretty weird sort of guy! As the morning progresses he begins to reveal more of his life story. It is one that speaks of a very claustrophobic relationship with an overbearing mother which (he feels) left him with an unnatural fear of women and overwhelmed by relationships. Hale is very open and honest. What a sad story!

After lunch I work another kitchen shift. All work is marked up on a timetable in the kitchen. There's either a shift of kitchen, garden or housekeeping each day, with lots of spare time and days off. Working in the kitchen is kind of tiring, especially in the heat of the day but I try to make it a pleasure. After all, any work can be a spiritual practice, if we let it...

That evening Peyla an English woofer with an amazing gift for channelling, sings with her magical silvery voice, in the Octagon. Peyla leaves Mana tomorrow and people here have told me how special her voice is, so I have asked her to sing for me, before she leaves. We are a small group that cluster around Peyla as she lights a candle to mark this sacred occasion. As soon as she starts to sing, it's like an intense electric charge of lightning shoots across my lower arms and legs, then into my body. Salty tears begin to flow down my cheeks, but I have no idea why I'm so moved. Her words are unrecognisable to me, they seem to come from an ancient place and resonate deep within. A connection, I know not where from.

It's like a foreign language, rich, aromatic and majestic. Peyla chants again and once more, tears flow freely and my lower body feels intensely charged. Afterwards we huddle around her in awe, trying to understand what the strange words mean as Peyla explains (as best she can) about her gift. Sweet and gentle Peyla with her long dark hair cascading over petite shoulders, lowers her eyes in reverence and whispers that she is merely a channel. Then she laughs with delight before going on to say that she never knows what will happen, when the channelling starts. All she knows is that it represents the Divine Feminine and it sometimes connects people with a long lost place within.

Suddenly, without warning, Peyla turns to me and places her hands together, reverently. Speaking in a deep, rich, alien, but authoritative tongue, she bows and addresses me with a string of unrecognisable words. Again as she speaks, I feel an intense energy moving throughout my body. It's like my mind becomes disabled as this powerful experience washes through me. It's 'charge' is so moving that tears flow, again. Automatically, I find myself bowing my head at one point, intuitively 'knowing' what she is saying and then I smile as we connect with the energy of love. It's a powerful moment.

After 'the voice' ends Peyla explains that the Divine Feminine wanted me to know that I am most loved, most blessed and wonderful. I thank her but there are no words to describe this experience or how to express the gratitude that's in my heart.

138

As I sit on the bed writing up my journal at the end of one very strange day, I suddenly recall my Angel cards this morning. *Communion and inspiration…*

CHAPTER 96

Sunday At morning meditation, joined in a circle by hands with fellow workers, I spend five blissful minutes listening to the sanctuary bells on the hill, before picking out my daily Angel card. The word on the card says *Love.*

I wonder if this could be linked with the love connection to the Divine Feminine, that I felt last night? I pick a second card and get *Romance.*

As I read out loud the meaning on the back of my card, I come over a little bashful as it says, *The angels have heard your heart felt desire for a loved one and are meeting these wishes.*

I'm in shock, as I recall my recent request to the Universe sent from an open heart.

I am working most of the day in the kitchen and Vera is kitchen manager, today. Despite her position, it feels like she's a bit uneasy with herself and a little shy, and this comes out in a bit of a bossy way.

I must say, that I'm finding some people here not as spiritually mature as I'd anticipated. So many seem to be struggling to 'hide' or mask some issue in their life, whilst trying to appear 'together'. It's a bit disconcerting this feeling of pretence that I'm sensing. I much prefer to be around people who are more 'real' than this. Or maybe it's that I don't know them well enough yet for them to be comfortable with me? Maybe that's it. I do hope so.

Another thing my intuitive energies are picking up around here is that there seems to be an undercurrent of bitching and griping amongst workers and staff, which I am not at all comfortable with. In the evening we take the minibus down to Coromandel town and watch The Drifters. It's a lovely warm evening and they perform on an open stage with the setting sun behind it. I have lots of fun singing along to golden oldies from my youth. Alcohol is freely available here, but I make an inner deal with myself not to have any, as my time at Mana is also about experiencing (more than just a weekend) of alcohol free time. The Drifters are amazing, regardless of their years! As they leave the stage and pass by our seats, I shake each of the band's hand to share my gratitude with them. What fun!

Throughout the evening it became pretty obvious that there is a 'coupling' occurring between Sarah (a wwoofer) and Rick (a resident). They keep doing subtle touches and glances back and forth to each other. On the journey home they sit close, holding hands in the bus. When we get back to the Centre and everyone is saying their goodnights Rick and Sarah signal to each other a meet up. Strolling back up to my cabin, I glance back towards the main building and see Rick having a cigarette before heading over to Sarah's cabin! So much for 'spiritually enlightened beings' - it's supposed to be a drug free zone here!

Back in the sanctuary of my room, I snuggle down underneath my cosy duvet. Behind a paper thin partition wall I hear Terry (the gardener), with his young German wwoofer girlfriend next door, talking to each other as they prepare for bed. He's 20 years her senior; and it's another unusual 'Mana-made' couple! I'm starting to wonder what my love and romance cards could mean, as it seems there's certainly plenty of it happening around this place! If my beloved is here then it's no one I can identify as of yet I must say, but new wwoofers (and residents) arrive next week so who knows? Today, I continue to struggle with my feelings of being disconnected from the group and start to wonder if I'll stay the full month...

CHAPTER 97

Monday I start the day with a lie in (as it's my day off) and Suzanne my roommate is also off too. We sit drinking Roobus tea and having long chats about Mana and its residents, which is helpful for me to gain greater understanding of the people and group dynamics of this place.

She's a wise old soul, this Suzanne. I like her a lot. I decide that I like Donna too, who helps manage the Centre. She's got a nice gentle and relaxed energy about her. We sit out on the veranda eating lunch together in the midday sun and talk about sweat lodges. Donna shares with me her experience of them and it's interesting. After lunch I do washing and use internet facilities to catch up on emails.

I'm enjoying relaxing and taking the day at my own pace. I spend a little time sitting in the beautiful Octagon meditation room. I look out of its vast dome window and meditate on the view. It's a 'sticky' sort of a day, and very soon my washing is dry. I have a bit of a headache that drags on and so I go lie down.

As I rest, my mind starts to wonder about Hale. How, after our friendly and relaxed time together yesterday he seemed very different towards me at breakfast today, more distant and almost awkward. He'd commented to me that he was considering leaving tomorrow, to move on to another retreat in Taupo. Hale had then asked if he did decide to stay would we be able to take regular time to study, together. I have now decided my answer is yes, but not yet done anything about letting him know.

I think about leaving it until tomorrow and then something inside tells me I need to speak with him today. So up I get from my rest and put the Krishnamurti book (he loaned me yesterday) in my rucksack, then walk slowly up the hill to his cabin. I'm not sure if Hale will be in, but he comes out to greet me in the heat of the day, dressed in cream hemp, long undies! It's clear that his hippy styles of flax, hemp and linen clothing go right down to underwear! Hale welcomes me in and politely thanks me for coming. I can't help noticing that his body (for its 57 years) is very lithe. His chest and stomach areas are full of dark, soft downy hair.

Hale pulls on white shorts smiles sweetly and sits on the bed, which dominates most of his tiny wooden cabin. I tuck myself into a corner chair nearest the window, and after offering me a glass of water, Hale begins to talk about whether to leave tomorrow or not. He comments that he's pleased I have come to study once more with him.

Moving off the bed he pulls up a chair close to mine, opens a book and reads Krishnamurti. But this time his energy feels different. As we wade slowly through the difficult text, Hale reads then pauses, to offer extra understanding and meaning to any difficult words. However, this time, almost all of his interpretation of the text somehow keeps referring back to a theme of, 'the human need for pleasure.'

I comment openly, (in my confusion) to him, about my observations and experience of this. He seems surprised, and says he didn't realise he was doing it. His genuine manner would lead me to believe that this is true. Feeling a little braver, I speak openly and frankly with him of how I experience him as making too many references to touch and sex and that it's beginning to feel like it's about his own need for intimacy. I tell him that this makes me feel scared. I speak honestly about how this tension is making me apprehensive about spending any further study time with him. That it seems to me that there is some unconscious 'unmet need' that's driving all this.

Hale listens with an astonished look on his face, and then thanks me for my honesty. So I go on. I tell him that I experience him as an interesting intelligent and reflective, spiritual guy but that the intellectual side is just one facet to him. That the other side revealed to me is of a 'needy little boy' who's afraid of women. He listens in awe and keeps on thanking me (for what I'm not sure). Men don't usually like my honest feedback, so this isn't quite the reaction I expect. Hale confides in me that yes, it's true this is how it's been with every single woman in his life since his first girlfriend in 8th grade at high school. Women are attracted to him and him to them. They date a few times but then his 'needy side' takes over, or he starts to become afraid and either they leave or he leaves them. As we spend time together talking openly about this, I realise that Hale's issue feels to me like a mirror (in some way) to my own, around feeling emotionally safe with men.

Hale agrees that he is in many ways still a little boy who just reads and intellectualizes things, but that now it's time for this to end. He feels ready to change. Hale thanks me once again and says how amazing it is for me to be in his life giving him this honest feedback. Hale talks once more of his indecision about staying or moving on, tomorrow. I sense he wants me to ask him to stay (which I do), but I say he must not make his decision based on anything to do with me. He looks happy as he tells me that was absolutely the right thing for me to say to him.

Hale acknowledges that his energy towards me did change after our first meeting, when he discovered he liked me as this caused fear to surface – and he moved away; because he didn't know how to be around me. (So that's what happened at breakfast!). I tell Hale that I can't be comfortable being his friend or feel safe with him unless he's aware of my concerns and how I experience his 'neediness'. It's like Hale really begins to 'see' these behaviours for the first time. He gets very animated and passionate in his new understanding as he exclaims that he's quite sure he wants to make changes now, not remain in this fear. That we must communicate honestly and openly with each other for this to happen. I agree.

I look at him then, and see quite a handsome guy with alive and vibrant eyes. His shoulder length grey hair falls in soft lamb curls around his chin line. A mischievous grin sits across pencil thin lips, revealing gold fillings amidst even white teeth. When his 'little boy' is not running the show, I see how Hale's gentle, yet energetic spiritual expression is amazing company. We talk long into the afternoon. He tells me how he had inherited a large amount of money from his father at a young age, but feels it might have been a handicap, as he's never had to work or gain maturity. Hale seems amazed at my frankness and grateful for my honesty, saying that most people (because of his money) just tell him what they think he wants to hear. Personally, I'm amazed at how positively and constructively he received it all. I tell him that I have said some pretty difficult things to him and not many men could take it. Again, Hale says he wants me to say what I see. We walk to dinner, friends again with all misunderstanding behind us. Our openness and willingness to listen and share together, creates an easy closeness between us now. The evening is relaxed and pleasant. A small group of us share discussions and

142

Krishnamurti together. Hale reads out aloud with presence and passion. I see how very charismatic he can be when he forgets his fearful self and shares his love of Krishnamurti.

CHAPTER 98

A second day off in such a short time of being here! (Thank you Universe) Yet again the sun blazes down so I decide to sunbathe and read on the deck of our cabin. Hale has decided to stay on at Mana so after lunch we go to the library to read. Today I see him a little differently from yesterday. I ask him what's wrong and he says he feels worried because yesterday, he told me about him doing heavy drugs and alcohol in the past and its legacy of Hepatitis C. Hale is worried that I may have decided I don't want to be around him anymore or will judge him for those things. I say no this is not the way with me, that I try to meet people where they are at. He's happy again.

Hale shares with me that he's a songwriter and has written 3 CDs worth. That his songs were recorded and ready to be released, when he fell out with the woman who wrote the melodies. Hale is turning out to be quite a creative guy. I like creative types.

We agree to meet at 3p.m. to take a walk up to the sanctuary on the hill together. Bev sees me leaving and asks where I'm going? More and more I am finding that Bev is a rather strange girl. I don't quite warm to her. She's English and has been travelling for many years but seems a bit of a lost soul really. I experience her as over tactile and it makes me uncomfortable. For some reason she has become very 'into' Hale. I sense she *knows* I'm meeting with him but I don't tell her where I'm going, as I don't want her tagging along.

I walk the (now familiar) path of the Goddess Trail following its magical, lush, green path. Hale is waiting at his cabin door. He looks quite ridiculous in see-through striped flax shorts and clumpy black lace up shoes. He's carrying a hessian bag, enormous umbrella, and wearing sunglasses with a straw hat – even more bizarre, as it's starting to rain! I smile to myself at this eccentric sight and think what an odd pair we must look as we wind our way slowly up the hill, side by side.

Today, Hale and I fall quickly fall into discussion. He is gentle and deeply sensitive in many ways. I can see why his spirit has not fared so well in this world. We continue to talk openly and honestly about a range of themes (mostly about him) but then he says, "Soon we will talk about you, because I want to know all about you."

143

I don't mind, talking about his stuff as I realise the mirror effect is often at work and so his stuff (in some way) is a reflection of my own. But I really would like to experience the expansive joy that Hale clearly has glimpses of, and I want to experience more of his zest and enthusiasm for life. We arrive at the beautiful sanctuary high on the hill with remarkable views across mountains and the ocean. The sanctuary is a place of deep silence and reverence. Once inside Hale paces, in silence, round and round its parameters then stands firmly on a large green stone in the centre. I look up and see a symbol of seven hearts intertwined to make one star with seven prongs adorning the west wall.

Hale had already spoken to me of human separateness being an area of pain for him, as he feels we are really all one. I look at the symbol of the hearts and it speaks to me. I beckon to Hale in silence, he smiles (it's like he understands what I'm thinking).

I hold out my hand and he places his own in mine. We stand, each with one foot on the greenstone, holding hands. It's like we are breathing in (through our feet) ever so slowly, the energy of this sacred place.

CHAPTER 99

I lie like a star, face up on the cool stone floor and view the sanctuary from below. Directly above, a stained glass symbol of the Divine Feminine casts its shadow across my body. Hale comes to joins me on the floor and we lay there for a long while, eyes closed and silent. I want to keep this experience pure and not taint it with words..

Once back in the 'world' we both find ourselves wanting to talk about it, so as we wind our way back down the hill, away from the peaceful sanctuary, we search for words to describe our experience. But somehow words don't work, as we limply verbalise the powerful experience of seeing reflections of each other (on the tiled floor) and feeling the sacred greenstone beneath us. Of our view of the illuminated ceiling and the energy we'd both felt. It's been quite delicious spending this time with Hale; his spirit seems so free today! Experiencing our collective energy and the vibrant power of Now makes me hungry for more.

Later, after dinner a small group of us go into the meditation room and Hale puts on one of his CDs. It's a new-age 'enlightened' American guy called Krishna Das who sings Sanskrit in deep vibrating tones. Our little group hold hands in a circle. We bend gently as we move round and round, with heads together, as we sway rhythmically in time with the mystical beat. Hale is on my left. I lean into him comfortably when he places his foot over mine and his cheek brushes gently against mine.

Round and round we go, the energy rising as we sing and hum to ancient sounds.

The music is rich, with a blissful peace about it. I have never heard this kind of music before. It's deep and very sensuous. Hale leans his head against mine as the tempo speeds up and pushes it deeply against my face, seeking contact with my skin. His eyes are animated and amazingly alive tonight. His quick whit caused much humour in our little group, over dinner. Bev has noticed the change in him and now seems to want a lot of his attention; trying to touch him in some way, as often as she can. I find myself making a conscious choice to stand back from this and not let it affect me.

13th February At breakfast Hale and I arrange to meet at his place after I finish work for an hour or so, to continue studying our latest piece of Krishnamurti. Today I'm on gardening duty and it's a lovely sunny day. I enjoy weeding the paths and flower beds around the main buildings. I silently make the intention to see every job I do at Mana, as part of my spiritual practice and to discover joy and delight in all work. With this mindset, the time passes with a gentle rhythm and peacefulness. At the end of my shift I stand back with pride to view my work.

At lunch I see Hale briefly and spend a moment chatting and sharing a friendly hug. Greeting everyone with hugs seems to be customary for most, at Mana. Although, I must confess, it took a bit of getting used to (embracing strangers) at first, now I'm relaxing into this way of greeting more and more. I love the warmth, the energy exchange and nice family feeling that it gives me – after months without regular hugs from family and friends.

CHAPTER 100

After work I take a shower, pack up my book and walk the Goddess Path. As I turn the final corner, I see Hale standing at the doorway, in his underwear (again!). This time, I'm very surprised to see this, as he knows I am coming! So I make a comment on it something like, "It's not seen by English people as socially correct to receive guests in underwear!" He laughs loudly as he pulls on shorts. Then, as he turns away, I see immediately that there's something very different about him today. His face seems pinched and pale; his movements slower and there are big spaces and pauses between his thinking and speaking. The eyes are different too, somehow more intense and large.

I ask if he's been taking dope. He says no more than usual. Hale has already told me that as the holder of a medical marijuana card, he uses cannabis on a daily basis for regulating his liver pain. And the other day I recall he'd commented on having taken a 'smoke' just before meeting me. I'm confused and not at all sure, (having no experience of cannabis at all) what this means. So I decide to just see how it goes and prepare to study.

Hale finds the chapter he's marked and begins to read but keeps pausing and looking across at me, with a display of agitation. Finally he asks, "Do you find me attractive?" I look up from the book and pause. I decide to keep communication lines honest and open, so I say that some aspects of him are attractive to me, yes. This seems to please him. Although, now I'm not at all sure where this might be heading and so I interrupt the study and ask outright what he wants from me? I mirror back to him information about his agitated state and suggest it might be best if I go, as we're not getting anywhere with our studying, today. I prepare to leave.

Hale becomes upset and asks me not to go. Feeling somewhat sad and disappointed, I shake my head and comment that I don't recognise this Hale. Quietly he says, "Maybe this is me?" I reply that, "I'm not sure if I've seen which one is really you, or how I can know." Glancing up at me with intense eyes, he mummers, "This is the way it is with an addict," then proceeds to tell me about women he's lost in the past, that couldn't accept his love affair with the 'green lady.'

Now an unpredictable and almost paranoid side of this man is being revealed to me; juxtaposed with the energetic, sweet and charismatic Hale I've met. An unsettled, confused and disturbed feeling begins to come over me and despite having looked forward to our study time together, I suggest he takes a rest now. But this suggestion doesn't seem to help either. Now Hale is somewhat distressed as well as agitated and asks (almost pleadingly) if I'll lie down with him. I refuse and begin to pack my book away, when all at once it's like his unstable state makes a big shift and the Hale I know is back.

His speech becomes faster and easier. Hale apologises profusely and thanks me for being direct and honest with him. This starts off a very animated discussion and sharing between us about our personal experiences, in relationships with the opposite sex. Hale asks, "Have you ever been hurt?" His intense eyes look searchingly into mine and before I know it I find myself sharing painful details about past loves and even adding a few childhood memories to the cauldron of emotional pain.

CHAPTER 101

A little shocked that all this has come out, I get up (again) to leave, feeling a little vulnerable now. Suddenly Hale blurts out a short but profound statement that stops me in my tracks. "I think it sounds like I am all your ex's rolled into one, and that you are now being given the experience of everything again, all together!"

Totally stunned by this disturbing statement, I am still deciding on how to reply when Hale continues on, with his bizarre assessment. Now, he informs me (almost in a whisper) that in his opinion our ability to be open and honest in this relationship gives it the ability to act like one amazing, intensive therapy and awakening treatment for us, because of the mirror effect it offers.

Crazy as it sounds it feels like this is true! When he's not high on dope Hale quite a wise dude and extremely intelligent, yet at the same time his life is so greatly limited by a fragile emotional state. Revealing more of the 'story', I hear about his over protective mother and her 'transference' of intense fear of the world, onto him. How, her inability to allow Hale to make decisions or take responsibility for himself has left him stuck in some sort of a Peter Pan time warp.

It's true, he seems to have somehow by-passed the growing up stage, and having enough money to 'pay' people to think for him has probably added to this. Hale's frank conversations about his past give me the image of a sensitive, insecure and confused adolescent. A rebellious young man that gets deeper and deeper into the heavy drug scene to find confidence and acceptance. I see a scene of 'shooting up,' of 'partying hard' and hanging out with drug using, rebellious hippies.

Most relationships with women lasting only a short while, before the warning, given by his mother: *a woman will only want you for your money* would ring loud in his ears. Hale's sad story moves on to speak of amazing courage and his journey back from a place of serious drug and alcohol addiction, following a fatal prognosis from a doctor. Years later, after daily AA and NA meetings Hale proudly tells me he became "Clean and sober," before concluding with the confession that his current use of 'Green Lady' is mostly from necessity, to help him handle life in this "Frikkin crazy world."

Wow! I admire his amazing openness and honesty. It feel like a breath of fresh air talking with Hale, as opposed to other men I've known who almost have to have emotional exchanges extracted like painfully bad teeth! I must admit though, that I do keep going off into fear places inside my head, as my mind races with all this new information. Hale notices this and keeps reminding me (with passion) to, "Come back, and come back, into the Now."

As Krishnamurti teaches, Now is all there is. We must die to the past, the past is gone. The future is not real. Only Now is real. I must meet Hale 'in the present' - not in memories from the past. What a challenging life lesson. Thanks Universe!

CHAPTER 102

Later that evening, down in the library a small group of wwoofers and residents (that Hale has drummed up) are gathered. The entertainment this evening is courtesy of Hale. He puts on a battered and ancient video he's discovered in the library here of his favourite buddy, Krishnamurti! We sit in chairs and around the floor listening intently as Hale works hard to translate the message contained in this complex (and poorly filmed) black and white video interview of his favourite guru.

Despite Hale's passion and numerous attempts to make the content accessible, most of the group are struggling to get past Krishnamurti's difficult delivery style (and to be honest) I'm finding it all a bit heavy too. So, in the midst of a 'solid' bit I excuse myself and leave the room to take a pee.

Suddenly Hale stops the video, gets up and (to everyone's surprise) follows me out into the corridor. Looking intently at me with a worried voice, he asks how I think it's going. I grope for kind and encouraging words for him, and say, "It's sort of good, Hale but a bit challenging for some." He nods and a serious look crosses his furrowed brow. How this man wants to get this message over! I so admire his passion.

When I come out of the loo, he's waiting. We share a smile, a hug and go back into the room, together. Bev watches our entry with interest then moves quickly to huddle close up next to Hale as he sits back down on the floor. When the video finally comes to an end, it's kind of an anti-climax for poor Hale. Everyone drifts off in dribs and drabs after only a brief discussion, mostly about Krishnamurti's unattractive delivery style. I try to add a positive comment to the 'pot' by saying that Hale's translation put it in ways that makes it easier for me to understand and has a more attractive and accessible delivery style for this message. People nod in agreement and Hale begins to ponder on this. After everyone has slipped away he comes to sit by me on the sofa and starts stroking my hand, gently holding sections of my arm as he talks. It's a tender, caring moment. I suggest that maybe he needs to take this message out on the road in his own style? Hale gets excited at this suggestion, and our conversation turns into almost urgent whispers as he tells me this is what he's often felt 'called' to do; to re-write Krishnamurti and put it 'out there'. I share his enthusiasm for the idea and add that maybe he could use a range of mediums, to get the message across; like his songs. I could go on talking for hours like this, us stroking each other's arms absentmindedly as we talk. Hale's bare foot gently, but firmly over mine as we sit.

It grows dark and we are still sitting there. Tanya comes back into the library, looks around, sees us alone there and goes out again. I wonder again, for a moment, what everyone must think of us. A most unusual couple! The long haired eccentric American hippie from Hawaii and the Julie Andrews look-a-like from England! Eventually, and with some reluctance (because it's such a delicious experience) I say maybe its time to say goodnight. Outside and hugs later Hale murmurs, "You're special. Thank you." I reply "You're special too." We continue this sweet round of gratitude with Hale telling me how grateful he is that I'm in his life. And me saying I feel pretty much the same about him.

We bid each other goodnight and go our separate ways. Hale up the Goddess Path to his cabin on the hill and me to my little wwoofer lodge. Once in bed, I can't sleep.

Thoughts and ideas are whizzing round and round in my head about this extraordinary guy, his complexity, his simplicity, his charisma, his cannabis use, his gentle beauty, his loving spirit. I wonder where on earth this strange and very unconventional relationship is going…

CHAPTER 103

February 14th Today I'm working until 4p.m. I offer to go to Hale's, to study for an hour after work, and he readily agrees. Almost immediately, I change my mind, and think I'm not sure if it feels okay to be meeting this often. So I say, "Actually, how about I just see how I feel?" Hale accepts this open arrangement and says that way feels right for him too. After I finish work I chat for a while with Suzanna. We talk about all sorts of stuff. I find myself making quite judgemental comments about Bev's touchy, feely behaviour towards Hale and I realise how annoying I find her. Suzanna comments that she's noticed Bev watching Hale and me a lot. I wonder how this must look to the group and again, what on earth people must make of my relationship with Hale. (Then I remind myself to not be so concerned with what other people think!). Suzanna is open in her observations and later I see how rigid and unkind I am to think this way of Bev. She is clearly insecure (and so am I!).

I decide to go up for a short while to see Hale (after my chat with Suzanna) but am not at all sure if he'll be in. But he is, and welcomes me in with one of his winning smiles, before showing me a new book, called *The Power of Now* by a German author called Eckhart Tolle. "Have you heard of it?" he asks. No. So now Hale urges me to read this book as he feels it will help me understand more easily, the work of Krishnamurti. Once again Hale speaks of his gratitude for the amazing mirror I am to him. He thanks me for the heightened self-awareness this has given him and enquires what he can do for me in return.

CHAPTER 104

Hale crosses the room to hand me the Tolle book and reads out loud an extract which (he tells me) sums up the entire book.

I do so love dialoguing with Hale around my spiritual growth. He has such a spontaneous and intelligent mind (when in this space) and it's very stimulating to be around. I tell Hale how gifted he is at being able to pick out the 'juicy' bits in books. He looks at me, pauses for a second and agrees. We then spend another delicious hour together, encased in such sweet mellow heat, from the driest New Zealand summer on record for fifty years…

Balancing his book on my lap Hale speaks in his velvet, rich tones with their American twang. Over and over he reminds us to be present. Be in the Now (and not in thought)! As he says this he looks so serious and intense. His beautiful grey eyes flash with passion. I can't resist verbalising my experience of his eyes to him. He pauses briefly, looks puzzled, then turns his focus onto my own eyes, "Oh, my God! I've never even seen them before, like this way," he exclaims. I suddenly feel shy and look away. It feels too intimate, almost as if I'm naked. Once again he repeats tenderly, "What can *I* do for you?"

I return the question back and make a comment that I'm not used to men wanting to know about my needs, that it's usually me meeting theirs! Hale laughs and says, "Well, you're doing pretty well here already! Just keep giving me more of this and being in the Now."

He asks a third time, "What can I do for you?" Without thinking, the words, "I'd just like for you to love me unconditionally," pop out.

"Wow!" He says, and repeats my request back to me adding, "Well, I guess that's pretty much the only kind of Real Love there is. The rest is just fake kinds, full of needs and expectations."

We both laugh and agree it's a pretty tall order! Now it's time for me to go. As I open the door to leave, I suddenly realise its Valentine's Day and turn back to share this with Hale. I comment that quite possibly the majority of people who are expressing their love today, don't know what Real Love is or how to give from a purely unconditional place (us included!).

CHAPTER 105

Hale decides to walk with me part way, down Goddess Trail. Everything around us seems pulsing and alive, as we slip in and out of, *no thought, no thought*. Then, talking takes over (almost like a bad habit) and we step out of the beautiful moment and into 'psychological time', as we become aware that our time together is almost over. I try to get 'more' by trying to make an arrangement to meet again, but Hale says that he'll need to use most of his time now, to prepare for his departure from NZ, in a few weeks' time. He informs me, that he'll take a two week return passage back to Hawaii, by boat. Hale goes on to say that it's already booked. I listen quietly.

As we walk, Hale keeps glancing over at me then suddenly asks if I'd like to accompany him on the trip, "So we can continue our studies together." I stop walking (quite taken back) then he adds quickly, "Or do you know anyone else who may be interested, as I needed to purchase two tickets to reserve the whole cabin; so there's one spare ticket available." I make some sort of stupid comment (can't even remember what it was now) as I'm quite taken off my guard with yet another, most unusual invitation! Hale turns to go and asks me to think about it. For a few sweet seconds more we enjoy being back 'in the moment' amongst our beautiful and magical surroundings of those rich green vines entwined with ancient creepers.

The next day Early this morning, while still in bed, I receive a text from a good friend who's taking care of my car, which is being housed at another friend's house. John kindly offered to make sure my car will be ready (on my return) to drive straight away. The text simply says: *Check your emails*. I'm puzzled. I go to breakfast and Bev is there, telling people about how she's seen Hale already that morning and how they have now arranged to meet each morning to share a friendly hug outside her campervan, before breakfast! I am acutely aware of my mind clicking into alert mode (not outwardly showing anything) but inwardly many thoughts and fears begin to run. *What is this man's game? Is he meeting her secretly? Would he have told me about this arrangement? What is her game? Could I get hurt here? Warning! Warning! Warning!*

I pause, take a mental step back and just observe all these thoughts parading by. Thoughts based on jealousy, fear, attachment, power and control. So I just watch, as they surface and try to 'feed'. I find myself looking at them in an almost curious and impartial way, and as I do, I feel their power reducing. Most amazing! I start to acknowledge these thoughts as part of my healing journey and self-awareness work and see how this is all part of learning to understand me! How quickly the ego wants to possess. I remind myself that Hale and I don't own each other. We are spiritual buddies.

CHAPTER 106

She is watching us, Hale agrees. Later he wants me to know that he didn't know how to handle her "Harmless suggestion for morning hugs." I tell him that he isn't in a relationship with me, so there is nothing to worry about. I speak of the importance in keeping our energies free from any attachment issues that may be trying to form. Hale agrees before stating that he's exclusive, when in sexually intimate relationships, but not before. I reply that this is how it is for me also. We both remind ourselves again, that we're not in 'that kind' of a relationship. Internally, I remind *myself* of this too, as I observe feelings of jealousy rising and the feeling of not being 'special' or 'loveable enough' to Hale, to be exclusive. I have seen these themes rise again and again in relationships with men, in the past. Now I want to really look at them and try to somehow heal them by bringing them out, into the light.

After breakfast I overhear Suzanna say that she's driving into Thames with Hale later on and then I hear her ask Bev if she wants to go too. I watch, as feelings of jealousy and insecurity start to rise. I hear Bev turn down the invitation – but not before she makes it publically known that she already knew Hale was going. Later on Suzanna asks if I'd like to go. I hear a little voice inside say *you were second choice...* I notice it and then drop it fast. I thank Suzanna for the kind invitation but decline.

Now, Suzanna tells me that Hale is going too. (Of course I know this but don't say so). Hale likes Suzanna a lot. She and he have lots of laughs and fun together. And I like Suzanna too.

Still, I continue to decline the offer and say it'll nice for them to have some fun time together, just the two of them, before Suzanna leaves on Sunday. Now she's beaming and then agrees. We embrace.

Feeling a little guilty now, I try to offer a "Sorry," to Suzanna for my harsh words to her the other day, about Bev, but she will hear none of it and exclaims, "Don't be hard on yourself Lynette, you are so wonderful a person!"

We embrace again and hug hard. Softly, she whispers, she thinks Hale really likes me, and I suddenly feel the need to assure her right there that ours is not a sexual relationship. Again, I look at this and ponder over why on earth I had to do that, for goodness sake!

I remember the need to check my emails. The one from John is there waiting. Very quickly, I realise that its contents bring a major healing opportunity for me. Unexpected freak flooding back home has caused wide spread flooding in unexpected areas. The home of Pauline (where my car is housed) has been waterlogged. She's now living in a caravan and her beloved cat has had to be put down, because of the stress and trauma of being evacuated by fireman in a dingy. Oh my goodness! Poor Pauline! Poor cat! Then another thought comes in. My car! My beloved cabriolet sports car. I'm in shock, as I read on. My car has been so seriously damaged (completely under water) it has been assessed as irrepairable. Water damage had saturated all its electrics. I log off the computer in a daze.

Vera and Donna are so kind and caring. They offer me the use of the office phone to make any necessary calls back to the UK, but I just can't think straight. I decide to go for a walk to try and get clear about what to do. I go into the woods and walk and walk. *This is not a big problem*, I tell myself. *My family are all well. This is a material issue that I'm being challenged with.* I am aware of a need to 'let go' of the urgent feeling that I have to 'do' something, rather than just 'be' – and also to let others (back home) 'do' for me. So I decide to simply thank the Universe for all its abundance and blessings and just look at the trees for a while. I return to the Centre and try to phone Pauline to reassure her that I'm not too worried about my car (I know she'll be feeling sad) as I left it in her care. I also want to offer comfort about the loss of her cat, but for some reason I'm not able to get the phone line to connect...

I think about the accelerated learning opportunity I have here, to learn to grow through attachment issues and the loss of material possessions, along with an opportunity to let go of the need to 'do'. To live in the Now and trust Universal guidance as I step into a field of uncertainty. How to have a feeling of security, alongside uncertainty? Goodness me, what a biggie! I do seem to be getting big challenges as well as big adventures on this trip!

CHAPTER 107

Suzanna and Hale go into Thames for the day and I go off to work. A lot of people leave Mana in a couple of days and this will bring big changes to the dynamics of our community. It is Suzanna and Tanya's last full day, today. Later, we will have girly time together and go for a swim. After work finishes, I arrange to study, with Hale. I'm getting on very well with *The Power of Now* and it really is opening doors to greater understanding for me. I'm learning about the importance of staying in the moment rather than going back into memory or forward into 'psychological time'.

As I leave the cabin to walk up to Hale's place, I sense Tanya wants to come too and even though a part of me is reluctant to 'share' Hale, I turn back to invite her along. She seems pleased to be asked and agrees to come. Hale is waiting impatiently at his door and looks a little confused that Tanya is with me. He wants to share new passages in *The Power of Now* but as Tanya is here, I suggest a walk. Hale looks a little annoyed and I quickly 'see' we have mirror issues of not wanting to share! He mentions again the book extracts he wants to show me. I suggest he brings the book along, so he does and we walk all together, up to the sanctuary. But it soon falls into a pattern of Hale chatting exclusively to me, even though I keep trying to draw Tanya in. We sit outside the sanctuary and Hale gets out his book; he's impatient for the lesson to start.

I realise again that it feels a bit exclusive, but when Tanya decides to go inside the sanctuary I'm ashamed to say I feel pleased. I share with Hale my sadness and frustration of all the un-giving traits I keep uncovering in myself and my desire to be rid of them once and for all. His advice to me is to just stay out of the mind, "Stop thinking!"

All of a sudden I realise I'm addicted to thinking, as I just can't seem to stop all the negative thoughts coming in! It's a horrible realisation when the implications of this fully dawns on me. Its reality feels menacingly scary, like a dark power that threatens to sabotage my growth. Hale becomes animated at my disclosure and his passionate message of support increases.

Stay with the teachings of Krishnamurti and Tolle just allow the mind chatter to fall away. He tells me that this stage is the "Last stand of the ego." I'm not so sure... Mine seems such a powerful ego. Feelings of desperation and a cold fear grip me tightly – despite the warm sun on my skin and I sob, "What if I can't do it Hale. What if I can't make it any further than this – I don't know if I can do it..."

Such a gut retching feeling, a scary void opens up inside, and a feeling of entrapment consumes me. Hale doesn't seem to know what to do with

154

my strong emotions or how to console me. He walks away and gazes out onto the sea far below. I can't look at him, as tears pour down my face and I sense the frustration and feeling of helplessness that emanates from him. Out of the corner of my eye I see him pluck at grass and throw it down. I look at the soft mountain vista and the sea line below, as fear continues to engulf me in a cape of darkness. Then, all of a sudden I come back with a jolt, into the present, gather my senses and start to speak calmly again. Hale edges nearer and asks if there's anything he can do for me. "Give me a hug?" I smile.

We hold each other tightly and a tiny sob escapes from somewhere deep inside me and then no more. I feel tired but comforted by his embrace. We share gratitude for each other in words and then Hale is focused again, looking for text to help me understand this. Hoping I'll gain a theoretical 'knowing' – from actual experience, offering his helpful teachings and guidelines; encouraging me to not 'give up'. I tell Hale (again) what an inspirational teacher he is and how he could share this gift with so many. He agrees.

Hale is holding my arm firmly and transferring this 'holding' up and down the arm as he talks. Moving up and down, feeling form and muscle. How deeply satisfying and comforting it is to have this non-sexual union with a man. We walk back to his cabin giving each other the occasional touch or reassuring word.

CHAPTER 108

Once inside the cabin we share refreshments and sit close. Hale begins squeezing my arm again as he talks. He asks if it's okay that he does this. I say I like it and that he seems to do it almost unconsciously as he talks. Hale confesses that it's not completely unconscious as he has awareness of the pleasure it gives him and wonders if I like it too? Once again Hale speaks of the amazing mirror that I am to him. Says I'm special. I disagree and ask him not to feed my ego! He agrees that we are all special and yes, perhaps not helpful to make another feel they're special. (I've mentioned to Hale that my ego wants to be special to him over his relationship with Bev). He tries to reassure me again, but I tell him that his relationship with her is not my business. He agrees. Hale walks with me to the start of the Goddess Path for my return journey to the Centre.

We hug farewell and I decide not to ask for a commitment over when we'll meet again and to leave it to Hale to decide, this time. As I walk away he calls, "When will I see you again? When is our next therapy appointment, so to speak, in this amazing laboratory experiment here?" I laugh. So pleased he's asked. "I can come tomorrow, after the girls leave."

There's a goodbye party for Suzanna and Tanya at Donna's home tonight. It's great fun! Much later, we go by minibus, at Tanya's request to the sanctuary. It's late and dark and quite eerie. In silence we arrange a circle of cushions and drape woollen blankets around us for warmth, in the chill evening air. We take turns to choose songs and chants until everyone is weary and can delay the farewell party no longer. Full of nostalgia to be saying goodbye to my two special friends, we three walk arm in arm down the hill to our little cabin for one last night, together. Back in the cabin Tanya and I take up our usual bedtime reading poses, while Suzanna pulls down her eye mask and is soon snoring gently. Tomorrow these sweet German girls leave my life. We have shared so much love, laughter and wise words together. I'll miss them but know that this feeling will not last long. I seem to 'let go' sooner and much easier these days…

The next day I phone my sister and we chat. I tell her about my concerns over no contact from Gemma. She promises to try and make contact to talk with her. I observe myself slipping back into old patterns of 'over protective mothering' and try to pull back from it. This really isn't my sister's responsibility and maybe I was a bit insistent about re-enforcing to her that I want her to do this, for me. Janet happily agrees but I hear the apprehension in her voice.

Sitting in the garden, I write *PRINCIPLES NOT PERSONALITY* in my journal. This is a Hale 'nugget of wisdom'. Be true to your authentic self rather than get bogged down with non-essentials or dramas from other people's lives. I need to keep reminding myself of my own personal responsibilities and principles – regardless of their compatibility with others…

Before breakfast the Mana workers meet for one last circle with Suzanna and Tanya. We hold hands and sit cross-legged with eyes tightly closed listening to the gentle peal of bells, ringing out their morning song. We choose our angel cards and say goodbye to the girls. As soon as they drive away I head up to Hale's cabin, impatient to be in his presence again. He's cooking lunch. We exchange a greeting and then he shares a concern. Is he taking me at too fast a pace with his Krishnamurti teachings? Hale informs me that I'm his first 'serious' student and it's important for him to have success, to increase his own confidence as a teacher!

We talk about this and other things and then he unexpectedly adds, "By the way, I'm not getting the feeling that you are my soul mate." It's completely out of the blue (but I'm getting used to that now)! I reply that strangely enough (even though what we share is lovely) I kind of get the same feeling about him too. I explain to him that we both come from very different 'worlds' and will return to them soon, but right now we seem to have something to give each other. He agrees and then goes on to talk openly about how strongly he feels that part of his own healing journey involves him being able to get closer to a woman. That despite his 'fears', the longing to experience love is sometimes so strong, he can't think about anything else.

I listen quietly as Hale tells me about the many therapies, treatments and counselling methods that he's tried in his lifetime, to conquer his fear of women. How he's spent thousands and thousands of dollars trying to heal it. I think how brave, to keep pushing through, with so many addictions, limitations and fears! My heart goes out to this wounded guy as he tells me he's not spent so much time in a woman's presence for years.

CHAPTER 109

I think it's time to talk about boundaries in our relationship and we both agree that it doesn't feel that taking our relationship to a sexual level (despite a mutual attraction to each other) would be helpful for either of us. And anyway, we have other things to concentrate on like spiritual growth. Our study time is so precious! Yet, despite our awareness of this, we idle the rest of the morning away talking about relationship stuff. I tell Hale that I think my ego is very clever at distracting me (and others) by using lots of words. He says that he's clever too and that he'll pull me back, if he discovers this happening. I reply, "We have met our match, huh?" Hale strongly agrees he feels this to be very true. I want to kiss him when he looks so intently at me with those piercing eyes and soft curly lashes, but I don't. We head down to the centre for lunch and he follows me down the Goddess Trail; giving back-rubs as I walk!

The next day I try to phone Gemma's on her landline, but it's the answer phone running. I leave a message. There's been still no reply from my last email... My mind is groping around inside my brain, trying to figure it out. As soon as possible I head up the path to Hale's cabin. I suggest we agree a stricter study schedule, as the ego seems to be sabotaging our sessions lately with all this chat about relationships. Hale likes this idea, so we decide on one hour study, followed by a thirty minute break, then an hour of mindfulness practice and then a final half hour of chat.

This works well and we both manage to keep bringing each other back, from the wanderings of our minds, back to the study to support each other's learning. It is so special and pure. Not about sex at all (apart from Hale saying he's having to keep pulling back an occasional thought that tries to wander off in that direction!). As we talk, read and discuss Hale likes to be in constant contact with the skin on my arm. It's a comforting touch, and it gives me a connected and healthy feeling, as it synchronises with his words.

After our study hour Hale asks if we can lie down on the bed to practice 'being in the moment' by looking at, and really 'seeing' each other. I'm unsure about this initially. It seems pretty intimate and there's a big glass window in front of his bed with a gravel road to other cabins running right by. Reservations apart, I lay next to him and we begin our task of observing each other's face, without allowing thoughts to attach to image. Drop the mind. Drop the mind.

Soon the room is still and so is my mind. I hear birds and outside noises, within my outer awareness. I feel Hale's skin gently touching mine and I can hear his soft breathing. Time stands still. I close my eyes and a deep peace descends. I don't think. I just 'Be'. I feel nourished by the union of our shared energy. I feel safe, secure, and at peace with myself and the world. Unexpectedly, Hale's lips make contact with my own. I just allow them to rest there, without any movement. It feels such a different kind of male female contact than I have ever known before. In the timeless space of Now all is perfect and simple. My mind is calm and my body at rest. There is only, 'what is'.

Hale's lips move against mine to form a kiss. Instead of wondering *where is this going?* I keep my mind empty. It's blissful. An eternity passes and I sit up and bring myself back into the world. We look at each other, kind of shocked and kiss again, but this time in a more 'worldly' way. Thoughts tumble back into my mind. Both of us comment on this delicious experience of spending time in the Now. Allowing life the freedom to unfold – without needing to control or plan it.

CHAPTER 110

There is a new closeness between us now, like we've shared something extremely intimately, (which we have). Hale offers a back massage and I accept, leaning back inside his open legs. From time to time, he breaks from his rhythmic movements, nuzzles forward and kisses my neck softly. It is sweetly pure and uncomplicated.

Hale muses, "How long it is since I last kissed a woman?" I reply, "Does it matter?" He quickly replies, "No, No", as he comes back into the Now.

I walk down the hill, in a heady, euphoric state. Before I leave, I joke, "Have we found a new kind of drug Hale?" He laughs and agrees it's true.

For hours I remain in a place of peaceful yet buzzy, energy state. I feel immense gratitude for the whole experience. Later there are some odd conversations going around the dining room that I sense are hinting at an inappropriate level of relationship between Hale and me. They point to the fact that he is a guest and I am staff. I begin to slip into a state of anxiety, as my mind starts to project all sorts of assumptions and criticisms onto it! Ah! How quickly the ego gets in and tries to destroy any happiness, by trying to head me off in a direction that may not even be real!

Olivia a new, American wwoofer helps me to access a different reality, points out my projections, and encouraging me to come back into the moment! Although only in her twenties Olivia is another young spirit that's clearly on a fast spiritual track. She shares my bedroom now in the little wwoofer lodge. Each morning and evening, I watch her pull up the quilt around her tiny, dark haired frame, and start and end each day with meditation. We become close friends in no time. Olivia tells me she loves my youthful ways and English accent, before playfully awarding me the nickname of *Foxy Mary Poppins*.

The next day Ed offers me a ride into Coromandel, as he has errands there. I have errands too. I post Gemma's birthday present and pick up three meters of cotton fabric for Olivia, in a haberdashery store. Her request as I left was to get her a "Thing of beauty." You see, Olivia makes most of her own clothes. She sits cross legged, sewing tiny stitches carefully, by hand! So I pick out a vibrant Maori print and hope she'll like the rich colours and dramatic patterns in the material. It's lovely to be out but also nice to be back, in the peaceful arms of Mana. It's strange how easily I accept the noise of town, but gained little pleasure in shopping or being amongst so much concrete!

After working a shift in the kitchen, I make my way to Hale's place with books tucked neatly inside my backpack and a bottle of water. The heat of the day is really intense, and soon I'm panting with perspiration. He's pleased that I've come, and says he wasn't sure I would. We talk again of our experience yesterday. Hale thinks maybe we should take things slower? Nice as it was, I have to agree with him. We begin to study and have an amazing study hour, but as we are concluding our last paragraph before break time a car pulls up and parks right outside Hales cabin. A new resident and a woman get out. Hale goes out to say hi and I pop my head out too, just to be friendly. As the couple hang about talking outside, it feels a bit like Hale and I are in a sort of goldfish bowl behind his huge picture window. In the end, I suggest we just continue with our reading. So sitting side by side, I read out aloud, whilst outside the couple go back and forth, unpacking their car. Hale seems agitated. "Why does he have to park his car there?" He snaps. I laugh and say, "There's Hale's ego speaking out again!" He laughs as he quickly recognises his impatience, too.

CHAPTER 111

Work again, today. I'm in the kitchen helping prepare and serve up a delicious dinner. Mana food is always varied and imaginative – a feast of organic colour; often adorned with edible flowers. Working fast and hard, I finish a little early so that Olivia and I can go down the hill to Dharma Gaya (a Buddhist Centre) and attend their weekly walking meditation. We remove our footwear after being graciously greeted by a petite and brown eyed nun with a shaven head. Her facial expressions are soft and gentle with huge doe eyes smiling back at us. As part of a silent crocodile we barefooted souls take fairy steps around the peaceful garden and lily pond. Mindfully, I follow in a pathway trodden by footsteps of the person in front.

Eventually the silent nun leads us, like Piped Piper, into a candlelit, darkened and musty meditation room, adorned with tatty silk drapes. We sit cross legged on plumped up floor cushions and pass round tiny silver cups of steaming herbal tea. Each one of us peer into each cup as we silently offer 'loving kindnesses' to each other and to the world – then pass it on. I have a strong 'knowing' feeling that old patterns are moving away. I notice a pain in my right upper breast bone and wonder what's shifting. Olivia is seated cross-legged next to me. The long chain of cups continues their journey around our circle. It's a strangely intimate and tender ritual. After every cup has been gifted with loving kindness, we drink from them in silence, and then silently leave the room. Outside, silence still hangs in the air like a sacred gossamer thread. Olivia and I walk hand in hand (not speaking) back up the hill to Mana under a magical, moonlit sky bursting with tiny silver stars. We continue to hold our silence for the rest of the evening and then retire to bed. It's simple beauty has transcended all use of words.

The next day I still have the pain in my breast bone when I awaken early, after a very strange dream. I dream that I'm in a backpacker's hostel in Australia. I come across a group of young English travellers huddled together. Some of the group are sweating profusely and I get a sense that they're 'doing' drugs. I peer closely at their distorted faces and suddenly realise that one of them is my daughter, Gemma. I ask her what she's doing here and why isn't she at university completing her studies? The dream is confusing and scary. I awake with a jolt and it feels so real.

This turns my mind back to thinking about Gemma and that deep down, I really don't feel happy at having received no contact from her for so long. I decide to ring again and this time I call her mobile (even though it's terribly expensive) as I need to make contact. To my surprise she picks up straight away. A little unsure as to how to explain my impromptu call, I tell Gemma that I love her and (in a jokey way) share the details of my dream. After a second or two of silence Gemma blurts out that I've actually dreamt more or less what she's living through right now, but hadn't wanted to burden me with it all.

Her many held back words tumble out fast now, and between sobs Gemma explains that she's thinking of suspending her studies, due to boyfriend related issues and not being able to concentrate on her work. I'm shocked and arrange to call her right back on a landline, so we can share a longer call, without my credit running out. For a long while we talk about Gemma's options and I'm trying my utmost to remain neutral and not influence her decision making process. My daughter reveals that another part of my dream is also partly accurate. Feeling so low and unhappy Gemma confesses she'd considered taking recreational drugs (with friends) for relief – but at the last minute had decided against it. A cold shiver runs down my spine. I feel so far away, and the mother in me that wants to 'rescue' my little girl (despite her being 22) begins to rise up, again.

It's a horrible, helpless kind of feeling and (briefly) it consumes me. I feel the need to ask if I myself have contributed in any way to stress or the burden of expectations around feeling she must take or complete her degree, to please me. To my relief Gemma says that she'd not ever thought that I had. After a long time, trying to stay in my professional coaching head and not give advice, she finally arrives at her own decision. I end the conversation exhausted but happy that my precious daughter had shared her difficult decision with me. Gemma says she's feeling a lot better now, and has a real sense of relief.

Later I reflect on what an amazing dream that was and how it gave me the insight and wisdom that something was wrong, to prompt that call. I'm so relieved I'd acted on the message my intuition gave me. How awesome is the Universe!

CHAPTER 112

Well, what a crazy day! I'm late going up to Hale's at our pre-arranged time but he is still waiting patiently and in a very happy mood. He pulls out a notepad from his breast pocket and says he has a list of things he wants to talk about. I smile to myself in amusement. I tell him about Gemma and he listens amazed that I encouraged her to decide for herself and not listen to what others might want of her. Hale comments on how different his own life might have been if his mother could have said that to him...

The emotional events of this morning have left me fragmented and weary. Hale expresses concern about my mental state; as I'm finding it hard to study. To try and cheer me up, he reports solemnly that as my teacher he needs to inform me I've passed the first semester of my Krishnamurti study course, "With flying colours!" But that he won't be grading me, as he doesn't want to encourage my ego!

Hale's intellect, wit and clever humour, make him attractive. Looking into his dramatic eyes with their ever changing shades, I muse over how he must have been quite a 'looker' in his youth. On his list of subjects to talk about is his invitation. "Have I decided what to do yet?" To gain more background around his unusual invitation I talk further about practicals and logistics such as flights back to the UK and possible options I might have. I still haven't decided, but my mind remains open as I keep checking in with my body to 'feel' for information and 'listen' for inner wisdom, to help me decide.

I've already got a pre-booked return flight home via a two day stopover in Singapore and don't know if it can be changed. Hale offers to purchase me a flight from Honolulu, (where the boat docks) back to Singapore, so I can pick up my flight path.

But I'm not feeling like making any decisions today and ask if we can discuss the subject later...

After lunch I go down to the meditation platform alone and try to ground myself. In the stillness, tears come and I experience a feeling of 'letting go'. The pain in my chest is easing now. I wonder if it was linked to Gemma's. What an extraordinary day!

CHAPTER 113

The course that's running at the Centre finishes today, so it's a busy time. Olivia is leaving tomorrow, too. We have shared a special world together and I'll miss her. She has confided in me of the difficulties in her own younger years when her mother got stressed. I tell her that I have been that kind of mother too! Olivia can't believe it. Coming onto her shift half an hour early to relieve me from my kitchen duties, Olivia tells me it's her goodbye gift to me. Sweet thing!

I leave and go to Hale's place. I find him with all his furniture outside. He tells me he's spring-cleaning the cabin. I read a chapter of Tolle while he finishes off. Hale says that he's been working all day. Work is something that's been alien to Hale, as he's always paid people to do work for him, so he hasn't followed the conventional work route, like me. Hale astounds me further when he tells me he walked up to the sanctuary that morning and has been writing songs again, as the words just keep flowing out. Hale feels certain that things are changing for him. He's buoyant and positive around an optimistic future with relationships. Despite the fact that Hale keeps saying how different it's been with me than other women, I still remain grounded in the reality that we come from different lands and will return to them very soon now.

After an excellent study session we lay on the bed. I'm able to stay focused and in the Now more than yesterday. Hale's energy is full of excitement as he runs a hand over my skin. We share a gentle yet passionate energy exchange that's sexually charged but without the intention for it to go anywhere. I touch Hale's beautiful shoulder length curls, feeling safe and understanding the importance of me communicating boundaries that feel safe for me. To move at a pace and speed that's right for me. To listen with deep awareness to what my feelings are trying to say, rather than ignore uncomfortable ones. I listen intently to my body for signs of what it wants. I get up off the bed, when the desires of the flesh begin to heighten – as something deep inside me says it's not ready.

We stand at the bedside and thank each other for special moments shared. Then I kiss him. Hale kisses me back urgently, then playfully makes a gesture of sweeping me back down onto the bed. We both laugh. It's a beautiful light and carefree laugh. Fun time over, Hale hands me another book and urges me to read it thoroughly. Says time is running out for our studies now, as he has only one more week at Mana. There's no mention of his invitation or the decision I have still to make...

I walk down the hill and mixed feelings tumble through my mind. Hale and I are clearly growing closer each day. The way things are going there's real chance that we could become sexually intimate on the trip. I wonder about the Hep C condition he carries but I also think about how it would be if we get real close and then have to say goodbye. There goes the mind again, running ahead in fear and psychological time! So I let it go and simply enjoy the lush green trees and giant green ferns that adorn the Goddess Path. I really don't need to think at all about any of these things, I just need to stay in the moment and let it reveal what action to take, when the time is right.

Olivia and I are playful at dinner. There's lots of tenderness between us, like mother and daughter. She says she'll miss me. We chat about her boyfriend that's waiting for her back in America. I confide in her about the decision I have to make about going with Hale or not. Olivia looks a little concerned at first, especially as she knows of his cannabis use and Hep C. Then she says that I just need to follow my own path. We go up to the sanctuary and it's a windy night. Olivia and I stand hand in hand looking out onto the far away estuary and rolling hills before going into the sanctuary to sing together. Al and Nora leave tomorrow also. Our little community of wwoofers is slowly dissolving.

CHAPTER 114

21st February I wake early. Olivia is leaving. She comes over to my bed to kiss me goodbye and asks me not to get up. But I do, as I've secretly arranged to borrow Ed's car to drive her down to the Mana gates, where she'll catch the bus. After parking the car we sit on top of her huge holdall, holding hands. Olivia smiles as she tells me again that I just need to follow my path. I agree, but I'm still unsure what that is right now! Olivia suggests I 'ask' for guidance and wisdom to know which way. I think this is a good idea. Then the bus pulls in. We hug each other tightly and sweet Olivia is gone. It's still early morning when I arrive back at Mana. I join the morning circle before breakfast and a new day begins.

As the meditation starts I close my eyes, and hear the sanctuary bells peal out. I feel tears rolling down my cheeks, but I realise they're tears of gratitude for the whole experience of everything that's happening to me right now and the people who are in my life. It is a special moment and I share it with the little group of workers.

Today I work until 4p.m. My period arrives, bringing with it a lot of pain and I already have 'the shits' from something I've eaten so it's a bit of a grotty and tiring day. After work, because it's raining and because I feel crap, I go to the library to read. Bev comes in and joins me. I start to write up my journal, whilst hugging a hot water bottle to my tummy for comfort. Hale comes in but neither Bev nor I look or get up. It's clear that we all feel a bit awkward. No one speaks. Then I break the ice, make a joke, and then go over to give Hale a hug. Bev jumps quickly up and hugs him too, holding on for a long time. I observe an ever so slight feeling of annoyance and then it's gone. Good. She does the hugging thingy a few more times. Once again, I sense a faint annoyance come and then go. There is so much learning here!

Everyone is preparing their own meals now that the courses at the Centre have finished and there's no set meals being prepared, for us to share. Terry the gardener comes into the kitchen and is noticeably hostile to Hale. This man appears such a lonely 'little boy' himself. It seems to me that Hale is a 'shadow' that reminds Terry of a part of himself that he doesn't like to look at...

The evening limps along. The rain continues to fall and Hale and I return to the library and we are soon talking about the boat trip, Hep C and all the other stuff that's coming up for us both around all this. That morning I had put it 'out' to the Universe that I'd really like some clarity on whether to go with Hale or not. And as the day goes on, it feels like a 'knowing' is settling on me, like the final piece of a jigsaw falling into place. I become aware that information is coming from a place of 'feelings,' not thinking. I ask my body the question *what happens if I go with Hale?* Then I stop and 'listen' with all my senses for the slightest feelings of discomfort (or comfort) so subtly hidden, inside. Then I ask my body *what happens if I don't go with Hale?* Again, I search inside for the answer via feelings that I feel. There's definitely a distinct feeling. I become aware that it's giving me a comfortable feeling around making the decision to go.

Later, I search the Internet for information on Hep C as I realise I have no information about it and that people's initial reaction almost always come from a fear base and not always helpful. I also search the Internet for flight options, if I end up in Honolulu without a ticket home. I decide to email my flight company back in UK who I booked my original tickets with for advice. I conclude from the information I find (on various sites) about Hep C that it's not highly contagious and simply needs protective levels of caution when (if) entering into a sexual relationship.

My decision is made. Tomorrow I will share it with Hale. Despite the continuing pain in my gut I sleep well. It rains continuously throughout the night, harder and then harder. Now my decision to leave NZ is made it appears that the long golden summer is over.

CHAPTER 115

I wake up late. The Centre moves at a much slow pace these days. No guests in the lodges (except Hale). No meals to be made, and the remaining wwoofers on minimum work schedules. It's still raining. After breakfast, Hale and I enjoy study time in the comfort of the library and share further discussions about his trip. It feels like I'm going now, even though I haven't actually said so in words. Partly, I guess because it feels a little crazy and a lot exciting, all rolled into one!

The little group of wwoofers have lunch together but there doesn't seem to be anyone left that I really resonate with. Hale wants me to walk up to his place after lunch. He whispers that he's hungry for hugs! I smile inside as I have that feeling too, but at the same time I feel bad about not inviting others who are spending free-time alone this afternoon. I really do have to work more on this feeling bad if I put my needs before others. I decide to go, and as we leave one of the 'gang' enquires where we're going and I feel obliged to explain. Why (??)

Hale and I walk through the rain, under his huge umbrella chatting away happily. I have to walk slowly, as my energy levels are right down, due to the stomach cramps. We spend a few relaxing hours laying on the bed listening to the rain and Krishna Das. It's nice. I tell him that I kinda feel like I've decided to come with him on the cruise – but I'm still getting used to this information. Hale jumps up excitedly, but at the same time urges me to keep processing, until I know for sure. At 4.45p.m. I return to the Centre, but no one's there. I head off to bed with a hot water bottle and camomile tea.

The next day I feel a little better. A member of staff has given me some sort of natural remedy, (which tasted disgusting) but helped. I eat bland food for the rest of the day. Bev is hugging Hale at breakfast, when he asks me if I'd like to study in the library later. I would. We've just begun our latest chapter when Katrina comes in to use the computer. It's obvious that Hale's feeling annoyed, as he planned to intersperse study time with sharing his latest thoughts. It's hard to just get up and leave the room though, so we carry on.

This shared community life has its challenges around privacy, that's sure! I confirm to Hale that I've finally decided – it's definite. Hale's face is animated as he speaks of the practical plans we must now make. Throughout the day both of us find our minds popping worry thoughts in to try and make us change our minds. Hale is concerned about the fact that if we grow close on the two weeks of the trip, that he has a Sufi residential camp to go straight on to, (with lots of support) but he's worried about me, flying home, all alone. What support do I have? His concern is touching.

Its Bev's last evening and she wants to walk up to the sanctuary to sing, like we've done for others, on their last night. Hale and I are reading in the library when she comes in to invite us. He turns down the offer straight away and without a second glance returns to his reading. Bev looks disappointed and turns to me. I smile kindly at her little-girl-lost face, as I explain that I don't really feel strong enough yet, to make the long walk up to the sanctuary. But as the small party sets out, I start to feel bad and my mind plays the: *what will people think* game again. A new wwoofer comes into the library, making it hard to talk privately, again!

CHAPTER 116

We wander into the Octagon but I feel uneasy as Hale pulls me towards him, calling me, "Daarrlin'," in his thick American drawl. It's sweet, but I struggle to relax in such a public place. I'm intensely aware now how very much I'm caught up in the mind-prison of *what people think*. I realise that I need to tell Vera, the coordinator that I'm leaving soon. I need to do this tomorrow but I find the thought of it hard to do and to explain that I'm going, with Hale. I get angry at this stupid limitation that I had no realisation was so powerful in my life. Frustration arises. I share another fear thought with Hale, "What if we get closer to a place of love and then struggle to let go of each other at the end of our trip, without great pain?" And then a horrible thought comes *What if you go home, Lynette and never find such a beautiful relationship, ever again?*

Hale looks at me and is shocked at how shut down my energy field has become and yet earlier he'd told me how attractive I looked. Now he says my state of fear is not at all attractive. I feel trapped, in a place of no return, and surrounded by a fear that I won't make it to the other side of this abyss. Hale holds me. We embrace. I feel scared and lonely and long to be with him tonight. I tell him I want him. Hale says we could sleep together (in the meditation room) tonight or at his place. I so want to, but don't feel okay about people seeing, hearing or knowing we have done this. There I go again! Hale is fine and says, "Look, if you're not sure, then it's a no. Unless both of us are sure of something, then it's a no-go-er." This is just what I need to hear. Hale takes it so slow and respectfully with me, asking how I'm feeling often, checking I'm okay. I've never know this level of care from a man, that I have feelings about, too. Hale tells me how much he's grown to care for me, and that he too had wondered how it will be; and yes, his mind has tried pulling him in too. He'd pondered over thoughts of how he doesn't travel much and doesn't want a long distance relationship. I say, "Surely, we could allow ourselves to just 'rise' in love and not fall, to allow this experience to give us real freedom through its gift of unconditional love – then take this back into our lives and future relationships?"

<u>The next day</u> I feel much better. Yesterday I spoke to Melanie to congratulate her on passing her driving test. It sounds like she and Gemma are getting on well, again. However, Mel sounds frustrated that Gemma is giving her studies up and not dealing with life issues very well. I tell her that we all deal with things differently and we all have our own paths to walk. I find myself gabbling on in a mother sort of way – getting a bit too 'advisory' and butting in far too much to what she's saying. I am *so* aware of this straight after the phone call, it's painful. Melanie was excited at the fact it's only weeks away from my homecoming. Both my daughters have been at my sister's for lunch, together, today and I'm pleased that everyone's getting on and supporting each other. There are so many opportunities for healing, and growth coming out of my trip, beyond all comprehension!!

CHAPTER 117

Hale pulls me to one side after breakfast to ask me two questions, "How are you today? Do you have second thoughts about going with me, after last night?"

I tell him I'm back in a balanced place (out of my mind!) and "Yes, I'm still coming." He takes some personal details from me to get my ticket for the boat sorted out. I tell Hale that today I'll start to tell people that I'm leaving. I know this is all part of my healing journey, so I go in the kitchen and tell Katrina, the first person I meet, that Hale and I are leaving together on Sunday. She looks shocked and quizzes me as to why I am doing this and "How do I know it's the right thing?" I try my best to explain my decision making method but she clearly doesn't get it! I guess it does sound kind of crazy. I go into the office and discover that Vera is away for two days. So I tell Donna I'm leaving - which is much easier to do. Initially, she's surprised but then wants to know more. Yet I only give her the date I'm leaving and then leave the office; as I feel too shy to say more! Instantly, I tell myself off and push myself back into the office, where I give her the rest of the story. Donna seems happy for us both and our use of the opportunity that's presenting itself. I'm so pleased with how this is received. Phew!

Then it's work. During lunchtime Hale appears. He's also told a few people and I tell him that Donna and Katrina know. He's happy today and informs me he's not taken a smoke for the last couple of days. Hale wants to sort out my flight home and is prepared to contribute up to $1,500 to get me a replacement ticket home. I say it will surely not be that much! He's going into Coromandel and asks me if I need anything. I say that I could do with some Tampax to give back to Katrina for ones she loaned me when I ran out last week. Embarrassed, he takes back his offer and mutters that maybe I could give her some money instead. I say of course I could but being stuck up here (miles from any shops) I thought it would be more helpful to replace them, but no worries. Men!

Bev is leaving. Hale says goodbye to her quickly, obviously distracted by other things and it's clearly not the grand finale she'd have liked. I do realise however, that Bev's many hugs have been of immense value to him. So necessary in the early stage of his emotional healing and growth, but Hale says he's no longer comfortable with them. He is learning (we both are) in our kindergarten class on relationships...

CHAPTER 118

So now people know and there's definitely a shift in how they see us. Mostly positive! Donna is warmer towards Hale and me and another member of staff shouts after us, as we walk past his house that evening, "Hey! I hear you two are taking a trip!" I shout back in a joking kind of way, "Yes, it seems so. Crazy things happen when you're open!" Saul laughs and shouts: "Email us and let us know how you get on!" Hale and I look at each other and beam. I joke as I call back, "We'll send you a copy of the book we might write." Hale laughs and adds it's imaginary title, "Fourteen Days to Enlightenment!"

We continue up the hillside to watch the sun set across the sea. The air is full of magic and beauty, with a soft view of sea, billowing clouds and far away islands. Walking arm in arm, we return to his cabin and Hale tells me he hopes I'll spend the night. I'm open to explore this, but although we're sharing a closer level of intimacy, it 'feels right' to head back to my cabin. So, down I go, underneath a full moon, down a dark (now spooky) Goddess Trail and back into my own little bed.

Each day Hale starts doing new things and stops doing other behaviours which aren't serving him. He's delighted with the opportunity of this new unfolding place that we meet each other in. Of course, this is exactly what I need to heal too... We share our fears openly, about being over conscious of revealing our bodies to each other and worrying that they won't be good enough. I see so clearly now how much I've internalised this into my very being. I'm aware how damaging it is, so I try to stay in the Now and just 'feel' the sensation, touch and emotions that are occurring without too much thinking. Hale says he is trying to do the same. We both know that if we can stay in that place, everything will be okay.

<u>The next day</u> It felt so right to return back to my bed last night, despite the pull to stay in Hale's arms. At 8 a.m. morning circle, it's just Terry and me and there is much learning and opportunity for growth given, through the message of Terry's card - if only he'll take it! Later, I notice that he's making an effort to be more accepting of Hale...

New people arrive. There's Rudi, a French Polynesian guy. Heaven sent to Mana! He's experienced the teachings of Krishnamurti, in person! Wow! What a peaceful guy Rudi is, full of wisdom and inner knowing. He lives on one of the islands our ship will be stopping at. What a coincidence (or not?). Another guest arrives, a woman from England. She seems very interested in Hale. He tells me he knows, "That look," in women. I'm aware that many women will be interested in Hale, when he heals his wound...

The new lady, Hilary, tries to spend time with Hale, but he keeps moving away. For days now, he just wants to be with me. We sit at the computer together and register my name on his cruise ticket and I'm glad that's sorted. Looking at the company website, I get a glimpse of the kind of boat we'll be travelling on. Hale hasn't really given many details and I haven't asked, but now I see that the site's called Celebrity Cruises and our boat carries a Five Star rating. Wow! There's loads of entertainment on board, yet Hale informs me he used hardly any of the facilities when travelling here. That he ate mostly in his room and spent the majority of time on his own. He smiles as he tells me that he believes this won't be the case with his spiritual buddy on board, and I agree!

We're both sensing it's going to be a lot of fun. How exciting for me to have this opportunity, and what great timing! Thank you, Universe.

How awesome is your synchronicity.

CHAPTER 119

Hale and I hike up to the sanctuary to watch the sun set again. Tonight it feels right to spend the night with him. We listen to Krishna Das and his magical voice surrounds us, in the darkness.

Lying in each other's arms, we gaze dreamily out onto a star filled night sky. Such a clear night with so many stars! I sleep easy in Hale's arms and we're both up at 6 a.m. (as planned) to watch the sun rise from the upper most part of the hill. Sleepily, Hale gathers up rice cakes and bottled water as we stumble out into the dim light of pre-dawn. Passing the huge crystal set in stone at the peak of the hill, we wonder at its power. I want to know its history. Who put it there and why? Hale is alive and animated this morning. In twenty years, he tells me he's never slept through the night with a woman before and has always had to leave the bed, during the night. Hale feels confident that maybe he can make a relationship work now, after so many years without one. He speaks of the nourishment last night gave him and my acceptance of where he's at. That his sleep was so peaceful that he didn't get up to pee (another first in as long as he can remember!). Hale is excited at making connections about how his mental wellbeing affects his body. As we wait for the sunrise he begins to talk of his wish to move house on return to Maui and the desire to change his reclusive life.

When this man's brilliance is shining and his life force is flowing (like this morning) Hale is handsome and sexy, when he moves into who-he-really-is and not those other states of *little boy* or *old man*. I love his beautiful spirit and yet at the same time feel a sort of detachment from him. The sun breaks through, in all its morning glory and the awakening of a new day is a wonder to behold. How special is this moment that we share together with such sweetness, innocence and awe.

Hurrying back down the hill to attend morning circle, I say goodbye to Hale, with a hug. Everyone is seated in their usual circle of cushions. As I sit down I notice my trouser bottoms are damp and muddy with morning dew from our walk. Katrina looks at me with her shrewd eye. She's obviously noted I didn't return to our cabin as she makes a comment about not hearing me come in last night. I pretend not to hear and change the subject in a way that allows me to successfully move the conversation away from it. I notice a slight irritation towards Katrina and then it's gone. I feel fine. At breakfast Hilary is wearing a see-thru white top with no bra. I guess it's for Hale's benefit. I watch as a glimmer of jealousy surfaces in my mind and a feeling of inadequacy. As I watch, it quickly subsides. Terry is making a real effort again, in his conversation with Hale and it's lovely to see.

A new wwoofer arrived yesterday and is allocated to my cabin. She's a German girl called Andrea. Leaving a husband back home (no children) she's decided to take time-out to lone travel. After telephoning hubby, Andrea shares her feelings of missing him. We attend the walking meditation together and enjoy its beautiful stillness.

CHAPTER 120

Early next morning I compose my email to everyone back home, to tell them about my next amazing adventure, with Haleakala the hippie! It is such exciting and mind blowing stuff to think I'm writing this, about me! Rudi is silent at breakfast, and sits away from the group. Hale dashes off after breakfast for a neck treatment with Saul, a body worker. I'm working with Andrea today and we share interesting conversation as we clean the retreat cabins and prepare them for the next guests.

I talk about my decision to go with Hale. She is supportive and intrigued, as are most at the Centre! I sense they're all gossiping about the news of level-headed Lynette going with dope smoking Hale across the Pacific on a luxury liner bound for Hawaii. Well I have to agree, that it is a pretty unusual piece of gossip and a bit of a fairy tale ending!

Rudi gives off vibes that he likes me but knows about my relationship with Hale and maintains some emotional distance. Hale and I watch a Krishnamurti video together, with Rudi, but Hale is too impatient to stay to the end and leaves early. Rudi and I remain until it finishes and discuss the contents. Rudi appears to be very wise in spiritual understanding. He's been meditating for years and his mind seems in a peaceful place. He doesn't use many words, I've noticed. Today, I watch as he chooses the solitude of eating alone, rather than joining the buoyant banter and noisy chatter in the main dining hall. An interesting man…

I spend time with Andrea and Stevie, (another English woman) who shares the same age and birthday as me! We have a naked sauna together and I feel very at ease. I observe this difference in me, as they both have big breasts and I'd usually be feeling self-conscious and comparing my body to theirs by now. Again, I see how social conditioning has affected my ability to love and accept my own body form, just as it is. I'm so glad this is finally moving away. It's been with me all my adult life… When we leave Mana there will be only Katrina and Andrea left in the little wwoofer family here. Such a contrast to when I first arrived. (It feels like a lifetime ago). Andrea reflects on this fact, and then makes the decision to move on herself. She asks to share our taxi to Auckland next Sunday. Then there was one…

CHAPTER 121

It doesn't feels like I need to sleep with Hale again, during our last few days at Mana and he's comfortable with this; now he's 'tried out' a night of sharing the same room, before the boat. We try to confirm my flight home via the Internet but it's not possible. I can't make contact with my flight company and so it seems I must leave Mana without knowing how I'll get home. I need to put all my faith in Universal guidance. Hale has promised to pay for my flights but I will have to set sail into the unknown without the security of a ticket that my mind so badly wants. I hold on to the belief that it has felt 'right' in intuition and body to make the decision to go with Hale so I must leave the rest with the Universe. I let go.

My friend is still in communication with me about my flood damaged car. He's liaising in my absence, with the insurance company. It seems like they are preparing to 'write off' my convertible and he's negotiating the best settlement deal he can for me. My mind could easily hook onto this and set off on a 'fear of lack' roller coaster around money as I'll arrive home without a wage and now, no car. I decide to let go, to detach from it all and once again, leave it in the hands of the Universe. I surprise myself at how easy I'm doing this with such 'biggies' like flights and cars. Maybe it's all part of preparing me for greater challenges...

There's much conversation and joking about our trip amongst Mana staff and I catch a sense of excitement from some. Others get caught up in the glamour and glitz of it all, as Celebrity cruise line has a reputation for opulence and luxury. They joke around how Hale and I might be perceived by the other guests on board and it is kind of a fun subject to speculate on, for sure!!

The weather has turned really awful, adding to the feeling that it's time to go. Hale and I had hoped to watch the sunset on our last evening, but foul weather rules it out. So I spend time on the Internet, before I lose contact with this world for two weeks. I answer emails from home as replies come in from those I've told about my next trip. They seem to share my excitement.

CHAPTER 122

My last day at Mana and I'm working all morning. Hale is animated at breakfast as he converses with Rudi who, on discovering we are leaving after lunch promptly decides he's going to leave too! Now we are four in the cab to Auckland. It's raining again, as I make my way up the familiar and well-loved Goddess Trail, sporting oversized wellingtons and a bright yellow umbrella. I go to say goodbye to Hilary. Yesterday, she gave me a 'Oneness Blessing' and it felt like another important part of my healing journey. Maybe it's no coincidence which people have been here, when I have; as they have all been part of my learning and healing at Mana. I share a goodbye hug and we exchange emails before I clomp, clomp back down to my cabin, through rain saturated forest and swirling mist. I get my bags together. It's almost time to go. How strange it feels. But still, a strong feeling of 'rightness' follows me around as I say my farewells. When our taxi arrives, we four musketeers pile in amidst shouts of "goodbye," and "good luck" but I feel no heart pangs or regret; just a feeling of gratitude and anticipation for the adventure ahead.

As we bump and wind along the coastal road, that takes us further and further away from dear Mana, Hale and I sit side by side in the back of the cab with Andrea on one side and Rudi up front. It's almost like a party atmosphere, as we joke and laugh together. Rudi keeps turning around to include us in his conversations with our intrigued driver, who wants to know the story of these four characters from four different parts of the globe!

Before long we're in Auckland, as the skyline of skyscrapers and freeways tell us that our journey together is over and it's time to say goodbye. The driver stops at the docks first, so Hale and I get out and say goodbye to Rudi and Andrea. We take a picture together to mark our friendships with promises of keeping in touch.

Once out of the taxi, with my faithful (if not somewhat battered) holdall by my side, I turn and look at the huge luxury liner that's in front of me. My home for the next two weeks… It is only then, that I fully comprehend how amazingly wonderful and incredible a thing this is, that the Universe has gifted me. After months of budget backpacking and economic eating, I now get to cruise across the pacific and enjoy a freebie of five star fun and pleasure. Wow!

CHAPTER 123

All around me there's a sense of urgency, hustle and bustle. I notice it so acutely, after the gentle, peaceful pace of Mana. It is *so* not attractive. Loads of people are pushing classy suitcases purposefully through a filtering system that's managed by smart, uniformed officers. They direct us efficiently towards the check-in area for the boat. Hale seems to immediately pick up on this urgent energy and a brusque, direct manner kicks in, as he navigates us confidently through, and onto the boat. Luggage is taken from us, and my battered holdall kinda looks out of place, but yet I don't feel any discomfort around the old *'what will people think'* routine. Who cares! My bag is my bag. It's not a reflection of the sum total of who I am, but if people wish to judge or measure my worth by it, that's up to them.

I reflect on the contents of it and how little there is in there that equips me for life on a luxury cruise; in either clothes or accessories! But this thought carries no anxiety with it at all, only feelings of amusement at how Hale and I will look – me in my casual backpacker attire and him in his hippy hemp linens, at formal dining.

We make our way to the cabin (sorry State Room, is its official name!) and I discover a beautiful room with its own sitting area and enormous picture window looking out onto the ocean. Once we've located our accommodation, we catch the lift up to one of the decks and look out across the docklands and huge skyscrapers of Auckland. It's almost time for our ship to sail. Crowds of family and onlookers gather on the docks to wave off loved ones and there's a real mood of anticipation and adventure in the air. The ship's funnels are stoking up and huge clouds of black smoke begin to pour out to signal our imminent departure. A four piece band plays softly on a corner stage, as toots of farewell fill the air and this enormous vessel manoeuvres slowly out to sea. I am leaving New Zealand!

The band starts to play a catchy tune as hundreds of people press against the rails on the boat's numerous sun decks. The sun is shining brightly and Hale is standing quietly in the shade, but I'm right at the edge of the deck, leaning over the side and looking down into the water. "Oh Islands in the sun…" I hear, as the lead singer bursts into song. The boat gives a final farewell toot, and I send out my own silent thank you to New Zealand for all its gifts and care during my stay. My heart is so full of gratitude, it feels like it's going to burst! There's no sadness. It feels so absolutely right and perfect to be leaving in this way, at this time. Looking down into the ocean, once again I reflect on my incredible departure on this magnificent boat, with Hale's companionship, as we begin our journey across thousands of miles of the Pacific Ocean, heading for Hawaii.

The rest of the band harmonise with the lead and they all sing, "Sail away with me into another world, and we rely on each other, ahaaa." The words hit me so directly that I turn back and glance over at Hale. Has he heard them too? At first he seems lost in thought, looking down at his feet but then suddenly he looks up, and we exchange a knowing smile.

I laugh, throw back my head and look away again, entranced by the magic and synchronicity of the Universe. I'm blown away with all the signs and messages that keep coming to affirm that what I'm doing is right; reassuring me of its presence and full support. It's so very wonderful and beyond anything that I can comprehend or understand.

The shore line fades into the distance and my next adventure begins.